500 YEARS OF NEW WORDS

Greetings from

Bill Sherk

a.k.a.

¡William Sherkspeare!

To my two wonderful children,
Jeffrey and Juliana

500 Years of New Words
By Bill Sherk

THE DUNDURN GROUP
TORONTO

Publisher: Anthony Hawke
Copy-Editor: Lloyd Davis
Design: Andrew Roberts
Printer: Transcontinental

Library and Archives Canada Cataloguing in Publication

Sherk, Bill, 1942-
    500 years of new words : the fascinating story of how, when, and why hundreds of your favourite words first entered the English language / Bill Sherk.

ISBN 1-55002-525-2

    1. English language--Etymology. 2. English language--History.
I. Title. II. Title: Five hundred years of new words.

PE1574.S53 2004   422   C2004-905468-6

1   2   3   4   5   08   07   06   05   04

 Conseil des Arts
du Canada   **Canada Council**
for the Arts Canada ONTARIO ARTS COUNCIL
CONSEIL DES ARTS DE L'ONTARIO

We acknowledge the support of the **Canada Council for the Arts** and the **Ontario Arts Council** for our publishing program. We also acknowledge the financial support of the **Government of Canada** through the **Book Publishing Industry Development Program** and **The Association for the Export of Canadian Books**, and the **Government of Ontario** through the **Ontario Book Publishers Tax Credit** program, and the **Ontario Media Development Corporation's Ontario Book Initiative**.

Printed and bound in Canada
Printed on recycled paper

www.dundurn.com

Dundurn Press
8 Market Street
Suite 200
Toronto, Ontario, Canada
M5E 1M6

Gazelle Book Services Limited
White Cross Mills
Hightown, Lancaster, England
LA1 4X5

Dundurn Press
2250 Military Road
Tonawanda, NY
U.S.A. 14150

500 YEARS OF NEW WORDS

TABLE OF CONTENTS

FOREWORD

by Dr. Frederick Sweet, Ph.D.

Bill Sherk and I share a mutual affliction. We are both incurable logophiles. In my case, this affliction carried me in the direction of what are generally known as the Dead Languages, Greek and Latin (I will grant that they are dead if others will grant that they remain remarkably vital). By contrast, Bill, a neighbour of mine in North Toronto, has discovered the rewards to be had in creating brand new words. If you haven't yet read Bill's splendid *Brave New Words* or its sequel *More Brave New Words* — in which you will be exposed to such creative neologisms as "accident-dent-dent-dent" (a chain-reaction car crash) or "parsipetrolambulist" (a person who walks in order to conserve gasoline) — you really should hunt up these volumes wherever they are to be found and settle back for a truly satisfying read. And while you're at it, try to find the books in which Bill indulges his second great love — his long-standing passion for old cars: *The Way We Drove: Toronto's Love Affair with the Automobile, 1893–1957* and *60 Years Behind the Wheel: The Cars We Drove in Canada, 1900–1960.*

In the present volume, which is a welcome update of an earlier edition, Bill has had the inspired idea of arranging new words chronologically over the past five centuries. He thus, in one swell foop, gives us both an insight into the origins of words and also an appreciation of the times that produced them. Never has history (Bill's academic discipline) been so painless or so illuminating. Open this book and open your mind to a reading and learning experience that will leave you richly satisfied and greatly entertained.

The 1500s

By the year 1500, England was beginning to shake itself loose from the Middle Ages. For fifteen years the strong-willed Henry VII had been sitting on a throne he took by force from Richard III in the Battle of Bosworth Field ("A horse! A horse! — My kingdom for a horse!"), and although old-timers still spoke of the Wars of the Roses, the English people were beginning to enjoy the blessings of peace, order and good government.

William Caxton had set up the first printing press on English soil in 1476, and a multitude of books poured forth from it, including the Bible. In 1497 Henry VII commissioned John Cabot to sail to the unknown lands across the Atlantic, and Cabot returned to tell about a "newe founde land."

Meanwhile, around the royal court, Henry's four children — two boys and two girls — were growing up. By 1503 one son would be dead, but the other would survive to become the most famous and the most feared of all English kings — Henry VIII.

By the year 1600, the people of England could look back on a century of turmoil, conflict, adventure and change. To obtain a divorce from his first wife, the strong-willed Henry VIII had broken all ties with the Roman Catholic Church and established a new Church of England with himself as Supreme Head. When Sir Thomas More refused to accept Henry as his spiritual leader, the king had his head chopped off (he also beheaded two of his six wives on a charge, real or fabricated, of adultery).

During the brief reign of Henry's son, Edward VI (1547–1553), England drifted toward the Protestant faith. During the equally brief reign of his sister, Queen Mary (1553–1558), three hundred Protestants were burned at the stake as Mary tried to re-establish the Roman Catholic Church in England. The country was heading for civil war.

In 1558 Princess Elizabeth became queen and calmed the troubled waters of religion with her new Anglican Church, a compromise solution that blended Catholic and Protestant faith and doctrine. A new English Bible and Book of Common Prayer gave the English people a heightened sense of pride in the majesty of their mother tongue, a majesty that reached full flower during the Elizabethan Age with Shakespeare, Marlowe, Ben Jonson, and the other poets and playwrights who drew their inspiration from the exciting times in which they lived. Francis Drake had returned home in 1580 from his thirty-five-month voyage around the world, a feat comparable to English-speaking astronauts landing on the moon in a future age of exploration. Eight years after Drake's epic voyage, English ships and guns (and favourable winds) helped to defeat the "invincible Armada" in the English Channel, a naval victory that paved the way for the growth of English sea power in the New World.

The forces and events that changed England and the English people during the sixteenth century are reflected in the English language itself. Thanks to the Renaissance of classical learning that began in Italy in the 1400s, a multitude of new words poured into English from Latin and Greek, including *drama, sincere, peninsula, circus, satellite, democracy, stigma* and *catapult.* Thanks to the religious struggles, words like *scapegoat, papist* and *puritan* became part of the everyday vocabulary. Recurrent outbreaks of disease contributed words like *smallpox, gonorrhea* and *virus.*

But the biggest influx of new words came from the geographical discoveries made possible by the daring sailors and navigators who set out from the seaports of England in search of glory, gold and God. The treasures they brought home from these voyages included more than the cargoes in their holds, for they also brought with them strange new words to describe their strange new discoveries: *parrot, torpedo, hurricane, typhoon, tobacco, alligator, obelisk, molasses, canary, penguin, mosquito, banana, coffee,* and many more. Scholars estimate that ten thousand new words entered the English language during the reign of Queen Elizabeth I alone. Small wonder Shakespeare felt so inspired!

1504 Coparcenary

This word is approximately five hundred years old and can be found in the 2003 edition of *Merriam-Webster's Collegiate Dictionary* with this definition: "1) joint heirship; 2) joint ownership." Apparently even older is *coparcener* (a joint heir), dating back to at least the fifteenth century.

Johannes Gutenberg constructed his first printing press in Germany in the 1450s, and William Caxton set up his first press in London in 1476. Before this time, anything recorded in English had to be written out by hand. Imagine copying the entire Bible by hand, as some medieval monks actually did.

The farther back we go in time, the less certain we can be of the precise date of a letter, document, book, or anything written or printed. For all entries older than the year 1500, *Merriam-Webster's Collegiate Dictionary* simply indicates the century it dates from, instead of the specific year.

All of which brings to mind one of the favourite stories of the Canadian author and retired auto mechanic Gord Hazlett: "A museum guide, leading a tour group, announced, 'This ancient mummy is two million and nine years old.'

"'How can you be so precise about something that old?' asked a skeptic in the crowd.

"'Well,' the guide said, 'I've been here for nine years, and it was two million years old when they hired me.'"

1505 Bounder / Hussy

For this year, you get two words for the price of one. The first refers to a man and the second to a woman. Both words are uncomplimentary.

First, *bounder*, with two definitions in Merriam-Webster: "1) one that bounds; 2) a man of objectionable social behaviour: CAD."

The word *cad* is fully capitalized in this definition to let you know that it can be found as a main entry elsewhere in the same dictionary. Following up, we find that second definition of *cad* relates to *bounder*: "a man who acts with deliberate disregard for another's feelings or rights."

The next entry after *cad* is the fully capitalized *CAD*, the acronym for "computer-aided design."

5

Now *hussy*, which also has two definitions in Merriam-Webster: "1) a lewd or brazen woman; 2) a saucy or mischievous girl." It derives from the Middle English *huswif* (housewife).

Dating from 1955 (only half a century ago!) is the term *househusband* for "a husband who does housekeeping usually while his wife earns the family income."

The word *husband* can be traced back to Old English *husbonda*, master of a house. It also means "house-bound" because, when a man marries, he is expected to spend more time at home.

1506 ADULTERATION

This word has plenty of company in the dictionary with other words beginning with the same five letters: *adult, adulthood, adulterant, adulterate, adulterer, adulteress, adulterine, adulterous* and *adultery*. All of these go back to the Latin *adultus*, the past participle of *adolescere*, "to grow up."

The main entry for *adulteration* lists it as a noun. The verb *adulterate* dates back to 1531, and, according to Merriam-Webster, carries with it a loss of innocence: "to corrupt, debase, or make impure by the addition of a foreign or inferior substance or element; esp.: to prepare for sale by replacing more valuable with less valuable or inert ingredients."

So does this mean that when we leave childhood behind, we say good-bye forever to our childhood innocence? Not necessarily. Some adults live long enough to reach their "second childhood."

1507 AMERICA

"In 1492, Columbus sailed the ocean blue." Generations of school children memorized that couplet in honour of the best known of all the European explorers who crossed the Atlantic and reached the Western Hemisphere five centuries ago. For someone so famous, you might expect the New World to be named after him — but to his dying day in 1506, Christopher Columbus insisted he had not found an unknown continent, but rather had reached an unexplored part of eastern Asia.

Instead, the honour fell to Amerigo Vespucci, a Florentine navigator who made four visits to the New World between 1497 and 1503 and who suggested the new lands be called *Mundus Novus* — New World. A German mapmaker named Martin Waldseemuller read Vespucci's account of his voyages and labelled the new land "America." When Waldseemuller later learned of the role Columbus had played in these discoveries, he dropped the name "America" from his maps and renamed it "The Land Unknown."

Despite the change, "America" caught on. Over the years, Vespucci has been accused of cheating Columbus out of an honour that should have been his, although Vespucci never claimed the New World should be named after him. The American poet and essayist Ralph Waldo Emerson wrote: "Strange that broad America must wear the name of a thief! Amerigo Vespucci, the pickle-dealer at Seville, who went out in 1499, a subaltern with Hojeda, and whose highest naval rank was boatswain's mate, in an expedition that never sailed, managed in this lying world to supplant Columbus, and baptize half the world with his own dishonest name." In fact, Vespucci *did* sail, not once but four times, and had nothing but respect and admiration for Columbus.

The legacy of the pickle dealer from Seville still lives, and not only on maps. A bumper sticker currently popular in the United States proudly proclaims: "America — a good old Italian name."

How fortunate that Waldseemuller chose Vespucci's first name. Otherwise, Americans would be Vespuccians (ves-POOCH-e-ans), living in the United States of Vespuccia.

1508 Pet

This three-letter word gives you three parts of speech rolled into one. As a noun, *pet* was used as early as 1508 as a term of endearment for an indulged (and usually spoiled) child. By 1539 its meaning was extended to include dumb animals. That was the year when the *Accounts of the Lord High Treasurer of Scotland* made reference to the wife of one Thomas Melville, who kept pets, including parrots, monkeys, peacocks and swans. As an adjective, pet was used in front of the child or animal to which it referred: a pet monkey, a pet parrot, and so forth.

Pet appeared as a verb as early as 1515, when it meant "to break wind," from the Italian *petto,* "to fart," presumably coined, like *fart* itself, by way of onomatopoeia. It later acquired the additional verb use "to fondle," which applied at first to pet animals, but was later extended to the fondling of someone's erogenous zones, as in "necking and petting." With the arrival of the Pill in the 1960s, *petting* as a term with sexual overtones began to fade away as many couples went straight from kissing to coitus.

1509 OBTUSE

Although this word has been traced back to the fifteenth century, the earliest specific year it can be dated from is 1509.

This word started out in English as a synonym for dull, stupid or insensible, as in "an obtuse fellow" or "an obtuse remark," from the Latin *obtundere, obtusum,* "dull" or "blunt." By 1570 it had come to mean an angle greater than ninety degrees, presumably because such an angle was dull and blunt instead of sharp and pointed.

That was the year when Sir Henry Billingsley, in his translation of *The Elements of Geometrie of Euclid,* wrote: "An obtuse angle is that which is greater than a right angle."

An angle of less than ninety degrees is known as an acute angle, from the Latin *acutus,* meaning sharp. I once knew a math teacher who had a favourite gimmick for any student who could not remember the name of that kind of angle. The student would be called to the front of the room to draw such an angle on the blackboard; the teacher would stand alongside and, while gently prodding the student in the belly with a wooden pointer, would say: "Let me know when the pain becomes acute." It worked every time.

1510 SPOKESHAVE

Although they built mighty temples, all-weather highways and designed an accurate solar calendar, the Native peoples of the New World knew nothing of the wheel until it was introduced to them by Europeans. The unknown genius of the Old World who built the first usable wheel probably had no idea what he (or she) was starting. The earliest wheels were probably round slabs of stone used for grinding grain, or sections of a log joined together by a crude axle. The wheel began to improve when the art of warfare in the Middle East and China made the construction of chariots necessary. At first, chariot wheels were made of solid wood, bound together by an iron hoop to prevent the wood from splitting when the vehicle bounced over bumpy roads. As technology improved, the solid wheel gave way to the lighter spoke wheel, which increased the chariot's top speed and made it easier to pursue or escape from the enemy. Once spoke wheels became widely used, the art of making and decorating the spokes came into its own — hence the need for the spokeshave, a tool for the shaping of spokes, from the Old English *spaca*, "spoke," and *sceafan*, "to scrape."

The spokeshave is far from being obsolete. Horse-drawn buggies are still widely used throughout the world and even in the United States, particularly in the Amish and other Mennonite communities in southeastern Pennsylvania, where buggy manufacturers are still busy building new ones, spokes and all. One buggy maker reports that business is so brisk, he works six days a week and still can't keep up with the demand.

1511 SANDALWOOD

Sandalwood is a hardwood rich in fragrant oils that is obtained from several species of tree in southern Asia. Although the word *sandalwood* first appeared in print in English in 1511 (the earliest example yet found), the word *sandal*, as a synonym for sandalwood, appeared as early as 1400. The wood itself is used for cabinet making and wood carvings, while the oil extracted from the wood is used in perfume and soap.

Where does the word itself come from? The *American Heritage Dictionary* traces it back to the Medieval Latin *sandalum, santalum*, which came from the Greek *santalon, sandanon*, which in turn probably came from the Sanskrit word *candanah*. This etymology apparently bears no connection to the other *sandal*, the word we use to describe the footwear that consists of a sole fastened to the feet by straps or thongs. That word has been traced back to the Greek *sandalon*, which perhaps came from the Lydian word *sandal* in reference to the shoe of Sandal, a Lydian god.

A history teacher named Leon Trechikavitz was marking essays on ancient Rome when the following sentence popped up: "The Romans wore scandals on their feet."

1512 TINNER

Although the word *tinner* (one who works in a tin mine) can be traced back to somewhere in the thirteenth century, we can pin it down to a specific year by 1512.

Tin, a word of Old English origin, was one of the ten elements known to the ancient world, the other nine being gold, silver, lead, iron, sulphur, mercury, copper, antimony and carbon. Tin was highly prized in the ancient world because, if you added copper to it, you could make bronze, a strong metal for weapons, tools and ornaments. The Phoenicians, who lived on the eastern shores of the Mediterranean, sailed far and wide in search of tin, and their travels took them to Britain, where the tin mines of Cornwall and Devon yielded their wealth. British tin was carried in Phoenician ships back to the Mediterranean more than six hundred years before the birth of Christ. It was sold and resold, and fashioned and refashioned, for it was far too precious to throw away once its original purpose had been fulfilled. Some of this tin found its way into the breastplates of the soldiers of the Roman army, and when Julius Caesar stepped ashore in Britain in 55 B.C., his men did not realize their breastplates were made of Cornish tin mined in Britain over five hundred years earlier.

For people who work in tin mines, we no longer use the word *tinner*. Now we call them tin miners, and those who fashion tin are called tinsmiths.

1513 DANDELION

Until its spelling became standardized (probably by the eighteenth century), *dandelion* appeared as *dent de lion, dentdelyon, dantdelyon,* and *dendelion.* The spelling may have varied, but the etymology did not. *Dent de lion* came from French, meaning "tooth of the lion," because of the tooth-shaped green leaves that surround the yellow flower.

Before this word crossed the English Channel from France to England, English dandelions were simply yellow weeds. By 1597 a new synonym had appeared for this plant: *pissabed,* so called because of the ability of the dandelion, if ingested, to make one urinate. In 1822, in *Good's Study of Medicine,* we are reminded that pissabed is not fit for polite company: "It (the dandelion) possesses unquestionably diuretic powers, and hence, indeed, its vulgar name of piss-a-bed." Lest you look upon *piss* as just another vulgar four-letter word, however, remember that it appears in the King James version of the Bible.

1514 Topgallant

A topgallant is the mast, sail or rigging directly above the topmast and topsail, so called because it makes a gallant show compared to the other sails.

I never encounter this word without thinking of one of the finest educational motion pictures ever made, *The England of Elizabeth.* Produced by the British Transport Corporation in 1957, this film chronicles the life and times of Elizabeth I, "the Virgin Queen" of England, from her birth in 1533 ("She had been but a baby when her mother knelt at the block") to her death nearly seventy years later.

After presenting a dazzling panorama of monarchs and monasteries, playwrights and Puritans, sailors and sea serpents, Bibles and bawdy houses, the film finishes by capturing the glory of the Elizabethan age with these stirring words: "In March, sixteen hundred and three, Elizabeth died. A bright day was done. A messenger upon a lather'd horse rides north to Scotland. Hail, King James. New king, new court, new manners and new ways, and all the old ones elbowed off the stage. And so, the sun went down upon the Elizabethans. An age had ended.

"But it was a time so bright, we're still aware of the shine and the splendour of it — a quickening time, when the winds that bore the ships about the world seemed to blow too through the high topgallants of man's spirit, and sent it voyaging in the lonelier ways where, without chart or compass, the poets sailed alone. The treasure they brought home from these voyages was the words and the music — such stuff as dreams are made of, outlasting the years."

1515 DRAMA

Plays performed in England in the Middle Ages almost invariably had religious overtones. But by 1500 the impact of the Italian Renaissance was spreading throughout Europe and reaching Britannia's shores. No longer were plays exclusively religious — now there was a growing interest in reviving the classical Greek plays of ancient times. Many old manuscripts of these plays had lain dormant in monasteries for hundreds of years. With the fall of Constantinople to the Turks on May 29, 1453, hordes of Greek scholars fled the city to seek refuge in Italy and points west. The documents they brought with them included the plays of ancient Greece, which were revived to the delight of Renaissance audiences throughout western Europe.

Because native English words were often inadequate to express the ideas in these plays, the natural solution was to anglicize the Greek words. *Drama* entered the English language in 1515 and was joined by *theatre*, *chorus*, *comedy*, *tragedy*, *orchestra*, *irony*, *prologue*, *dialogue*, *epilogue*, *episode*, *critic* and *climax*, all of which come from Greek.

1516 UTOPIA

Just nine years after the Western Hemisphere was given the name "America," the English scholar and statesman Thomas More wrote *Utopia*, a description of life on an imaginary island. Written in Latin but with a Greek title — utopia literally means "nowhere," from the Greek *ou*, meaning "not," and *topos*, "a place" — More's book paints a picture of the perfect society as he saw it. No one owned any private property or money. Gold was made virtually worthless by being used for chamber pots, and diamonds and pearls were given to children as toys. Fifty-four cities were scattered throughout the island, separated from each other by at least twenty-four miles of countryside. Everyone held a general belief in God, but individual creeds were tolerated.

If More himself had been more tolerant of the religious changes Henry VIII was ramming through Parliament in the 1530s, he might have lived longer. As Lord Chancellor, Sir Thomas More wielded great influence, but was still expected to kowtow to the king. When Henry VIII asked him to take an oath to the Act of Supremacy, which replaced the pope with the king as head of the Church of England, More, a staunch Roman Catholic, refused. He was then charged with treason, tried, convicted and beheaded.

The title of More's book lives on, and received a fresh new twist around 1950 when Sir Winston Churchill coined the term *queuetopia* for all those new socialist countries plagued by interminably long lineups.

1517 STARTUP

A startup was originally a kind of boot worn by peasants, but the word was later used to describe a gaiter or legging (from the phrase "start up," as in "a shoe that starts up to the middle of the leg").

This word is now classified as obsolete, probably because the boots and gaiters and leggings it used to describe are either no longer worn or are called by other names. And although the *Oxford English Dictionary* says it first appeared in print in 1517, no one knows quite when it died. Although most of the entries in this book are words that are still flourishing today, *startup* and a few other archaic entries have been included to remind us that some words fall by the wayside as time marches on. Should your curiosity be sufficiently piqued that you want to read a book devoted entirely to old English words that are no longer with us, grab a copy of Susan Kelz Sperling's best-selling *Poplollies and Bellibones*.

1518 SMALLPOX

Although smallpox was killing people before 1518, that's the year in which Henry VIII gets the credit for first mentioning it on paper: "They do die in these parts (Wallingford) ... of the small pokes and mezils." Reports of epidemics from the 1400s testify to the catastrophic effects of this disease, which swept the world in recurring waves and took millions to an early grave. The Spaniards carried smallpox to the New World in the early 1500s, where it is said to have been responsible for the death of half the Native population of the

Americas (some tribes, including the Mandans and Assiniboins of the upper Missouri valley, were nearly or completely exterminated). Its effect on the European settlers in America was often just as severe, as a visit to any colonial American cemetery will show. By the eighteenth century, smallpox was so widespread that nearly everyone in Europe and Asia had had the disease at some point during their lifetime.

While smallpox was often fatal (following a high fever, headache, backache and rash), many victims did survive, only to find their faces horribly pockmarked for life. The word comes from Old English *smael*, meaning "small," and *pox*, the plural of *pock*.

In 1796 an English medical student named Edward Jenner began working on the cure that would save hundreds of millions of lives. Jenner had noticed that milkmaids very seldom contracted smallpox and thus came to believe, quite correctly, that infection with cowpox, a much milder form of the pox, would protect a person against a subsequent smallpox infection. He inoculated a young boy with cowpox by taking the disease from the hand of an infected milkmaid and injecting it into the young lad's arm. Six weeks later, the boy was inoculated with smallpox and remained healthy and normal. The cure worked. Since then, millions of people have received smallpox vaccinations, and the disease has been virtually eliminated from Europe, North America and most other parts of the world.

1519 TRUEPENNY

A truepenny is an honest person, comparable to a coin of genuine metal. The penny itself, also called the cent or copper (because it is made partly of copper), is a coin of small value introduced into England in the eighth

century by Offa, King of Mercia, who patterned it after the European coin *novus denarius* (the *d* of which, prior to decimalization in 1971, was the symbol for the English penny). Unfortunately, you can't buy much with a penny anymore — not even a Canadian penny. It now costs about two cents to mint each one.

The nickel got its name because nickels were long made of the metal (nickel-plated steel is now used). The dime comes to us through French from the Latin *decimus*, tenth, because it is one-tenth of a dollar. The quarter got its name because it is one-quarter of a dollar — and the dollar originated in Germany in the 1500s, near a silver mine in the Joachim Valley. These first dollars were made not of paper but of silver; you can read the story of the dollar on page 42.

Both gold and silver coins have been debased with inferior metals ever since the invention of coinage, and you must exercise care in trying to get coins that are really worth the value stamped on them. The word *coin* itself can be traced back to the Latin *cuneus*, a wedge, because the die that made the coins looked like a wedge. The word entered the French as *coign* and then English as *coin*, at first referring to the die itself and later to the money the die produced. The word *money* goes back to the Roman goddess Juno Moneta, whose temple was built on the Capitoline Hill (making her the first capitalist) and who became the guardian of Roman finances. Her second name, Moneta, comes from the Latin *moneo*, meaning "I warn," because she would blow the whistle on anyone who tried to steal government funds. The Roman mint was set up in her temple so that she could keep an eye on every coin stamped out.

1520 Torpedo

In 1520 a torpedo was a fish with a cigar-shaped body and tapered tail; only much later did it become a self-propelled submarine missile that explodes on impact with a ship or other target. The fish we call a torpedo is noted for its ability to emit electric shocks, a feature that a chap named Andrewe was well aware of when he wrote these words in 1520: "Torpido is a fisshe, but who-so handeleth hym shalbe lame & defe of lymmes that he shall fele no thyng." And that quote explains the origin of the word, which comes from the Latin *torpedo*, meaning stiffness or numbness. By the end of the 1500s *torpedo* had broadened its meaning to cover anyone or anything that causes numbness. It was this definition that Oliver Goldsmith had in mind in 1762 when he wrote: "He used to call a pen his torpedo. Whenever he grasped it, it numbed all his faculties."

In 1807 Robert Fulton, the inventor of the steamboat, designed and built submarine explosives to destroy enemy ships. These "floating bombs" were towed or allowed to drift toward the target, and then they exploded on contact. Although they were called torpedoes at first (probably because of their shape or "sting"), they were really mines. The first modern self-propelled torpedo was developed around 1875 by a British engineer, Robert Whitehead, who employed steam propulsion and a gyroscope to send it to its target. Forty years later, during World War I, his new weapon came into its own as submarine-launched torpedoes sent hundreds of ships to the bottom of the sea.

1521 PERNICIOUS

In 1521 Bishop John Fisher wrote a pamphlet entitled *Sermon ... made agayn ye pernicyous doctryn of Martin Luther*. This is the earliest example listed in the *Oxford English Dictionary* of the word *pernicious* (a synonym for "destructive" and "ruinous," from the Latin *per*, meaning "thoroughly," and *nex*, "death by violence"), although the word must have been in circulation before 1521 in order for Fisher to use it in his title. You will notice that the spelling of *pernicious* has changed since Fisher's day, along with *doctryn* and *agayn*, the latter being the sixteenth-century version of *against*.

Martin Luther, a German monk, triggered the Protestant Reformation on All Saints' Eve (Hallowe'en) in 1517 when he nailed to the front door of the Castle Chapel at Wittenberg a list of ninety-five protests against the Roman Catholic Church. When Bishop Fisher four years later wrote his sermon "agayn ye pernicyous doctryn of Martin Luther," he had high hopes of stemming the Protestant tide, especially in England. How could he foresee that, twelve years later, his own king, Henry VIII, would sever all ties with the Church in Rome — not because of Martin Luther but because he wanted a divorce from a wife who had failed to produce a male heir to the English throne?

1522 Pit-a-pat

Back in prehistoric times, when word coiners had no Greek or Latin roots to fall back on, most new words were coined through onomatopoeia. *Pit-a-pat*, the sound of a rapidly beating heart, light and rapid footsteps, or any similar series of alternating sounds, probably has a history as old as language itself. Its earliest appearance in print has been dated at 1522, when Sir Thomas More wrote: "Some wretches yet scant can crepe for age … walk pit pat vpon a paire of patens." In 1601 the Elizabethan poet Ben Jonson set the word in a romantic context: "You shall have kisses … goe pit-pat, pit-pat, pit-pat, vpon your lips, as thick as stones out of slings." In 1693 William Congreve, an English dramatist noted for his lewdness and wit, wrote: "Agad, my heart has gone apit pat for thee." And the great Charles Dickens, in *Barnaby Rudge*, uses onomatopoeia to convey the relative size of two approaching figures: "Tramp, tramp, pit-pat, on they come together."

A slightly modified version of pit-a-pat was used by Margaret Mitchell when she created the character of Scarlett O'Hara's Aunt Pittypat in *Gone with the Wind*. The aunt was well named because her heart was always beating rapidly, especially when Union soldiers began shelling and burning Atlanta. Frantically mopping her brow, she wailed, "Yankees in Georgia! How did they ever get in?"

1523 Dilemma

A dilemma (from Greek *dis*, meaning "twice," and *lemma*, "proposition") is a choice between two alternatives, both of which are equally unappealing. This is the meaning the word *dilemma* has carried with it ever since it appeared in a religious book in England in 1523. The word was no doubt well known when Sir Francis Bacon used it ninety-nine years later in writing about Archbishop Morton, a tax-collecting genius during the reign of King Henry VII (1485–1509) who turned that grasping and greedy ruler into a very wealthy monarch. Under what came to be known as "Morton's fork," if you were living high, you were taxed heavily because you could obviously afford it. But if you were living humbly, you must have been saving your money instead of spending it, and you therefore could spare some money for the taxman. No matter your standard of living, you had to pay up; neither alternative appealed. Bacon described this arrangement as "a dilemma that bishop Morton … used to raise up the [taxes] to a higher rate," and a good choice of words it was.

1524 PESTER

Appearing in print as early as 1524, *pester* (to tangle, overload, obstruct, annoy, trouble or plague, from the Latin *pestis,* "a plague") has been a popular word for more than four hundred and seventy-five years. In a letter to Viscount Lisle on August 29, 1536, Sir John Russell wrote: "You are daily pestered with business" (an observation most of us can sympathize with today). In 1562 a very relieved Englishman commented upon the peace that Queen Elizabeth had brought to her country after the turbulent reigns of the axe-happy Henry VIII, the boy-king Edward VI and Bloody Mary: "Howe was this Realme pestered with straunge rulers, straunge Gods … and howe is it now peaceablye ridde of theym all."

Someone who pesters is a pest, and among the most pestiferous of all creatures, in the eyes of man, are the insects. And because chemical sprays were developed in the twentieth century to keep these pests under control, a new word entered our language around 1950: *pesticide.*

1525 PARROT

Although parrots were first introduced into Europe from the tropics around 400 B.C. and some ancient Romans had parrots as pets, the news of this bird's existence apparently did not reach England until after the discovery of the New World. The more than three hundred species of parrot (from the French *perroquet,* meaning "parrot") are widely distributed through the tropical regions of the world, with the Amazon parrot — bright green and yellow with dashes of red, blue and black — being perhaps the most familiar today. This is the parrot that is often caricatured as sitting on the shoulder of an old sailor and learning a vocabulary too salty for polite company.

Parrots have been popular as pets for many centuries, partly because of their gaudy colour, partly because of their longevity (some parrots have lived eighty years or more), but especially because of their ability to imitate human speech. If you are teaching a parrot how to talk, you need patience. Start off with one or two words, then work these into subsequent lessons with lots of repetition. It is useless to reward Polly with a cracker after each new word he or she learns because parrots, unlike mammals, do not learn by association. They will fail to see any connection between the word and the food. Of course, some parrots, despite the most painstaking efforts on the part of their owners, will refuse to say anything.

1526 Dictionary

Although the term *dictionarius* was used by English writers as early as the thirteenth century, it described lists of Latin words and phrases. The first recorded use of *dictionary* in an English sentence took place in 1526, in reference to a book compiled by one Peter Bercharius in the fourteenth century: "And so Peter Bercharius in his dictionary describeth it." In 1538 Sir Thomas Elyot published his Latin-English *Dictionary* — and the word *dictionary*, from the Latin *dicere*, "to say," began appearing in book titles from then on.

Most of the early dictionaries of the English language were restricted to difficult words. The first all-inclusive dictionary of the English language was compiled by Dr. Samuel Johnson between 1747 and 1755. Although he thought of himself as a "harmless drudge," he was not without humour, as evidenced by his definition of window: "an orifice in an edifice." He included far more words than any lexicographer before him, but refused to include any vulgar terms. The story goes that a pair of very proper ladies approached the great doctor at a literary tea and said, "We see, Dr. Johnson, that you do not have any naughty words in your dictionary." To which he replied, "And I see, dear ladies, that you have been looking for them."

The greatest dictionary of all time got under way in the latter half of the nineteenth century in Oxford, England. The first volume was released in 1884, the tenth in 1928, precisely forty-four years later. (One of the original typesetters was still at work on it when the last volume was printed.) In 1933 it was reprinted as a twelve-volume set, and a supplementary volume was published. A second supplement, consisting of four volumes, came out between 1972 and 1986. A revised edition, running to 22,000 pages spread over twenty volumes and containing more than 615,000 words, was published in 1989. A third edition is currently in the works.

In 1980, the Oxford lexicographers made a successful grab for the lucrative American dictionary market with the publication of the very first *Oxford American Dictionary*. Sales have been brisk, thanks in part to the blurb on the front cover: "The most authoritative paperbound dictionary." But by a curious oversight, the word *paperbound* is not in the dictionary itself.

1527 Hockey

Although the word *hockey* entered the English language as early as 1527, probably from the Old French *hoquet* — meaning "crook," from the shape of the stick — the game itself is much older than that. It was played in ancient Persia and was as widely dispersed as the Americas and ancient Greece. A wall in Athens contains a description of the game dating back to the fifth century before Christ — although it was probably not until the nineteenth century that the game shifted from dry ground to an icy surface.

And where did the word *puck* come from? It dates back to before the twelfth century, meaning "an evil spirit" or "mischievous sprite." Its modern link to ice hockey dates back only to 1891.

1528 Congress

Thousands of new words flooded into the English language during the 1500s, and they came chiefly from two sources: via ancient Greek and Latin from the Mediterranean, and from Native words learned in the New World. One of these new words began in ancient Rome, popped up in sixteenth-century England, then took root in America — and that word is *congress*, from the Latin *congressus*, "to meet." When it first appeared in print in England in 1528, it simply meant a meeting or interview. By 1589 it had acquired the additional meaning of sexual intercourse. In 1774 it began its long political career in the New World with the formation of the Continental Congress in the British North American colonies. This congress provided the spark that triggered the American Revolution. The Congress that serves as the legislative branch of the United States government first met on March 4, 1789, in New York City (the nation's capital was shifted the following year to Philadelphia, and ten years after that to Washington, D.C.). The members of the upper house of Congress are known as *senators*, a word that comes from the Latin root *senex*, meaning "old man." That root also gives us the word *senile*, a fact to which senators are not likely to draw your attention.

1529 PERIWIG

If you wear a wig, you are wearing an abbreviated word. Just as the word *bus* is short for *omnibus*, the word *wig* is short for *periwig*. It appeared in print as early as 1529 and, because the spelling of English words did not become standardized for another two hundred and fifty years, there were more than twenty different ways of spelling it.

One of the most famous wigs in British history sat on the head of Mary, Queen of Scots on February 8, 1587, the day she was beheaded for treason at Fotheringay Castle. After three blows of the axe, Mary's head fell into a basket, from which it was to be plucked by the executioner who would hold it aloft before a crowd of witnesses. But Mary had not bothered to glue the wig properly to her nearly bald scalp, and when the axe-man hoisted what he thought was her head into the air, all he held was a handful of hair.

One of the pleasures enjoyed by those word lovers who browse through the *OED* is the opportunity to read the quotations that illustrate the history and usage of every word listed. Under *periwig*, the quote from 1579 sounds as though it was written by a misogynist: "Take from them their perywigges, their paintings (etc.) ... and thou shalt soone perceive that a woman is the least parte of hir selfe." The quote from 1656 tells you where you can buy one: "I bought me a perewige (off) of my barber." Jonathan Swift, around 1710, gives you the price: "It has cost me three guineas to-day for a periwig." And a quote from 1598 warns of the hazards of wearing one: "Th' unruly winde blowes off his perwinke." But my favourite of all these quotes was written in 1639 by a chap named Fuller, who turns the noun into a verb: "Map-makers rather than they will have their maps naked and bald, do periwig them with false hair, and fill up the vacuum with imaginary places."

1530 SCAPEGOAT

In her fascinating book, *More about Words*, Margaret Ernst tells us how *scapegoat* was coined: "The word scapegoat was invented by [William] Tyndale in 1530 to express what he believed to be the literal meaning of the Hebrew phrases in Lev[iticus] 16:8, 10, 26: 'The goote on which the lotte fell to scape.' In the ancient ritual of the Day of Atonement, two goats were brought to the temple. One was chosen by lot to be sent away alive into the wilderness, bearing away on his back, symbolically, the sins of all the people. This was the scapegoat. The other unfortunate beast was offered up in sacrifice."

Six years after coining *scapegoat*, Tyndale must have felt like the goat that didn't get away. He had translated the New Testament from Latin into English back in 1525 and, through a middleman, had sold some copies to the Bishop of London, who promptly burned them (the Roman Catholic Church adamantly opposed any translations of the Bible lest people — Heaven forfend! — start reading it on their own).

Tyndale was certainly onto a good thing while it lasted, with the Archbishop of London eager and willing to buy and burn the Bibles as fast as Tyndale could get them printed. Talk about a guaranteed market! But a man to whom Tyndale had loaned money turned him in. He was strangled, then burned at the stake for his crime.

Incidentally, nearly a hundred years after Tyndale went up in flames, the so-called *Wicked Bible* went on sale. Not only was it printed in English, but the word *not* was missing from the Seventh Commandment, making it read: "Thou shalt commit adultery."

1531 Encyclopedia

The first "walking encyclopedia" was probably Aristotle, the Greek philosopher and tutor of Alexander the Great whose wide-ranging curiosity made him an expert on philosophy, government and natural science. But if Aristotle had published an encyclopedia, it would have contained some errors. He believed, for example, that men have more teeth than women, that the direction of the wind plays a role in determining the sex of an unborn child, and that heavy objects fall faster than lighter ones. On that last point, he was not proven wrong until Galileo came along in the early 1600s.

The first written encyclopedia we know of was compiled by Marcus Porcius Cato (234–149 B.C.). The oldest encyclopedia to survive in its entirety is the *Historia Naturalis* of Pliny the Elder, who died in Pompeii during the eruption of Mount Vesuvius in the year 79. When the word *encyclopedia* (from the Greek *enkuklios paideia*, "all-round education") first entered the English language in 1531, it simply meant a course of instruction ("the circle of learning"). By 1644 it was being used in reference to the encyclopedias of the ancient world. Modern encyclopedias did not appear until the eighteenth century. Leading the way in the English-speaking world was the *Encyclopaedia Britannica*, which began as a "dictionary of arts, science and general literature" and was first published in Edinburgh between 1768 and 1771.

Anyone who reads an encyclopedia from A to Z will certainly acquire a well-rounded education. As a young lad, the prolific author Isaac Asimov set himself the task of doing just that, but his mother sold the set when he was halfway through F. And then there's the story of the fellow who bought a book called *How to Hug*, thinking it would be filled with amorous advice for someone looking for a little romance. When he got the book home, he opened it only to discover he had purchased Volume Seven of the *Encyclopedia Americana*.

1532 Ambidexter

Today, we are more familiar with the adjectival form of this word — *ambidextrous*, describing someone equally skilful with both hands, from the Latin *ambi*, meaning "both," and *dexter*, "on the right hand." Back in 1532 it was used as a noun, *ambidexter*, to describe a person who took bribes from both sides. By the end of the 1500s, *ambidexter* had acquired its more modern meaning, and people began using other words (some of which are unprintable) to describe people who take bribes from both sides.

Although *ambidextrous* has now been part of our language for several hundred years, some people are still not sure of the meaning. In her Pulitzer Prize–winning novel *To Kill a Mockingbird*, Harper Lee describes a rape trial in the courtroom of a small town in Alabama: "Mr. Gilmer asked him one more question. 'About your writing with your left hand, are you ambidextrous, Mr. Ewell?' 'I most positively am not, I can use one hand good as the other,' he added, glaring at the defence table."

1533 SINCERE

Caveat emptor means "let the buyer beware." Your chances of getting stung with shoddy merchandise were just as good in ancient Rome as they are today. The workmen in marble quarries in those days would often rub wax into the cracks and flaws in marble columns and pillars to make them look whole. The wax would wash off in the first rainstorm, by which time the sale had usually been made and the irate customer was left holding the bag (or in this case, the wax). This sneaky trick came to the attention of the Roman senate, which passed a law stating that all marble purchased by the government must be *sine cera* — without wax. From this law and this root comes our modern word *sincere*, which means "without deceit."

1534 PAPIST

After twenty years of marriage to Catherine of Aragon, King Henry VIII of England was getting restless. After several miscarriages and stillbirths, his wife had failed to produce a male heir for the English throne. Now she was too old to bear children, and Henry wanted a divorce so that he could marry the younger (and presumably more fecund) Anne Boleyn. But the Pope in Rome said no. Henry then spent the next six years trying to get the Pope to change his mind, to no avail. Finally, his patience exhausted,

Henry persuaded the Archbishop of Canterbury to annul his marriage to Catherine and marry him to Anne. The following year, in 1534, Henry induced Parliament to pass the Act of Supremacy, which removed the Pope as the head of the Church in England and put Henry in his place.

The age-old connection between England and Rome had been severed — and Henry's subjects who still harboured Roman Catholic sympathies quickly found themselves in trouble. Because the Catholics still looked to the Pope, and not to Henry, as their spiritual leader, the term *papist* was coined as a term of contempt to be hurled by Henry's followers at those Catholics who refused to switch their allegiance.

1535 BLOODTHIRSTY

The English priest Miles Coverdale wrote in 1535: "Odestroye not my soule with the sinners, nor my life with the bloudthurstie." Since then, the word *bloodthirsty* has been applied to pirates, Vikings, wolves and any other creatures that seem to revel in the shedding of blood. Coverdale might have been surprised, however, to learn that the early Christians in Rome — the very people who nurtured the faith that Miles himself embraced — were suspected of engaging in bloodthirsty, cannibalistic rituals. The rumour apparently got started when someone eavesdropped just outside a Roman house where some Christians were meeting in secret to celebrate the sacrament of Holy Communion. The eavesdropper's eyes must have widened with horror when he hear these words from within: "Take, eat, this is my body …. Take, drink, this is my blood…"

1536 RUBBER

Although the word *rubber* was used as early as 1536 for a hard brush or cloth used to rub something to make it clean, the substance we call "rubber" today did not acquire that name until the late eighteenth century. The story of rubber goes back to the day Columbus stepped ashore in South America and found the natives bouncing balls made of an elastic substance totally unknown in Europe at that time. The natives made the balls by cutting the bark of a certain tree and scooping up the milky liquid that oozed out. The natives called the bouncing stuff *cahuchu*, or "weeping wood," a name that the French modified to *caoutchouc* and the Spanish to *caucho*. We would probably have a similar term in widespread use in English today had not the English chemist Joseph Priestley noticed, around 1770, that this elastic substance was useful for rubbing out pencil marks. He called it "rubber" and the name stuck.

Rubber was also used at that time as a waterproofing material, but with two serious drawbacks. The rubber was stiff and brittle when cold, soft and sticky when warm. An American inventor named Charles Goodyear tackled the problem and came up with the answer in 1839 when he accidentally spilled a mixture of rubber and sulphur on a hot stove. After holding his nose and cleaning up the mess, he discovered he had a rubber that stayed flexible when cold, yet dry and firm when warm. He called the new product "vulcanized rubber," after Vulcan, the Roman god of fire, because the heat of the fire brought the rubber and sulphur together to make what Goodyear was looking for. You can see Goodyear's name on television today whenever the Goodyear blimp floats across your screen, but poor Charlie had his problems. His serendipitous (see page 170) discovery paved the way for our modern rubber industry, but Goodyear himself spent the rest of his life fighting to defend his patent rights and died heavily in debt.

1537 SCRABBLE

The earliest English example of this word, which comes from the Dutch *schrabben*, "to scratch or scrape," can be found in a translation of the Bible that was published in 1537: "And he ... scrabled on the dores of the gate" (1 Samuel 21:13). Nearly four hundred years later, in 1931, the word *scrabble* became a proper noun and trademark when unemployed American architect Alfred Mosher Butts invented Criss-crosswords. Jim Brunot, who bought the rights to the game from Butts, changed the name to Scrabble, to reflect the digging for the letters on the part of the players. Since the day Butts had his brainstorm, more than fifty million Scrabble sets have been sold, and the game continues to sell at the rate of one million copies a year. If you play the game to win, you should memorize the eighty-three two-letter words that qualify for use in the game. See how many you recognize: *aa, ad, ae, ah, ai, am, an, ar, as, at, aw, ax, ay, ba, be, bi, bo, by, da, de, do, ef, eh, el, em, en, er, et, ex, fa, go, ha, he, hi, ho, id, if, in, is, it, jo, ka, la, li, lo, ma, me, mu, my, na, no, nu, od, oe, of, oh, om, on, op, or, os, ow, ox, oy, pa, pe, pi, re, si, so, ta, ti, to, un, up, us, ut, we, wo, xi, xu, ya* and *ye.*

1538 PENINSULA

Latin being the ancient language of the Italian peninsula, how appropriate that the word *peninsula* should come from the Latin *paene,* meaning "almost," and *insula,* "island." If you look at a map of the Mediterranean, you'll see three large peninsulas (or *peninsulae,* if you prefer) hanging down from the underbelly of Europe: the Iberian, the Italian and the Balkan. The Balkan is actually a peninsula *with* a peninsula, because the Peloponnese peninsula juts out from the Balkan peninsula proper and is connected to the mainland by the narrow Isthmus of Corinth. Actually, the Peloponnese is no longer almost an island — it *is* an island, and has been ever since the Greeks realized an age-old dream a few years ago by building a canal through the isthmus.

At the eastern end of the Mediterranean, you find exactly the reverse: a peninsula that used to be an island. When Alexander the Great invaded the Persian Empire in 334 B.C., his line of march took him along the eastern end of the Mediterranean Sea. When he reached the city of Tyre, which had been built on an offshore island, he tried repeatedly to capture it, without success. Finally he ordered his men to build a giant causeway from the mainland to the island, across which his troops could march to the very walls of the city itself. After ferocious fighting, the city fell. Alexander and his army are no longer there, but the causeway still is, making the City of Tyre a twenty-three-hundred-year-old peninsula.

1539 PARASITE

The word *parasite,* from the Greek *para,* "beside," and *sitos,* "food," originally applied to people who sponged off others for their food and other means of livelihood, but particularly food. The meaning was extended to the field of biology by 1727 to describe any animal or plant that lives in or on another organism and feeds directly upon it — a tapeworm, for example.

Incidentally, you may have wondered why the citizens of Paris are known as Parisians. It's because they don't like being called "Parisites."

1540 HEREDITY

When this word from the Latin, *heres*, "an heir," first appeared in print, it was a legal term that referred to property that was handed down to one's heirs. A quotation from 1540 illustrates this use: "This Richard was a manne … well worthie the princelie hereditee of his father which hee soberlie governed." It was not until 1863 that the word *heredity* acquired the meaning it has today: the genetic transmission of physical and behavioral characteristics from parents to offspring. And why did that new definition pop up in 1863? Four years earlier, Charles Darwin had published his best-seller, *On the Origin of Species*, in which he set forth the theory that forms of life on earth were not divinely created, as the Book of Genesis claimed, but evolved out of other forms of life through a process of natural selection dictated by the characteristics passed along from one generation to another. Darwin's book triggered a great debate between science and religion and between heredity and environment, a debate that continues to this day.

Darwin himself could look to his own family for evidence to support his theory of biologically inherited characteristics. His grandfather was a famous British physiologist named Erasmus Darwin (1731–1802) and his son was Sir George Howard Darwin (1845–1912), a British astronomer and mathematician.

1541 ABDOMEN

Abdomen is the fancy word for *paunch*, *belly* or *guts*. You could get by without this word when referring to the human body, but it's an absolute necessity when talking about insects, because they are divided into three parts: head, thorax and abdomen. Which reminds me of the young lad in school who kept his English and science notes in the same binder. When it came time to write the science exam, he defined an insect as "a bug which is divided in three participles: the head, thorax and abominable cavity, to which are found the five bowels — *a, e, i, o* and *u*."

1542 Geographer

A colleague of mine in the teaching profession, Lyn McMurray, had a teacher in high school who always asked the class, "Who put the 'G' in geography?" I never did find out what answer he was looking for, but it may have been inspired by his students' reaction to intriguing geographical information.

For example, he may have said to his students, "If you travel far enough in one direction, you will reappear from the opposite direction." His students may have responded to this startling geographical fact with "Gee!" (a contraction of *gosh*, which in turn is a euphemism for *God* as a swear word). Or maybe "Gee whiz!" or even "Gee Willikers!"

In any event, the word *geography* goes back to the fifteenth century and is defined by Merriam-Webster as "a science that deals with the description, distribution, and interaction of the diverse physical, biological, and cultural features of the earth's surface."

It is not surprising that the word *geographer* popped up by 1542, exactly fifty years after the first voyage of Columbus to the New World. The idea that the world was flat died off slowly, and even people who were willing to accept that the Earth was round had trouble swallowing the notion that, not only was it round, but it was moving!

Just one year after *geographer* appeared, Nicolaus Copernicus, a Polish astronomer, lay on his deathbed. A copy of his new book, *De Revolutionibus Orbium Coelestium*, was brought to him just before he died. In this book, he advanced the idea (which he found in an ancient Greek manuscript) that the Earth orbits around the sun.

1543 Alcohol

When Julius Caesar visited Egypt in 48 B.C., he lingered there for nearly a year, so captivated was he by the charms of Cleopatra. Those charms were no doubt intensified by the fact that Cleopatra was in the habit of darkening and lengthening her eyebrows with antimony paste, and the Arabic word for powdered antimony was *al-koh'l*. This word eventually came into English to describe any fine powder or extract. It was not until well into the eighteenth century that *alcohol* came to be applied to the intoxicant in certain beverages, and by the nineteenth century, this meaning had almost totally replaced the original definition.

Alcoholism became a recognized disease by the 1850s, and the noun *alcoholic*, for someone so afflicted, followed soon after. And thanks to *that* word, author Wayne Oates used the word *workaholic* in the title of his book in 1971 to describe anyone whose addiction to work resembles an alcoholic's addiction to alcohol.

The word *drunk*, by the way, has more synonyms than any other word in the English language. In his fascinating book *Words*, the American author Paul Dickson lists no fewer than 2,231 of them — and they stretch all the way from page 247 to page 296 in the chapter entitled "Soused Synonyms."

1544 VENTER

Venter, from the Latin *venter*, meaning "abdomen" or "belly," is a legal term that first appeared in print near the end of the reign of Henry VIII to refer to one of two or more wives who produced offspring for the same husband. Henry himself had three venters, each of whom bore him a child: Catherine of Aragon, who gave birth to the future Queen Mary; Anne Boleyn, who bore the future Queen Elizabeth I; and Jane Seymour, who gave birth to the future Edward VI. Out of Henry's six wives, only the first three bore him offspring, and, oddly enough, none of his three children had any children of their own.

Incidentally, the Latin root *venter* that gives us this entry, also gives us the word *ventriloquist* (see page 108), because people who can speak in that fashion were at one time believed to be speaking from the belly instead of the throat.

1545 DANDRUFF

Although everyone today knows what this word means, no one knows where it came from. Several distinguished linguists have tried in earnest to track down its origin, but, according to the *OED*, no satisfactory explanation as to its etymology has ever been found.

We do know, however, that *dandruff* first appeared in print in English in 1545 (and, no doubt, on the scalp of an Englishman much earlier than that), when Raynold wrote in *Byrth Mankynde*: "They that haue blacke hayre haue more store of Dandruffe then others." Remedies for dandruff began appearing in English as early as 1601, when a chap named Holland translated the writings of the Roman historian Pliny: "The juice of Garlick being taken in drink clenseth the head from dandruffe." That's a great solution, Pliny. Now pass the mouthwash.

1546 HONEYMOON

The practice may be much older, but the word itself has been found in print no earlier than 1546, during the second-last year of the reign of Henry VIII, who had been married six times.

Contrary to popular belief, Henry VIII did not behead all six of his wives — only two of them. A mnemonic helps to remind us of the fate of each of the six: divorced, beheaded, died, divorced, beheaded, survived (the last one, Catherine Parr, outlived him).

1547 ABORTION

A contentious issue today, the word *abortion* has been traced back to 1547. The word took on more frequent use as the verb *abort* after the beginning, in 1957, of the race for space. The most famous mission to the moon to be aborted in mid-flight was Apollo 13 in April 1970. By great good luck, all three astronauts returned safely to Earth. Their voyage was later immortalized by Hollywood in Ron Howard's 1995 film, *Apollo 13*.

1548 SATELLITE

With the revival of classical learning during the Renaissance, thousands of Latin words poured into the English language, and *satellite* was one of them. When this word first appeared in print in English in 1548, it was used to describe a practice popular in ancient Rome: prominent politicians often hired "satellites," or hangers-on, to follow them through the streets to make themselves look important.

In 1611 *satellite* took on a new meaning when the German astronomer Johannes Kepler applied the term to the four largest moons of Jupiter, discovered the year before by the Italian astronomer Galileo. Kepler's choice was a good one because those moons follow the mighty planet Jupiter around the sun just as faithfully as those hangers-on in the streets of Rome.

1549 BLOCKHEAD

In bygone centuries, hats and wigs, when not being worn, were often mounted on a block of wood of the same shape as the head of the person who wore them. Because these blocks of wood had no brains inside, it was not long before people of low intelligence began to be called "blockheads." English author John Olde helped to start the new trend when, in 1549, he wrote about "blockheaded asses … (and) doublefaced frendes."

The American cartoonist Charles M. Schulz, creator of the *Peanuts* comic strip, was equally fond of this word. One of his characters, a brassy little medusa named Lucy, always called Charlie Brown a blockhead (and, come to think of it, Charlie's head does look like a hat block). Another character, Linus by name, always carried his blanket around with him for security, thereby coining the term *security blanket*, which is now in the dictionary.

1550 VACUUM

In 1550 Thomas Cranmer wrote, "Natural reason abhorreth vacuum, that is to say, that there shoulde be an emptye place, wherein no substance shoulde be." According to the *OED*, that passage is the first recorded use of the word *vacuum*, Latin for "empty," in the English language. Cranmer didn't exactly coin the word; he just pulled it straight out of Latin and stuck it into English. By the mid-1600s, *vacuum* came to be applied to a space from which the air had been pumped out (Robert Boyle and men of his ilk were busily experimenting with such things at the time).

By 1903 the modern vacuum cleaner was ready to make its debut. In the *Westmount Gazette* on May 30 of that year, we find: "There is a machine at work, called the 'vacuum cleaner,' which gives them all, in turn, a thorough spring cleaning." Of the countless millions of vacuum cleaners that have been manufactured since 1903, most have to be lugged from room to room. But now there are models whose vacuum motors are installed permanently in the basement of a house. You simply attach a hose to a little opening in the wall of each room and then flick a switch. You've heard of central heating? Now there's central suction.

1551 Smug

Smug appeared as early as 1551 in a translation of Thomas More's *Utopia* into English: "They be so smugge and smoethe, that they haue not so much as one heare [hair] of an honest man." In 1648 John Beaumont wrote: "His soft smug words tickle your wanton ear." In both these quotes, *smug* is used as a synonym for "neat," from the Low German *smuk*, which means "neat." But the meaning was gradually shifting to describe a self-satisfied and respectable air. In his diary on March 28, 1669, Samuel Pepys penned these words: "To the office with Tom, who looks mighty smug upon his marriage."

If you look up *smug* in the *OED*, you will discover it is followed by *smuggle* — "to convey [goods] clandestinely into [or out of] a country or district, in order to avoid payment of legal duties…" But on the next page you will find another definition for *smuggle* you may have been unaware of: "to cuddle, fondle, or caress." In support of this definition, the *OED* offers several quotations, including these: "This precious Saint … hath been seen to … kiss her many times over, as if it had been part of her Penance to be most filthily smuggled" (1679); "You may smuggle and grope" (1709); "He Smuggled her, and Squeez'd her" (1719). If your smuggling produces the results you are looking for, you will probably feel quite smug (just like Tom).

1552 BLACKMAIL

According to the *OED*, the word *blackmail* was first used to describe "a tribute formerly exacted from farmers and small owners in the border counties of England and Scotland, and along the Highland border, by freebooting chiefs, in return for protection or immunity from plunder." The earliest recorded use of the word dates back to 1552, when England and Scotland were still two separate countries and the ruins of Hadrian's Wall still stood as a silent reminder that even the Romans themselves could not conquer the wild and unruly land that is now synonymous with kilts and bagpipes.

But *blackmail* was not the only word born out of the bloodshed along the English-Scottish border. Some dictionaries still include the term *cornage* (based on the Latin *cornu*, meaning "horn"), a form of landholding found in northern England in bygone centuries under which the tenant farmer was required to sound a warning blast on a horn whenever he saw a band of angry Scots charging in for the kill. The word *carnage* (a bloody massacre) comes before *cornage* in the dictionary, but along the English-Scottish border it was usually the other way around.

1553 DOLLAR

Our word *dollar* can be traced back to *Joachimstaler*, a German coin first minted near a silver mine in Joachimsthal, Bohemia, in 1519. (*Joachimsthal* literally means "Joachim Valley," just as *Neanderthal* refers to the Neander Valley in Germany, where the remains of Neanderthal man were first discovered in 1856.) The coins from Joachimsthal were called *thalers*, *dalers*, *dallers* or *dollars*, and the word reached England by 1553. It was slow to catch on in England itself because the English were using pounds, shillings and pence — but it was liberally applied by the English to describe several foreign currencies, including the Spanish peso, a gold coin that circulated widely in the British North American colonies prior to and during the American Revolution.

When the Treaty of Paris was signed in 1783, Britain officially recognized the independence of the United States of America, and the fledging republic proceeded to establish its own currency thanks, largely, to the urgings of Thomas Jefferson, who favoured a decimal currency based on the dollar. His proposal was adopted by the Confederation Congress in 1785, and the first American dollars were minted in 1794. Strange, is it not, that the dollar is not the unit of currency in the country that gave birth to the word? The Germans used the *Deutschemark* until 2002, when it adopted the euro.

Incidentally, the dollar sign ($) was not, as many people believe, derived from the letters *U* and *S* (for United States) being superimposed one on the another. This symbol was in use even before America was colonized, and apparently dates back to the *pillar dollar* in Spain. This coin, also known as a "piece of eight" because it was worth eight *reales* (a *real* being another old Spanish coin), bore on its surface the letter *S* as a partial representation of the figure eight, and two vertical strokes representing the Pillars of Hercules, the ancient name for the Strait of Gibraltar.

1554 MAYPOLE

Since prehistoric times, people have held festivals to celebrate the return of spring. During the Middle Ages, the people of England set aside the first of May as a day of rejoicing. Flowers adorned doors, windows and gateposts, gifts were exchanged, and the fairest maid of the village was chosen Queen of the May. Somewhere along the way, the maypole was added to the festivities (the term itself has not been found in print earlier than 1554, although the practice of erecting such a pole likely goes back to an earlier date).

Each village erected a maypole and attached to the top long ribbons, which the villagers held while they danced around in a circle until the pole was covered in bright colours. Each pole was cut as high as the mast of a ship of one hundred tons.

Although it is widely believed that all the maypoles in England were cut down during the Puritanical rule of Oliver Cromwell in the 1650s, such was not the case. One Puritan eyewitness reported that May Day 1654 "was more observed by people going a-maying than for years past; and, indeed, much sin committed by wicked meetings with fiddlers, drunkenness, ribaldry and the like [with] … shameful powdered-hair men, and painted and spotted women…"

1555 HURRICANE

Many of the new words born during the exploration of the New World were inspired by the strange new forms of life encountered there. Hurricanes, an equatorial phenomenon unknown to Europeans, served as an outstanding example of the hitherto unknown dangers that lay in wait for those unsuspecting adventurers. This word comes to us by way of the Spanish adaptation, *huracan,* of a Native Caribbean word for those catastrophic storms defined by the *American Heritage Dictionary* as follows: "a severe tropical cyclone with winds exceeding seventy-five miles per hour, originating in the tropical regions of the Atlantic Ocean or Caribbean Sea, travelling north, northwest, or northeast from its point of origin, and usually involving heavy rains. See synonyms at *wind.*"

When you turn to *wind,* you discover why the *American Heritage Dictionary* is one of the best on the market. Not only does it give you a list of synonyms, but explanatory notes on how each synonym differs from all the others in the list. Under *wind,* you find *wind, breeze, zephyr, blast, gust, gale, whirlwind, tornado, twister, cyclone, hurricane, typhoon* and *waterspout.* You discover that *hurricane* originates in the West Indies, whereas a *typhoon* (from the Chinese *ta feng,* "big wind," first appearing in English in 1588) applies to windstorms in the western Pacific and China Sea. The term that covers them both is *cyclone*: "the general term for a system of rotating wind, often hundreds of miles in diameter, that travels widely, brings driving rain and often great destruction." This term is much newer than the other two, not appearing in print until 1848. It is based on the Greek *kuklos,* or "circle," because of the circular path of the wind.

Also in 1555: *bookkeeper*

1556 COACH

Athletic coaches and railway coaches can both trace their linguistic origin back to a small town in central Europe. It all began hundreds of years ago in Kocs, Hungary, where some of the first passenger vehicles, or *coaches,* were manufactured. The town gave its name to the carriages and, gradually, the term *kocs*, or "coach," came to be applied to carriages built elsewhere as well. The word first reached England in 1556, but received a fresh new twist in the early nineteenth century when students in English universities began calling their tutors "coaches," possibly because the assistance they rendered conveyed the students through their examinations. And because athletic instructors could carry their students to victory on the playing field, they came to be called coaches, too.

1557 Bullet

When *bullet* first appeared in print in English, it described a cannonball of metal or stone. The cannons in use back then often had a tapered barrel, because cannonballs varied in size. You simply shoved the ball down the barrel until it got stuck, then you lit the fuse.

If the barrel was made of wood, as they sometimes were, and the ball was really wedged in tightly, the back of the cannon would sometime exploded in one's face. A few years after 1557 the word *bullet* was being used the way it is today, to describe a small ball of lead fired from a pistol or other gun of small calibre.

Bullet comes from the French *boulette*, meaning "little ball," and *ballot* comes from the Italian *ballota*, also meaning "little ball." A bullet looks like a ball, but a ballot is simply a sheet of paper we mark on election day. It comes from the Italian word for "little ball" because balls have often been used in elections. The ancient Greeks voted by dropping a white stone ball into a container when they favoured a candidate and a black stone ball when they didn't. Even today we speak of someone being *blackballed* from a club.

1558 Twangle

The verb *twang*, "to pluck a stringed instrument," first appeared in print in 1542, when Henry VIII (who, some say, composed "Greensleeves") sat on the throne of England. Sixteen years later, in the year that Queen Mary died and left the throne to her half-sister Elizabeth, the more melodious synonym *twangle* joined the English language. Both words are examples of musical onomatopoeia, along with *pluck, strum, pick* and *plunk*, all of which apply to stringed instruments. *Pluck* and *pick* go back to the Middle Ages, but *strum* and *plunk* are relative newcomers to English. *Strum* first appeared in print on the eve of the American Revolution, in 1775, and *plunk* had its debut thirty years later, in 1805.

1559 SUPERCELESTIAL

When William Cunningham first used this word in 1559 ("… the marvellous course and sundry motions, of the supercelestiall bodies"), he was referring to things that he believed were situated above the canopy of the heavens — in other words, above the sky itself. The word is a combination of the Latin roots *super*, meaning "above," and *caelum*, "heaven." In 1672 William Sterry placed the carpenter from Nazareth high above the sky: "Jesus Christ is a supernatural, supercaelestial Spirit [today we would say *superstar*], far above the nature of Souls or Angels in the first Creation."

The ancient Greeks had a feeling for supercelestial matters, believing that the Earth itself is composed of four elements — air, fire, earth and water — with the fifth element reserved for things heavenly. That's where our word *quintessence* (the highest or best) comes from. It's based on the Latin root *quintus*, for "fifth" (the Romans having borrowed many of their ideas from the Greeks) and refers to the fifth, or heavenly, element of creation — hence, the best (as in the phrase "the quintessence of good taste").

1560 DING-DONG

The earliest example of *ding-dong* in print occurred around 1560 with this sentence: "In the midst of his play he hears the … bell goe ding dong." The first ding-dongs were applied to doorbells, dinner bells or fire bells. But as time went by and clocks became more musical, *ding-dong* had its meaning extended. In *Clock and Watches*, published in 1860, we find this sentence: "… the clock [will] strike 3 ding dongs and one bell more."

Ding-dong is the unofficial trademark of Avon, a company that sells beauty aids door-to-door. The company was founded by D.H. McConnell, who began selling books door-to-door in 1886 but found there were fewer doors slammed in his face if he sold perfume. On the company's fiftieth anniversary, he changed the name to Avon because he was such an ardent admirer of William Shakespeare and his hometown of Stratford-on-Avon.

1561 GROTESQUE

Although *grotesque* is now used as an adjective, it first entered the English language as a noun to describe a type of decorative painting or sculpture that portrayed human or animal forms fantastically interwoven with foliage and flowers. In its earliest use, dating back to 1561, both the meaning and spelling differ from the way we use the word today: "Item, twa paintit broddis the ane of the muses and he uther of crotescque…" Around 1640 the spelling changed to *grotesque* from the original Italian, and this spelling has been retained ever since.

More recently, the word *grotesque* developed a new twist which I frequently heard on the streets of London in the early 1960s. Anything one disapproved of could be described by the slangy new adjective *grotty*.

1562 DIABETES

Although the disease is probably much older than the word, diabetes, from the Greek *dia,* meaning "through," and *bainein,* "to go," first appeared in print in English when William Turner in 1562 wrote: "It is good for the flixe to the chamber pot called the best Physicianes Diabetes, that is when a man maketh water oft and much." In 1649 a chap named Culpepper described diabetes as "continual pissing," the word *piss* being considered vulgar in our time but perfectly respectable back then. In 1690 the Earl of Gainsborough "died lately of a diabetes," as did many others until the discovery of insulin in the 1920s.

Incidentally, the word *piss* was used by Chaucer in his *Canterbury Tales* (first published in 1388). It appears in an old proverb that medieval monks were allegedly familiar with: "Money makes the pot boil, though the devil piss in the fire." It's difficult to say exactly when *piss* became a vulgar word, but probably its last appearance in polite society took place when French Premier Clemenceau made his famous remark about British Prime Minister Lloyd George at the Versailles Peace Conference in 1919: *"Ah, si je pouvais pisser comme il parle!"*

1563 ARCHITECT

Look at any topographical map of the world and you will see two geographical features directly related to the etymology of the word *architect*. In the Arctic, Pacific and Mediterranean, you will see clusters of islands called *archipelagos,* from the Greek *archi,* meaning "chief," and *pelagos,* meaning "sea." This term was first applied by the Greeks to the island-dotted Aegean Sea, which was, for them, the "chief sea."

Elsewhere on that world map you'll see mountain ranges: the Alps, Rockies, Andes and Himalayas. Those mountains were built by tectonic forces (from the Greek *tekton,* meaning a worker or builder) deep within the Earth's crust that shift, grind, buckle and push new crust upward to form new mountains.

Architect, therefore, means "chief builder."

The word first appeared in print in English in 1563 (according to the *OED*) in John Shute's book *The First and Chief Grounds of Architecture.* The 1560s were an exciting time to be an architect in England: wealth was pouring into the country from overseas trade and plunder; meanwhile, a lot of money that formerly left the country to fill the coffers of the Catholic Church in Rome, was now available as well, owing to the religious changes brought about by Henry VIII. The new money in circulation was lavished on palatial country estates, many of which were built on lands formerly occupied by the more than eight hundred monasteries that Henry confiscated when he made himself head of the Church of England. A new class of Englishman was emerging — rich, busy, vibrant and full of boundless optimism. The courtier, the merchant, and the bluewater sailor home from the sea all built their mansions as fast as the money could pay for them.

Over this feverish building boom reigned the Virgin Queen, Elizabeth I. So intense was the loyalty and devotion she inspired in her subjects that many of the new country estates were built with an E-shaped floor plan in her honour. Of course, many nobles no doubt did this in order to curry royal favour.

1564 African

It is not without significance that William Shakespeare was born in the very year that the word *African* first appeared in print in English. The name "Africa" itself had been around much longer, and in fact was the name of the old Roman province in northern Africa before it was applied to the entire continent. Shakespeare drew much of his poetic inspiration from the English mariners who were sailing westward to Virginia, eastward to Cathay and southward to Africa. Yet, while his young mind was being nurtured by tales of far-off exotic places, there was a darker, sinister side to the glory and excitement of overseas discoveries. Sea dogs like John Hawkins were raiding the coast of Africa in search of slaves. At first, Hawkins purchased — and sometimes stole — slaves from the Portuguese slave-catchers along the African coast, making his profit when he sold his cargoes of human flesh to the Spanish colonies in the West Indies. Then he tried capturing slaves himself to eliminate the Portuguese middlemen, but in the battle that ensued he lost a number of his own men. Gradually, many of the Africans along the coast became middlemen themselves, capturing slaves from the interior and selling them to the European ships anchored offshore. When English subjects of a later century became disgusted with the commerce in human flesh, slavery was abolished throughout the British Empire by an act of Parliament in 1833.

A friend in the old-car hobby, Donald Thomas, passed away peacefully on December 31, 2002, after a lengthy illness. Soon after his death, his good friend Mike Chernoski published in *Old Autos* a poem Don had written some time ago:

WORDS FROM THE SOUL
A voice in the wind whispered to me
If you're free, hard work can be fun.

So I made up my mind in that moment
That I was going to run.
So I ran until I found freedom
In a land where all men are free.
Oh, yes, I'm still hardworking.
The fun is that I'm free.

1565 TOBACCO

Tobacco was first brought to England from the Spanish West Indies in 1565. It was an instant success, judging from the words of an Englishman named Harrison: "In these daies ... the taking-in of the smoke of the Indian herbe called Tabaco, by an instrument formed like a little ladell, whereby it passeth from the mouth into the hed & stomach, is gretlie taken-up & used in England." Not everyone in England, however, took up the habit. King James I, who ruled from 1603 to 1625, regarded smoking as "a custom loathsome to the eye, hatefull to the nose, harmfull to the brain, dangerous to the lungs, and in the black stinking fume thereof, nearest resembling the horrible stygian smoke of the pit that is bottomless."

Tobacco was cultivated by the Indians of North and South America long before the arrival of Columbus, and they smoked it for both ceremonial and medicinal purposes. Europeans developed a taste for the "stinking weed" after Jean Nicot, French ambassador to Lisbon, sent some tobacco seeds to the queen of France, Catherine de Medici, in 1559. Nicot became immortalized when the word *nicotine* was coined in his honour, yet he would have preferred a different kind of fame. He laboured for forty years compiling the world's first French dictionary, and before he died in 1594 his mammoth work of scholarship had been completed. But he is chiefly remembered today for *nicotine*, a word that isn't even mentioned in his dictionary.

1566 SEASICK

Although English sailors and fishermen had no doubt been throwing up on board ship all through the Middle Ages, the word *seasick* did not appear in print until this quote from 1566: "I am even yet so Seasicke that I faynt as I go." Shakespeare himself used the word in 1611 when he wrote *The Winter's Tale*: "... the shepherd's daughter ... began to be much seasick." In 1701 the Irish-born English playwright George Farquhar wrote, "Look ye, Captain, I shall be Sea-sick presently." And in 1826, a Miss Mitford used the word in a way no one else has done before or since: "She ... pined for the water, and was ... in a new sense of the word, sea-sick" (meaning she longed for the sea in the way others become homesick).

Incidentally, have you ever noticed the similarity between the words *nausea* and *nautical*? The former comes from the Greek root *naus*, for "ship," and the latter from the Greek root *nautes*, meaning "sailor." Apparently, not all ancient Greeks were hardy sailors. Some of them, it would seem, spent some time retching in the rigging. Both these Greek roots closely resemble *nesos*, the Greek word for "island," and this similarity is not surprising. A Greek *nautes* would need a *naus* to reach a *nesos*. And he might feel nauseated while doing it.

1567 LOTTERY

Although lotteries date back to ancient times, the first one in England was chartered by Elizabeth I in 1567 to raise money for the repair of harbours and other public works. In 1612 James I granted permission for a lottery to help support the fledgling colony of Virginia in the New World. Fifteen years later, a series of draws raised money for the construction of an aqueduct into the city of London. In both England and the United States, lotteries were used to finance a variety of worthy projects, including the construction of the British Museum, the installation of guns for the defence of Philadelphia, and the building of a road over the Cumberland Mountains (an undertaking supervised by George Washington). Corruption and abuses led to their abolition in England in 1826. The U.S. Congress brought them to an end in 1895; the idea was not revived in the United States until 1963, when New Hampshire launched a state lottery that proved to be such a financial success that several other American states have since organized lotteries of their own.

1568 ALLIGATOR

According to an early European explorer, alligators were so plentiful from the swamplands of Florida to the mouth of the Mississippi that you could cross some rivers simply by stepping on their backs. The Spanish called these fearsome creatures *al lagarto,* "the lizard," which evolved over the years through *allagarto, alagarto, alegarto, alligarta, alligarter* and *allegater* to *alligator.* In 1568 John Hortop wrote, "In this river we killed a monstrous Lagarto or Crocodile." For the next four centuries the killing continued, with as many as a quarter of a million alligators slaughtered each year so that their hides could be turned into purses, shoes and handbags. In the late 1940s stringent laws were passed to protect the alligator, which is now staging a dramatic comeback from the brink of extinction.

Although crocodiles are found in the southeastern United States and in parts of South America, Africa and Asia, the alligator is found only in the southeastern United States and along the Yangtze River in China. Why the alligator would thrive only in two so widely separated places is a mystery that has never been solved.

If you happen to meet one of these reptiles in the wild and aren't sure whether it's an alligator or a crocodile, take a close (but not too close!) look at the snout. Crocodiles have a narrower snout and an enlarged fourth tooth which is exposed when the mouth is closed. The word *crocodile* comes from the Greek *krokodilos,* "worm of the pebbles," because of its habit of basking in the sun.

1569 OBELISK

When Napoleon led the French army into Egypt in 1799, he pointed to the pyramids and roused his men with these stirring words: "Forty centuries look down upon you." His men might have been less than eager to follow him into battle had they stopped to consider that the pyramid was the symbol of darkness and death for the ancient Egyptians (which is why all pyramids were built on the west bank of the Nile, toward the setting sun).

Napoleon should have pointed to all the obelisks, for they were the symbol of light and life as personified by the sun god Ra (perhaps because the obelisk, a word of Greek origin, is similar in shape to the rays of the sun).

We will never know how many obelisks the ancient Egyptians built, but many of them are still standing — and not just in Egypt. The largest of the Egyptian obelisks was brought from Thebes to Alexandria by Constantine the Great around the year 330, then to Rome by Constantius, who placed it in the Circus Maximus. It reaches over one hundred feet in height and weighs more than four hundred and fifty tons. Two of the best-known obelisks stand on opposite sides of the Atlantic Ocean — one on the banks of the Thames and the other in New York City's Central Park. Both are nearly seventy feet high and weigh more than two hundred tons (the London one being somewhat smaller and lighter due to weathering and chipping, having lain on the ground in Egypt for several hundred years before being erected in England). These obelisks are know as Cleopatra's Needles, although the queen of the Nile was born fifteen hundred years after they were built.

1570 Pistol

If you have ever wondered where this word comes from, the *Encyclopaedia Britannica* gives you three etymologies to choose from: *pistol* may have come from Pistoia, a city in Italy where the weapon allegedly originated; it may have come from *pistole*, an ancient coin, the diameter of which, some say, matched the bore of the earliest handguns; or it may have come from *pistallo*, meaning "pommel," the horn on the front of a saddle, because mounted troops carried the weapon in that location. In any event, the word was first used in English in 1570 by Sir Humphrey Gilbert, who wrote, in *Queen Elizabethes Achademy*, "To teache noble men and gentle-men … to skirmish on horsbacke with pistolles."

But these firearms we call pistols were in use in England several decades before Gilbert put the word in print. During the Middle Ages, the only firearms for quite some time were cannons, which had to be lugged around from battlefield to battlefield. Then the hand cannon, or shoulder weapon, was introduced; but it cannot be classified as a true pistol because its user needed both hands: one to hold it, the other to ignite the charge.

Around 1515, an unknown gunsmith invented the wheel-lock, which made a spark when it struck the flint. Now soldiers no longer had to carry a live flame to ignite the powder in their guns. They could fire the gun with one hand, leaving the other hand free to brandish another weapon. Wheel-lock guns were the chief firearms used in the cavalry of Henry VIII and Francis I, only to be replaced by the more efficient flintlock pistol, which appeared in the mid-1500s.

1571 ATHEIST

In 1571 an English writer named Golding wrote about "the Atheistes which say ... there is no God." The word, from the Greek *a*, "not," and *theos*, "a god," first appeared in an England that was just beginning to accustom itself to the new religious settlement imposed by Queen Elizabeth I in 1559. When Henry VIII died in 1547, his nine-year-old son Edward took over, only to die six years later, after his guardians had advanced the cause of Protestantism. Next in line was Mary (1553–58), who earned the title "Bloody Mary" by burning three hundred Protestants at the stake in a futile attempt to restore the Roman Catholic faith in England. When Elizabeth ascended the throne in 1558, England was teetering on the brink of civil war, and it is to Elizabeth's great credit that she solved the crisis with an ingenious solution: a new Church of England that would be part Catholic and part Protestant. Elizabeth was not overly concerned with things theological, and although atheism would never be encouraged, she preferred to keep one's creed a private matter. She had "no desire to make windows in men's souls," only to keep peace in her realm.

1572 PURITAN

Although Elizabeth I's new Church of England was a satisfactory compromise for most of her subjects, extreme Protestants objected on the grounds that Elizabeth had not gone far enough in purifying the Church of England of all traces of Roman Catholicism. And because these critics wanted a pure form of worship, they became know as Puritans. They wanted to be rid of bishops and priests, and even objected to the use of music in church services. "The service of God," they argued, "is grievously abused by piping with organs, singing, ringing and trawling songs from one side to another; with the squeaking of chanting choristers disguised in white surplices."

Although Elizabeth managed to keep the Puritans under control, her successor, James I, was not so lucky. He threatened to "harry them out of the land" if they did not conform to his rule, and thousands of them took the hint by sailing to the New World. James' son, Charles I, was bothered by them even more. After ruling for eleven years without calling Parliament — many members of which had become Puritans — Charles was finally forced in 1640 to summon them together to ask for money. That set off a chain of events that led to the English Civil War, which ended with Charles' defeat and execution by beheading.

Since those days, the excitement has died down. The word *puritan* has lost its capital letter and today is used to describe anyone who is unusually strict in morals and behaviour.

1573 WHIPLASH

This word was used as early as 1573 to describe the lash of a whip. By the nineteenth century it had acquired a figurative use, as shown in this 1894 remark: "Nothing escapes the whiplash of the college wit."

But it took the automobile and the twentieth century to give this word the meaning it has today: injury to the neck and spine of a motorist hit from behind by another vehicle. Whiplash injuries sometimes do not make themselves felt until several days or weeks after the accident, and if you jump at a quick cash settlement, you may regret it later. The headrests that are now a mandatory feature of automobiles offer you your best protection against whiplash.

1574 DEMOCRACY

In 1574 an Englishman named Whitgift wrote, "In respect that the people are not secluded, but have their interest in church-matters, it is a democracy, or a popular estate." Whitgift spelled the word *democraty*, but gradually the *t* changed to a *c*. Standardized spelling of English words did not become widespread until the mid-eighteenth century, when Dr.

Johnson's famous dictionary, published in 1755, helped to fix many spellings that are still observed today. When Whitgift wrote *democraty*, he was living in an England that had had the printing press for less than a hundred years, and printers often spelled the same word several different ways on the same page in order to fill a certain number of spaces on each line.

Democracy is often defined as "government of the people, by the people and for the people," a phrase attributed to Abraham Lincoln in his Gettysburg Address. But did Lincoln in fact originate this immortal phrase? Several years earlier, Theodore Parker had written, "Democracy is direct self-government, over all the people, by all the people, and for all the people." Lincoln had a copy of Theodore Parker's speeches, given to him by his law partner, William Herndon. A few years earlier still, Daniel Webster, in a famous speech known as the Reply to Hayne, said, "The people's government, made for the people, made by the people, and answerable to the people." A third of a century earlier, James Monroe expressed the same idea. And where did Monroe get it from? Five hundred years before Monroe was born, John Wycliffe had written that "this Bible [which he had translated from Latin into English] is for the government of the people, by the people, and for the people." And nearly two thousand years before the age of Wycliffe, Cleon of ancient Athens spoke of a ruler "of the people, by the people, and for the people." What ancient source inspired Cleon to speak those words, no one knows.

1575 SKEPTIC

Comments written in the margins of books are collectively known as marginalia. During the Middle Ages, when copies of the Bible were laboriously handwritten, the monks who produced them often worked under a vow of silence. When the urge to communicate became too great to ignore, these monks often wrote notes to each other in the margins of the Bibles they were copying. In the copies that survive today, we can read the messages they furtively scribbled to one another.

When *skeptic* first appeared in an English sentence in 1575, it was just a query scribbled in the margin of a letter written to a chap named Randolph by a fellow named Buchanan. From that humble beginning, *skeptic* became a permanent addition to the English language. It comes from the Greek root *skeptesthai*, meaning "to consider" or "to investigate." The ancient Greek philosopher Pyrrho and his followers called themselves Skeptics because they doubted the possibility of real knowledge of any kind. The most skeptical of all Americans living today apparently come from Missouri, long famous as the "Show Me State" because its inhabitants have a reputation for needing to see something before they will believe it.

1576 CANARY-BIRD

When the Romans first reached the Canary Islands, which lie sixty-five miles west of the coast of Spanish Morocco, they found them to be infested with wild dogs, and so they named this newly discovered land the *canaria insula*, "the island of wild dogs." (The English word *canine* comes from the same Latin root.) When barbarian hordes overran the western half of the Roman Empire in the fifth century, the Dark Ages descended upon western Europe and the Canary Islands were forgotten until they were rediscovered in 1270. By the mid-1400s, the Spanish began occupying the islands, which still bore the original name. The yellow songbird that was found in abundance on the islands was named the canary-bird, and word of this bird reached England by 1576, when *canary-bird* entered the English language as the name of a bird named after islands that were named after dogs. The name was shortened to *canary* in 1592.

By an interesting coincidence, the word *bow-wow* (to represent the barking of a dog) entered the English language in the same year as *canary-bird*. You would think *bow-wow* could be translated "as is" into any other language, but such is not the case. If you travel around the world, you'll find that dogs bark differently in different languages. According to the eminent American linguist Dr. Mario Pei, writing in the September 9, 1967, issue of *Saturday Review*: "Corresponding to our assorted bow-wow, woof-woof, yip-yip and arf-arf we find French *oua-oua* (pronounced 'wah-wah'), Italian *bu-bu*, Spanish *guau-guau* or *jau-jau* (pronounced 'how-how'), Rumanian *ham-ham* (with *a* of 'father'), German *hau-hau* or *wau-wau*, Russian *vas-vas* or *vaf-vaf*, Arabic *'au-au'* (constrict the throat at the start), Vietnamese *gau-gau*, Turkish *hov-hov*, Chinese *wang-wang*, and Japanese *wan-wan*. Even ancient Sanskrit had *bhuk-bhuk*."

1577 CATAPULT

The catapult, from the Greek *kata*, "against," and *pallein*, "to hurl," has been used as a weapon of war since ancient times. When Archimedes first saw one at Lacedemon, he reportedly exclaimed, "O Hercules, now manhood is come to an end!" Just before the onset of ancient battles, it was customary for both sides to use a catapult to hurl insulting messages tied to stones and rocks. During the wars between Rome and Carthage, women often cut off their long hair and twisted it into ropes for the catapults. The ships of the Byzantine navy were equipped with catapults on deck to hurl flaming balls of pitch (the dreaded "Greek fire") into the enemy rigging. And in the first few weeks of World War I, some catapults were wheeled out of museums and put back into action on the battlefield until the production of guns and bullets could catch up to wartime demand.

The most destructive use of the catapult throughout all of history took place in the middle of the fourteenth century. The Black Death, or bubonic plague, which swept across Europe in the late 1340s, first broke out on the Crimean peninsula in a fortress besieged by Italian troops. When the commander of the fortress saw his men and animals succumbing to this horrible disease, he decided the Italians should suffer the same fate. Dead and dying men and horses were catapulted over the walls, into the ranks of the unsuspecting Italians, who fled in panic and sailed for home as fast as the winds would carry them.

But they were too late. The plague broke out on board, and when they landed in Italy, it spread like a cancer up the Italian peninsula, over the Alps into France, across the English Channel, and onto the British Isles. One person in four went to the grave, and as people tried to flee from what they believed was the wrath of God, they carried the sickness into new towns and villages, creating further panic and spreading the disease in ever-widening circles.

In the midst of all the suffering and death, one little village in England — Eyam by name — had its finest hour. Recognizing the highly contagious nature of the disease, the local village priest persuaded the three hundred and fifty inhabitants of Eyam to hold their ground and hope for the best. They did, and when it was all over, two hundred and fifty of them were still alive to bury the hundred who had died. The priest was one of the lucky ones.

1578 Penguin

A week before Christmas in 1577, Francis Drake set sail from England with five ships for a secret destination: the Pacific Ocean, where no English ships had ever sailed before. His objective was to launch a series of lightning attacks on the Spanish treasure ships carrying gold and silver from the Incan Empire in Peru to the Isthmus of Panama. So successful was Drake in sinking Spanish ships and capturing Spanish gold that he dared not return home by the same route he had come. After sailing as far north as San Francisco Bay in a vain attempt to find a water route through North America, he struck west across the Pacific and so sailed around the great globe itself, returning home in England after thirty-five months at sea. Of the original five ships, only one, the *Golden Hind*, returned to England heavily laden with captured booty. He shared it with his queen, Elizabeth I, and received a knighthood.

His voyage accomplished something else as well. In order to reach the Pacific, Drake sailed through the treacherous Strait of Magellan and noticed some flightless seabirds, which he called "penguins," from the Welsh *pen*, meaning "head," and *gwyn*, "white" — probably suggested by a Welsh sailor on board. Drake even named an island in honour of the new bird.

1579 Violin

Edmund Spenser introduced the word *violin*, from the Italian *violino*, into the English language when he wrote in 1579: "I see Calliope speeds to the place, where my Goddesse shines: And after her the other Muses trace, with their Violines." In 1713 a rare use of the word *violin* cropped up when it was used as a verb meaning to entice or seduce by violin-playing. The lady in question remains anonymous, but her fate can still be read in the pages of the *OED* under the verb form of *violin*: "Was not Madame W. plaid out of her Reputation, and violin'd into a Match below her Quality?" She sounds like the woman who said she was going to marry a concert pianist and then ran off with a piano player.

1580 AMNESTY

In writing about the Greek author Plutarch in 1580, Sir Thomas North mentions "a law that no man should be called in question, nor troubled for things that were past ... called *Amnestia*, or law of Oblivion." From this Greek word *amnestia*, "a forgetting," we derive our modern word *amnesty*, a pardoning of past offences. When you grant someone an amnesty (as President Carter did for the draft dodgers who left the United States during the Vietnam War) you are promising to forget about past wrongs. This is why amnesty is closely related to *amnesia*, a loss of memory. And if you ever have your mind go blank while writing an examination, you are suffering from *examnesia*, a new word proposed by Lois Grant of Calgary, Alberta.

If you look closely at the original Greek root *amnestia*, you will find it divides into the prefix *a*, or "not," and the main root *mnemon*, "mindful." In other words, if you forget about something, you are no longer mindful of it. That root *mnemon* gives us the modern word *mnemonics* (pronounced ni-MON-iks), which is the study and use of techniques that aid the memory. If, for example, you confuse stalactites with stalagmites (those clumps of limestone that hang from the ceiling or stick up from the floor of a cave), just imagine that the letter *c* in stalactite stands for ceiling and the letter *g* in stalagmite stands for ground.

Also in 1580: *goodbye, lexicon*

1581 DIARY

One of the earliest English writers to use this word was the poet, dramatist, playwright and leading man of letters Ben Jonson (1572–1637), when he wrote: "This is my diary, Wherein I note my actions of the day." The word is based on *dies*, Latin for "day." The most famous diary by an English author was the one kept by Samuel Pepys (pronounced peeps) between 1660 and 1669. In graphic detail, Pepys describes, among other things, the ravages of the plague in London in 1665 and the destruction wrought the following year by the Great Fire. But his snooping contemporaries were not able to read his diary, because Pepys wrote it in a shorthand that was not deciphered until 1825.

1582 MOLASSES

William Shakespeare was a youth of eighteen in the year 1582, when *molasses* first appeared in English. Shakespeare had at least thirteen different ways of spelling his own name, and if you knew only one way to spell a word back then, you were considered not very bright. *Molasses* gave you the chance to wallow in a orthographic orgy of variant spellings, including *melasus, molossos, malosses, mallassus, mellasses, mullasses, mollossus, melasses* and, of course, *molasses*. All these versions appeared in print until the spelling of English words became standardized around the middle of the eighteenth century. Each of its various versions is based on the Latin word, *mellaceus,* "honey-like."

When the American author Theodore Dreiser wrote *An American Tragedy* in 1925, he gave to *molasses* a fresh new twist: "'You're the cutest thing here,' whispered Clyde, hugging her fondly. 'Gee, but you can pour on the molasses, kid, when you want to,' she called out loud."

1583 MOSQUITO

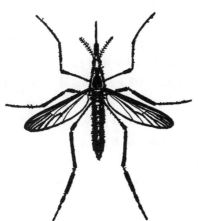

In *Hakluyt's Voyages,* published in 1583, M. Phillips writes: "We were also oftentimes greatly annoyed with a kinde of flie, ... the Spaniards called them Musketas." The Spanish word took its inspiration from the Latin *musca,* "fly."

It was not until 1897 that a certain type of mosquito was identified as a carrier of malaria (a word that entered English via the Italian *mal aria* in 1740 and which literally means "bad air," because of the malodorous exhalations of swampy regions).

Vaccines and pesticides have brought that and other types of mosquitoes under control, but we would do ourselves a disservice if we wiped out the mosquito altogether. This pesky bug is found all the way from the tropics to the Arctic and provides a convenient source of food for many birds, animals and fish, some of which might not survive if the mosquito were not around. If these predators of the mosquito did not survive and thrive, they would not be around to eat other insects, either, and we could easily be overwhelmed with pests far worse than the lowly mosquito.

1584 SPANGLED

"Oh, say, can you see, by the dawn's early light / What so proudly we hailed at the twilight's last gleaming…" When Francis Scott Key wrote those words in 1814 and set them to music, he called his song "The Star-Spangled Banner," officially adopted by the U.S. Congress in 1931 as the national anthem of the United States. *Spangled*, an adjective, was first used in print (according to the *OED*) in 1584 by a chap named Lodge: "Spangled hobbie horses are for children." *Spangle*, a noun based on the Old English word for "buckle," first appeared around 1420 and, the *OED* tells us, described "a small round thin piece of glittering metal (usually brass) with a hole in the centre to pass a thread through, used for the decoration of textile fabrics and other materials of various sorts."

It took a lot of glittering to produce the national anthem of the United States — a whole night of it, in fact. Francis Scott Key was a Washington lawyer when the War of 1812 broke out between the United States and Britain. In September 1814, the British burned Washington and then began shelling Fort McHenry, one of the forts that successfully defended the city of Baltimore. Key witnessed the all-night bombardment and was delighted to see the American flag still flying over the fortress in "the dawn's early light." He promptly sat down and wrote "The Star-Spangled Banner," revised it the next night in a Baltimore hotel, and had it printed anonymously under the title, "Defense of Fort." On September 20 it was published in a local newspaper and quickly became popular throughout the nation. We can thank Key for the words, but we ought to thank the British for the inspiration — and the music. "The Star-Spangled Banner" is set to the tune of an old English drinking song, "To Anacreon in Heaven."

1585 Eyebrow

Although the English-speaking peoples had hair above their eyes even in Anglo-Saxon times, they used the word *eagebru¢* (I-bre) instead of *eyebrow*. When James Higgins in 1585 defined the word *supercilium* as "the ridge of haire above the eye lids or the eye browes," he won for himself everlasting fame as the first English writer to use the word *eyebrow* in print (at least until we uncover an earlier example).

If the quotations in the *OED* are any indication, artificial eyebrows were at one time quite popular, and were apparently made of mouse-hide. In 1718 the English poet Matthew Prior wrote: "If we don't catch a Mouse To-night, Alas! no Eye-brows for To-morrow." And in 1703 in *The Tender Husband*, the English playwright Richard Steele makes hubby sound like a male chauvinist pig: "Pry'y thee, wench, bring me my black eyebrows out of the next room."

You may have noticed that some people have, not two eyebrows, but one, because of the hair that grows just above the bridge of their nose. In other words, they sport one long eyebrow that runs from one side of their face to the other. But you will look in vain in the *OED* for a word to describe such people. Fortunately, such a word has recently been invented: cybrow, from the one-eyed Cyclops in Greek mythology.

1586 Symposium

This word first appeared in English in 1586 as the title of one of Plato's translated dialogues, *Symposium*, in which he discusses his concept of ideal love, thus giving rise to the expression *platonic love* or *platonic relationship*. Plato must have been sitting around drinking with some friends when he wrote it, because that's what *symposium* means in Greek: a drinking party accompanied by conversation and intellectual stimulation. How many university professors realize the origin of this term when they instruct their students to attend a symposium?

Incidentally, Plato's real name was Aristocles. His friends called him Plato because of his broad shoulders, and the Greek root *platus* means "broad." From that same root we get *plate, plateau, platform, platypus* and the North and South Platte Rivers in Nebraska.

Also in 1586: *bamboo*

1587 MASQUERADE

The *OED* offers two possible origins for the word *masquerade*. It may have come from the Spanish *mascara* (and the lady who wears mascara is disguising her real appearance), which many etymologists believe came from the Arabic *maskharah*, meaning "laughingstock" or "buffoon." Other scholars claim *masquerade* comes from the Persian *mascarar*, then up through the Old French *mascurer* to the modern French *machurer*, "to blacken (the face)." The Old English derivative of that same Persian root may be *maescre* or *macula*, meaning a spot or blemish. From that last root we get *immaculate* to describe something without spot or blemish.

Regardless of the true origin of the word *masquerade*, the word *immaculate* is fascinating in its own right. It is just one of many English words widely known with its prefix but rarely known or used without it. Some people keep an immaculate home, but would you call a sloppy house "maculate"? Perhaps not, but you could, because *maculate* has been around since 1490 as an adjective serving as the opposite of *immaculate*. *Maculate* is also a verb, which the *OED* defines as "to spot, stain, soil, defile, or pollute." Other words famous for their prefixes are *impeccable* and *disgruntle*, but you can also find *peccable* and *gruntle* in the dictionary.

1588 TYPHOON

It took courage to sail through uncharted waters in the 1500s, especially in light of stories warning about sea serpents, whirlpools and sailing off the edge of the world. English sailors who ventured into the waters of the Far East often encountered storms more ferocious than anything they had known back in England. In the account of *Frederick's Voyages*, written in 1588, T. Hickock describes the fury of one of these storms: "I went to boord of the Shippe of Bengala, at which time it was the yeere of Touffon...."

This Touffon or cruell storme endured three dayes and three nightes." In 1614 Samuel Purchas reported, "the winde, which they call Tufan is so violent, that it driveth ships on the land [and] overthroweth men and houses."

As late as 1848 the spelling of *typhoon* differed from what it is today: "The increased temperature on the southern coast during … June and July operates … to produce violent storms along the seaboard, called tyfoons, from the Chinese *ta-fung*, or great wind." By 1900 the *f* had changed to *ph*: "The typhoon of the western Pacific Ocean is in many respects the counterpart of the West Indian hurricane."

It is ironic that these storms take place in the Pacific, the ocean whose very name is a synonym for "calm" and "peaceful."

Also in 1588: *caravan*

1589 ANAGRAM

After the defeat of the "invincible" Spanish Armada in July 1588, the English turned their attention back to more peaceful endeavours. *Anagram*, a word or phrase formed by transposing the letters of another word or phrase, appeared in print the following year, offering sure proof that the English were having fun with their mother tongue even then. *Anagram* is based on the Greek roots *ana gramma* — literally, "again a letter."

It is not known whether Queen Elizabeth I, who was on the throne at the time, whiled away her idle hours with anagrams, but we do know that Queen Victoria once stayed up all night trying to figure out this one: T E R A L B A Y. You'll find the answer on page 71.

Also in 1589: *pantomime*

1590 BEDROOM

When Shakespeare first used *bedroom* in *A Midsummer Night's Dream*, he was not referring to a room with a bed in it, but rather to a bed with a lot of room in it! And this was centuries before the arrival of king-size, queen-size and Hollywood beds. The current meaning of *bedroom* first appeared in print in 1616, when it began to replace the rather quaint *bedchamber*.

1591 PICKPOCKET

Pickpockets were busy at work hundreds of years before the hit musical *Oliver!* popularized the song, "You Got to Pick a Pocket or Two." Back in the sixteenth century, when the word *pickpocket* first broke into print, the streets of London were dirty, dark and dangerous. They were also crowded, crooked and full of people with money to spend. Spanish gold and exotic luxuries were pouring into London from the far-flung corners of the globe — with prices and wages climbing steadily for over a hundred years. In 1591, just three years after the defeat of the Spanish Armada, the word *pickpocket* began showing up in print to describe an activity as old as money itself.

Just below *pickpocket*, the *OED* lists *pickpocketry* as a synonym for plagiarism. And that makes a lot of sense, because if you plagiarize another author, you are reaching into his book (or pocket) and stealing his valuables for your own use. If you're going to do this anyway, pick stuff from several authors at once. Then it's no longer called plagiarism, but research.

1592 QUEUE

What five-letter word can be shortened to only one letter but still be pronounced correctly? The answer, of course, is *queue* (pronounced kyoo). It appeared in print as early as 1592 as a heraldic term for the tail of a beast, coming from the Old French *coue*, which in turn came from the Latin *cauda*, meaning "tail." By 1748 *queue* had acquired a second definition: a long plait of hair hanging down from the back of the head, so called because of its resemblance to the tail of an animal (and now known as a pigtail). In 1837 the English writer Thomas Carlyle used the word the way we use it today: to describe a number of people lined up at a ticket office or checkout counter, presumably because the lineup resembles the shape of an animal's tail.

Also in 1592: *bookworm*

1593 Useless

In frequent use since 1650, the word *useless*, from the Latin *usus*, "to use," and the Old English *laes*, "less," was first used by William Shakespeare in "The Rape of Lucrece":

> The aged man that coffers up his gold
> Is plagued with cramps, and gouts, and painful fits,
> And scarce hath eyes his treasure to behold,
> But like still-pining Tantalus he sits,
> And useless barns the harvest of his wits;
> Having no other pleasure of his gain
> But torment that it cannot cure his pain.

Notice how Shakespeare used *barn* as a verb, thereby turning *useless* into an adverb. He also makes reference to Tantalus, a character in ancient Greek mythology who revealed some of the secrets of Zeus and was condemned to a rather unusual punishment. He was plunged into water up to his chin, while overhead dangled succulent fruits from the branches of a tree. But whenever he bent over to drink or reached up to eat some fruit, the water receded and the fruit was withdrawn. That's why Tantalus has given us the word *tantalize*: to tease or torment someone by keeping just out of reach something which they ardently desire.

Also in 1593: *embargo*

1594 Cognac

Cognac, named after the small town in France famous for manufacturing brandy, is a liquor that people have been drinking for hundreds of years. The word appeared in English as early as 1594 in the quote, "Take small Rochell, or Conniacke wine." If you drink too much, you will get tipsy, as Charles Dickens implies in a letter he wrote on February 20, 1858: "His handwriting shakes more and more ... I think he mixes a great deal of cognac with his ink."

When you drink cognac, you are drinking a type of brandy. And what is brandy? It is a liquor obtained through the distillation of wine. The word *brandy* first entered the English language as *brandywine*, *brandewine* or *brandwine*, from the Dutch *brandewijn* — from *branden*, "to burn" — because the process of distillation requires the application of heat. The word *distillation* comes the Latin term *distillo*, which can be split into *de*, "down," and *stilla*, "a drop." When liquid is distilled, it is heated until it turns into a vapour; the vapour is collected in a separate container, where it is allowed to condense back into a liquid, drop by drop. And when we *instill* the young with wisdom, we are putting it *into* them drop by drop.

1595 AUCTION

Auction, a Latin word, first entered the English language in a 1595 translation of *Menaechmi*, a play written by the Roman playwright Titus Maccius Plautus two hundred years before the birth of Christ: "The auction of Menaechmus ... when will be sold slaves, household goods, etc." Slaves were a common commodity in auctions held in ancient Rome. In fact, so plentiful were slaves that the butchers' stalls in Rome often had slave meat for sale along with bacon, beef, mutton and veal. But the auction did not begin with the Romans, for evidence has been found of auctions in ancient Greece back to the time of Homer, eight hundred years before Christ.

By the seventeenth century trade auctions were popular in Europe as a quick and efficient means of disposing of products, especially perishable items imported from overseas colonies. Nearly every major European city conducted them, and the idea soon spread to America. The first recorded auction in the American colonies took place in 1662 in New Amsterdam (which the English captured from the Dutch two years later and renamed New York). Slave auctions were a common sight in the American South right up to the outbreak of the Civil War, with a good field hand fetching fifteen hundred dollars or more. Bidding at auctions in previous centuries was often governed by a candle burning an inch, or a sand-glass running out, or a running boy reaching a goal, with the last bidder becoming the successful purchaser. More recently, the bidding generally stops when the auctioneer brings down his hammer, signalling his belief that the peak bid has been reached.

1596 Stigma

In ancient Greece, a stigma was a mark on the skin made by a branding iron. Branding was practised through the Middle Ages to Elizabethan times and thereafter, criminals usually being branded on the forehead or hand with a letter to indicate the nature of the crime: *D* for "drunkard," *A* for "adulterer," *C* for "counterfeiter" and so on. But the level of literacy was not high in merrie olde England, and the Newgate prison calendar tells of a hangman who burned only the letter *T* for "thief" on the palm of every criminal because that was the only letter of the alphabet he knew.

1597 Banana

The first bananas to reach England could have come from the Spanish West Indies or from the Far East. The banana appears to have originated in southern Asia in prehistoric times and spread to the islands of the Pacific when immigrants carried them from the Asian mainland. They were found on all the tropical Pacific islands by the time white men first visited them. The name itself is West African.

Bananas were introduced to the Western Hemisphere by Friar Tomas de Berlanga, who brought them from the Canary Islands to Hispaniola in 1516. Soon they were growing in Mexico and thriving so well that many later visitors mistakenly thought the banana was indigenous to America.

Today more than a hundred million bunches of bananas are shipped around the world every year. With their high nutritive value, bananas greatly enrich our diets. They have also enriched our language, as witness the song title "Yes, We Have No Bananas," the political term *banana republic*, the tasty *banana split* at your local malt shoppe, the Bic Banana felt-tip marker, and the financially hard-pressed widow who promises herself that her next husband will be "a rich old man with one foot in the grave and the other foot on a banana peel."

Also in 1597: *scrotum*

1598 COFFEE

According to an ancient Ethiopian legend, the first taste of coffee took place when a goatherd in that country watched his goats eat some bright red berries from a tree growing wild in a pasture and then frisk about. "Why should my goats have all the fun?" he asked, then tasted the berries himself. The rest is history.

It's possible that coffee is indigenous to both Ethiopia and Arabia. Coffee is based on an Arabic word, *qah wah*. The Arab physician, Rhazes, mentions coffee as early as the year 900 and by the thirteenth century the Arabs were using coffee as a beverage. It was introduced into Turkey in 1554, into Italy in 1615, and into France in 1644. It probably reached England around 1650 (although the English had been hearing about it as early as 1598). The first coffee house opened in London in 1652. The Arabs continued to earn big profits because they exported only the coffee beans, not the seeds. Finally, the Dutch got their hands on some seeds in 1690, planted them in Java, and broke the Arab coffee monopoly.

Today Brazil is the biggest exporter of coffee in the world. It's a beverage enjoyed by hundreds of millions of people every day and is perhaps the only six-letter word in the English language that can still be pronounced correctly even if every single letter is misspelled. Think about that the next time you have a cup of kawphy.

Also in 1598: *sexless*

1599 VIRUS

The earliest recorded use of this word in English appears in a letter written in 1599 by a chap named Hugh Broughton: "You ... haue ... spit out all the virus and poison you could conceive, in the abuse of his ... person." At that time *virus* was a synonym for venom and came directly from the Latin root *virus*, "poison." Its meaning has changed since then. Now, according to the *Oxford American Dictionary*, a virus is "a very simple organism (smaller than bacteria) capable of causing disease." That definition would have been impossible in 1599 because, with the microscope not yet invented, the people of Elizabethan England had no idea such things as bacteria and viruses existed.

Incidentally, other words that first appeared in print in this final year of the 1500s include *bandage, leapfrog* and *macaroni*.

Answer to anagram on page 65: betrayal

The 1600s

At three o'clock on the morning of March 24, 1603, Queen Elizabeth died after ruling her beloved realm for forty-five years. A messenger mounted a horse and rode north to Scotland to tell King James VI that he could now call himself King James I of England. So began the century during which the Stuart family guided the destiny of the growing English nation.

To establish the Anglican Church on a firm theological foundation, James I, early in his reign, commissioned some fifty scholars and church-men to produce a new English Bible that would be used as the one single authorized version of the Bible, first published in 1611 and still one of the best-selling books of all time. Carried by English men and women to the four corners of the globe, its impact on the language over nearly four hundred years has been beyond measure.

Two other events took place during the reign of James I (1603–1625) that were to have a profound effect on the future course of the English language: the establishment of the first permanent English colony in the New World at Jamestown, Virginia, in 1607, and the landing of a shipload of pilgrims at Plymouth Rock in Massachusetts in 1620. A steady stream of new words — from the Natives of America and from the Spanish colonies to the south — poured into England from the new lands overseas: *tomato, raccoon, desperado, cockroach, vanilla, skunk, pumpkin, wigwam, rattlesnake, rum, siesta, barbecue, barracuda* and *woodchuck*, to name a few. From the Orient came *sampan, tea, punch, amuck, bungalow, maharajah* and *chopsticks*. And from Europe itself came such words as *ghetto, toreador, denim* and *champagne*.

The growth of English colonies in America, which began under James I, accelerated during the reign of his son, Charles I (1625–1649). In 1629, Charles refused to meet with Parliament and proceeded to rule England on his own. The taxes and religious uniformity he tried to impose prompted fifty-five thousand of his subjects to seek new homes overseas during the single decade of the 1630s. The inevitable showdown between king and Parliament took place in 1640 and led, within two years, to the outbreak of the English civil war, which ended with the beheading of Charles I on January 30, 1649. For the next eleven years, England was ruled by the Puritan government.

With the restoration of the monarchy in 1660 under Charles II, two developments already in progress were given a big boost: overseas exploration and the growth of modern science. The overseas scene was enlivened in 1664 by the English capture of New Amsterdam, which was promptly renamed New York. On May 2, 1670, King Charles granted a charter to the Hudson's Bay Company to promote the exploitation of the fur trade in the interior of North America. And in 1681 the king granted a charter to William Penn for the establishment of Pennsylvania, a new colony that quickly became a haven for a wide variety of religious dissenters, including Quakers and Mennonites.

Modern science received the official royal blessing in 1660 when King Charles granted a charter to the Royal Society, an organization of learned men who proceeded to study and advance the entire field of human knowledge through the pursuit of science. This interest in science marks the big difference between the sixteenth and seventeenth centuries. The new words that entered English in the 1500s were chiefly the result of overseas exploration, with relatively few words reflecting an interest in science. But the 1600s changed all that. In the pages ahead, you will meet *telescope, pendulum, meteorologist, euthanasia, submarine, autopsy, antenna, siphon, phosphorus, serum, missile, archaeology* and *acupuncture*. You will also meet new technological and architectural terms: *derrick, tank, turnstile, condom, cesspool, skylight, vestibule* and *arena*. And lest you think the 1600s were all work and no play, you will meet *cosmetics, serenade, ventriloquist, zest, plaything, pigtail, witticism* and *backgammon*.

Not everyone, however, in seventeenth-century England welcomed these new words, especially if they were — heaven forbid — based on

Greek, Latin or other foreign languages instead of good old Anglo-Saxon roots. Alexander Gil, the headmaster of St. Paul's School, considered the adoption of these linguistic imports to be downright unpatriotic. In his *Logonomia Anglica*, written in 1619, he pleaded with his fellow countrymen to resist the "new mange in speaking and writing": "O harsh lips! I now hear all around me such words as *common, vices, envy, malice*; even *virtue, study, justice, pity, mercy, compassion, profit, commodity, colour, grace, favour, acceptance*. But whither, I pray in all the world, have you banished those words which our forefathers used for these new-fangled ones? Are our words to be exiled like our citizens? Is the new barbaric invasion to extirpate the English Tongue? O ye Englishmen, on you, I say, I call in whose veins that blood flows, retain, retain what yet remains of our native speech, and whatever vestiges of our forefathers are yet to be seen, on these plant your footsteps."

And yet Gil himself was guilty of the very thing he was complaining about. The second word in his book title, *Anglica*, is Anglo-Saxon, but the first, *Logonomia*, comes from Greek.

1600 DERRICK

When your surname enters the English language without a capital letter, you have achieved a special kind of immortality. Goodman Derrick, a hangman at Tyburn, sent countless criminals to their final reward with a quick yank of the noose, and his skill at swinging his victims from the gallows earned him a place in the dictionary. Any hoisting apparatus that uses a tackle at the end of a beam is called a *derrick* from its resemblance to the gallows used by Derrick himself.

And thus Goodman Derrick entered the English language as an *eponym* (a word based on someone's name). Some of his eponymic cohorts include Captain Charles Boycott, the Earl of Cardigan, Nicholas Chauvin (the world's first *chauvinist*), the Earl of Chesterfield, Lord Sandwich, Dr. Joseph Guillotin, Jean Nicot (who gave us *nicotine*) and Ambrose E. Burnside, an American Civil War general whose surname was reversed when his side-whiskers came to be known as *sideburns*.

1601 REGURGITATION

The noun *regurgitation*, from the Latin *re*, for "back," and *gurges*, "gulf," appears in English as early as 1601 and the verb *regurgitate* as early as 1653, when a fellow named Trapp wrote in his *Commentary on the Book of Job*, "The Whale that swallowed Jonah found him hard meat, and for his own ease was forced to regurgitate." The word *vomit*, as both noun and verb, is much older. Back in the days of Julius Caesar, wealthy Romans who wined and dined all night long often made use of a *vomitorium*, a room adjacent to the dining room where gluttonous epicures disgorged the contents of their stomachs so that they could keep on eating hour after hour. One Roman even had a slave whose job it was to tickle his master's throat with a feather whenever his stomach was full.

In recent years, two new synonyms have been added to *vomit* and *regurgitation* — namely, *upchuck* and *barf* (see the entry for the year 2000 on page 310). And for those occasions when only a little swallowed food comes back up, Dee Durie of Freehold, New Jersey, has coined the word *regurgiburp* — a belch with substance.

1602 CUSTODIAN

This word (from Latin *custodia*, "guarding") is at least four-hundred-and-a-bit years old, and is defined by the eleventh edition of *Merriam-Webster's Collegiate Dictionary* as "one that guards or protects or maintains; especially: one entrusted with guarding and keeping property or records or with custody or guardianship of prisoners or inmates." The word *custody* is even older, dating back to the fifteenth century.

In the 1980s, a Canadian neologist living in Manitoba came up with the word *bustodian* (for a security guard in a brassiere factory).

1603 EUREKA

The Greek word *eureka* (meaning "I have found it!") first appeared in English in 1603 in a translation of Plutarch by Philemon Holland. Plutarch was telling the story of the Greek scientist Archimedes (c.287?–212 B.C.), who was given a problem by his benefactor, Hiero, the ruler of the Sicilian city of

Syracuse. Hiero wanted Archimedes to discover a way of determining whether the king's crown was made of pure gold or had been partly debased with silver. Pondering the problem one day as he was preparing to take a bath, Archimedes noticed that some of the water overflowed as he stepped into the tub, and this gave him the answer he was looking for. He knew that gold and silver had different densities, and therefore pieces of gold and silver of equal weight would displace different volumes of water. He could use this principle to determine the proportion of gold in Hiero's crown. Reportedly leaping from the bathtub and forgetting to put on his clothes, Archimedes ran naked through the streets, shouting: "Eureka!"

1604 Tomato

Like *potato*, the word *tomato* is a Native American word (from the Nahuatl *tomatl*) brought back to Europe by Spanish explorers. The first written record of the *tomate* (as the Spanish called it) dates back to 1554, and the earliest mention of it in English dates back to 1604.

After the tomato came to the attention of Europeans, two misconceptions arose concerning it: some believed it was an aphrodisiac, while others thought it was poisonous. Its reputation as an aphrodisiac gave rise to the term "love apple," and in fact the French still refer to it as *pomme d'amour*. Its allegedly poisonous nature, a notion more prevalent in the New World than in Europe, discouraged its consumption as a food in North America where, for a long time, it was grown only as an ornamental garden plant. Not until the early 1800s were North American tomatoes grown widely as food.

Also dating from 1604: *lemonade, leprechaun*

1605 Cosmetics

In 1605 Sir Francis Bacon wrote, "[The] art of decoration [of the body] ... is called cosmetic." Bacon was using a word of Greek origin (from *kosmeein*, to arrange or adorn) to describe what millions of women and men do to their faces and bodies every morning. The word *cosmetics* covers a whole countertop of other words devoted to the art of giving Mother Nature a helping hand. *Lipstick* as a word has been traced by Merriam-

Webster to 1880, although sticks for reddening the lips had been around for hundreds of years before that (and before these came along, women bit their lips to redden them). *Mascara* comes to us from the Spanish *mascara*, meaning "mask." *Rouge*, of course, comes straight from the French word for "red" and is usually applied with the fingers; eye shadow is often applied with a *pencil*, a word that comes from the Latin *penicillus*, meaning "small tail," from which we also derive the words *penicillin* (see page 272) and *penis* (page 115).

Human beings have been painting and powdering themselves at least as far back as cave days. We have evidence that prehistoric men and women were buried with red ochre smeared on their bodies, perhaps in the hope that the blood-red colour would bring them back to life.

Also dating from 1605: *chit-chat, fanfare*

1606 MISSILE

This word first appeared in English when the texts of the Roman biographer Suetonius were translated by Philemon Holland: "Scattered also aboard there were for the people Missils [sweets, perfumes, etc.], during the whole time of those Plays." The Romans themselves referred to these gifts as *res missiles*, literally, "things thrown." By 1611 the word *missile* was being used for anything thrown, and by 1656, when Geoffrey Blount defined it as "a dart, stone, arrow, or other thing thrown or shot," it was taking on the military connotations it bears today.

We have all heard of *ICBMs* (Inter-Continental Ballistic Missiles), cruise missiles, guided missiles and heat-seeking missiles. The *American*

Heritage Dictionary draws a distinction between a ballistic missile and a guided missile: the former is a missile powered and guided in its ascent, but which then falls freely toward its target; the latter is capable of being guided through the full course of its flight. Both missiles share the same Latin root: *mittere, missus,* "to send." That root has sprouted many branches in English, including *admission, commission, dismiss, emissary, emission, intermission, permission, remiss, remit, remittance, submit, submission, transmit, transmissible, transmission, transmitter, mission* and, of course, *missile* itself. Isn't it odd that a peace mission and a guided missile share the same Latin root?

1607 ARCHAEOLOGY

When the Turks captured Constantinople on May 29, 1453, bringing the thousand-year-old Byzantine Empire to an end, hordes of Greek scholars fled west to Italy with ancient manuscripts tucked under their arms. Their arrival in Rome and other Italian cities fanned the flames of the Renaissance, that great rebirth of ancient Greco-Roman culture that swept across western Europe in the 1400s and 1500s.

By the early 1600s, enough people in England were studying ancient artefacts to give birth to the word *archaeology,* from Greek, *archalos logos,* "ancient discourse." It would, however, be many more years before archaeology began to approach the status of the science we know it as today. The father of modern archaeology is generally considered to be Johann Winckelmann, whose careful, systematic excavations of Pompeii in the mid–eighteenth century helped to establish the principle that a lowly pottery vessel was archaeologically just as valuable as a crown of gold. Wickelmann's career unfortunately came to a sudden end when he was stabbed to death in a wayside inn in 1768.

When the late British actress Margaret Rutherford was asked why she and her husband had enjoyed such a long and happy life together, she explained: "Well, you see, my husband is an archaeologist, and the older I get, the more interesting he thinks I am."

See *carcheologist* (page 310).

1608 RACCOON

Just one year after the first permanent English colony in the New World took root at Jamestown, Virginia, the North American Algonquian Indian name for the raccoon was added to the King's English. Because the first few years of the new colony were known as "the starving time" (with nearly half of the settlers dying of disease or malnutrition), there must have been many a raccoon that ended up as colonial stew. The Natives went after the raccoon for its fur, and the newly arrived European settlers maintained that tradition. The raccoon is considered one of the most nervous of all woodland creatures, and probably with good reason: raccoon fur arrives on the market at the rate of one million pelts a year.

The raccoon's reputation for cleanliness stems from its habit of washing food before eating it. But it has acquired this habit out of sheer necessity, not for any innate love of cleanliness. A raccoon has hardly any saliva, and therefore must moisten food before eating it.

1609 QUARANTINE

When *quarantine* first appeared in print in English, it was used as a legal term for "a period of forty days during which a widow, entitled to dower, had the right to remain in the house of her deceased husband." By 1663 it had acquired its more familiar meaning: "A period [originally of forty days] during which persons who might serve to spread a contagious disease are kept isolated from the rest of the community" (*OED*). It was in that year that Samuel Pepys wrote in his diary: "Making of all ships coming from thence … to perform their 'quarantine for thirty days' … contrary to the import of the word [which] signifies now the thing, not the time spent in doing it." Although *quarantine* is based on the French term for "forty days," the period of time a person actually spends in quarantine varies with the virulence of the disease. When the first astronauts to walk on the moon returned to earth, they were quarantined for seventeen days as a precaution against any unearthly germs they might have brought back with them.

1610 Desperado

The *American Heritage Dictionary* defines *desperado* as "a desperate, dangerous criminal, especially of the western U.S. frontier," and gives the etymology not as Spanish but as pseudo-Spanish. Why? Because *desperado* rarely if ever appears in Spanish itself. It was apparently coined from the word *desperate* and given a deliberate Spanish flavour, perhaps because the English and Spanish were not on good terms when this word first appeared in 1610.

English-Spanish hostility took firm root in the New World and continued long after the colonies spawned by these two European powers became independent nations. Mexico freed itself from Spanish control in 1821, only to lose a large chunk of its land to American settlers who had moved into the part of Mexico that became the independent republic of Texas in 1836. Twelve years later, the United States took California — and, in fact, the entire southwest — from Mexico as the fruits of victory in the Mexican War. The Mexicans later coined the term *gringo*, an epithet hurled at foreigners in general and Americans in particular. The Americans responded with an equally disrespectful word: *wetback*, a Mexican who is in the United States illegally, so called from the practice of entering the country by swimming across the Rio Grande.

Incidentally, if you like playing with words, you'll love *desperado*. Shuffle the letters around and you can make more than a hundred other words, using each letter only as often as it appears in *desperado* itself.

1611 Ghetto

The first record of this word appearing in English has been traced to 1611, in a book by Thomas Coryat called *Coryats Crudities; hastily gobled up in five months travel*: "The place where the whole fraternity of the Jews dwelleth together ... is called the Ghetto." Although not all etymologists agree on where and how the word first originated, the most convincing version is set forth in Willard Espy's fascinating book *O Thou Improper, Thou Uncommon Noun*: "[This] symbol of restriction and oppression by reason of racial origin came into being in 1516 when the city of Venice expelled its Jews to the nearby Island of Ghetto, which was the site of a foundry, ghetto in Italian. A ghetto is a quarter in a city, especially a thickly populated slum area, inhabited by a minority group or groups, usually as a result of economic or social pressure."

1612 ASTERISK

Although this word has been dated to the fourteenth century, the year 1612 is apparently the earliest specific year its use can be pinned down to.

The asterisk, from the Greek *asteriskos*, "little star," has long been a favourite with lexicographers reluctant to spell out in full those vulgar four-letter words that have only in recent years lost their asterisks. Some people, alarmed at the rising tide of foul words in books and magazines, regard the dropping of the asterisk as a moral disaster, which brings us to another word based on the same root. Back in the days of alchemy and astrology, it was believed that things went your way because the stars were in favourable conjunction. But if things suddenly went against you — in other words, if disaster struck — it was a sign that the stars, *aster,* were not (*dis*), in your favour.

1613 CENSUS

When *census* first appeared in English, it referred to certain types of taxes, especially a poll tax (a tax on persons instead of property). By 1634 its meaning had broadened to include the registration of citizens and property for taxation purposes (as in ancient Rome). By 1769 it had acquired its modern meaning: an official enumeration of the population of a country or district. A census has been taken every ten years in the United States since 1790, in France since 1791, and in Great Britain since 1801.

Also dating from 1613: *basement, squid*

1614 INCUBATION

In 1614, in his *History of the World,* Sir Walter Raleigh wrote, "Whether that motion ... and operation, were by incubation, or how else, the manner is onely knowne to God." Raleigh is suggesting that the world may have been formed by God brooding or moving over the primeval chaos that preceded creation. In 1677 Sir Matthew Hale offered a different slant on the question of creation: "Some assign a natural determined cause of the first production of Mankind, namely, the due preparation of the fat and slimy Earth after a long incubation of Waters."

But it was Sir Thomas Browne in 1646 who first used *incubation*, from the Latin *incubare*, "to brood," the way we use it today: to describe the hatching of eggs by sitting on them: "Incubation alters not the species … as evidently appears in the eggs of Ducks or Partridges hatched under a Hen." But have you ever wondered how a hen or other bird can lay several eggs over a period of several days, yet manage to get all those eggs to hatch on the same day? It's because the hen waits until the last egg is laid before sitting on them.

1615 TEA

Like the beverage itself, the word *tea* comes to us directly from the Orient — *d'a* is its Chinese root. According to the *Encyclopedia Americana*, the first mention of tea in the English language was by R. Wickman, an agent of the English East India Company, in a letter from Japan in 1615. By the end of the seventeenth century, tea was a booming business for England, as its ships plied the waters of the world to bring back the leaves that yielded this intoxicating beverage. Tea helped to build the British Empire, and tea almost destroyed it. When the East India Company encountered financial difficulties in the early 1770s, the British Parliament (many members of which had invested their money in the concern) decided to rescue it from bankruptcy. The company was given preferential treatment in the importation of tea into the American colonies, thus forcing many colonial importers out of business. The result was the Boston Tea Party on December 16, 1773, during which three hundred and forty chests of tea were dumped into Boston Harbor in protest. The chain of events that followed led directly to the American Revolution.

When did the British custom of afternoon tea originate? Not until around 1840, when the Duchess of Bedford started the trend. Thanks to her, Britain now consumes one-fifth of the world's tea, and tea is to Britain what apple pie is to America. Tea sells well in the United States, too, but sales were sluggish at the 1904 World's Fair in St. Louis because of a heat wave. An enterprising Englishman named Richard Blechynden, unable to sell his hot beverage in the warm Missouri climate, poured it over ice, and voila! The world got its first taste of iced tea.

1616 TANK

Although *tank* — a word of unknown origin — appeared in print in England in the early 1400s as a synonym for a wild carrot or parsnip, that use of the word died out, apparently before the end of the 1500s. When *tank* reappeared in English in 1616 to become a permanent member of the language, it was spelled *tanque* and referred to a pool or cistern used in the East Indies for holding water: "Besides their Rivers, ... they have many Ponds, which they call Tanques, ... fill'd with water when that abundance of Rain fals." By 1690 it described an artificial receptacle for holding a large quantity of water or other fluid and was mentioned in that year by John Dryden in *Don Sebastian*: "Here's plentiful provision for you, Rascal, sallating in the Garden, and water in the tanck." But in the early years of the twentieth century, *tank* acquired a new and deadly meaning.

When World War I broke out in August 1914, soldiers marched off to the battlefield thinking they would be home by Christmas. How wrong they were. No one realized at the time that the rules of war had changed. No longer could you rout the enemy with a simple "Char-r-r-rge!" Now both sides could mow down advancing troops by the hundreds with a new weapon, the machine gun. Long before Christmas, the western front was a zigzag of trenches stretching from the Belgian coast to the Swiss border. The war had become a deadlock, with the lives of countless soldiers being squandered in a vain attempt to pierce enemy lines. The Germans resorted to poison gas in the spring of 1915 to try to break the impasse, but had to abandon it because any sudden shift in the wind meant gassing one's own troops.

The British were working on the problem, too, and in 1915 built the first armour-plated motorized vehicles with caterpillar treads for crossing trenches. Winston Churchill was an early and eager advocate of these new vehicles, the development of which was a well-kept secret. The first of these vehicles were shipped to France in crates labelled "Tank" to deceive German agents into thinking they were water tanks. The name stuck.

1617 Cult

When this word first appeared in printed English in 1617, it meant "worship of a divine being," from the Latin *cultus,* "cultivation" or "worship." In ancient Egypt, for example, there was the cult of Osiris, the cult of Amon, the cult of Ra, and many others to reflect the devotion of faithful worshippers who paid homage to their favourite gods. By 1679, when William Penn, the founder of Pennsylvania, used the word, it referred to any religious sect: "Let not every circumstantial difference or Variety of Cult be Nick-named new Religion."

Today, the word *cult* has an odious connotation for parents. Some young people are drawn into cults by a highly sophisticated process of indoctrination, which can produce drastic changes in the thinking and attitudes of an impressionable new recruit. Distraught parents have sometimes hired professional deprogrammers who literally kidnap a young person from the cult he or she has joined and try to restore that person to his or her original set of values and attitudes. This parentally inspired kidnapping prompted *Time* magazine into coining a new word to describe it: *cultnapping.*

1618 Toreador

The earliest quote in which *toreador* appears in English tells us that these caped and fearless men of the ring had more than bulls on their mind: "The Conde de Cantilliana, that excellent Toreador, hath stolen away the wife of a Procurador de Corte." Of the two words we have in English to describe these fellows — *toreador* and *matador* — the first gives more recognition to the bull (*toreador* comes from the Latin *taurus,* "bull"), whereas the latter is based on a Spanish adaptation from the Latin *mactare,* "to kill."

Incidentally, did you know the continent of Europe got its name with the help of a bull? Europa was the beautiful young daughter of the king of Phoenicia, and Zeus, the lusty lover from Mount Olympus, was completely captivated by her charms. To abduct her, Zeus changed himself into a handsome white bull and began to mingle with her father's herd. Europa was so taken with the bull's gentleness that she climbed onto his back. Zeus then dashed into the sea and swam with Europa to the island of Crete, where she bore him three sons. Thanks to the ancient Greeks, her name was eventually given to the continent we now call Europe.

1619 TELESCOPE

It has been said that the first telescope was invented by Hans Lippershey, a spectacle-lens maker in Holland who one day happened to hold up a convex lens in one hand and a concave one in the other. When he held them in line and looked through both at a distant church steeple, he was amazed to see it appear much closer than with the naked eye. He quickly constructed a tube to hold the two lenses in place, and that was, very likely, the world's first telescope. The time was around 1609.

The great Italian scientist Galileo soon got wind of Lippershey's magical eyeglass and built one of his own. He turned it toward the heavens and saw many sights never before seen by man, including the four largest moons of Jupiter (a solar system in miniature) and the rings around Saturn. What to call the new instrument was anybody's guess. A fellow astronomer, Johannes Kepler, suggested *perspicillum, conspicillum, specillum,* and *penicillium.* In Galileo's letters from September 1, 1611, onward, he used the Italian term *telescopio* (from the Greek *tele,* "afar," and *skopein,* "to see"), although there is some doubt as to whether he or someone else coined it. Its very first appearance in English has been credited to a chap named Bainbridge, who in 1619 wrote, "For the more perspicuous distinction where of I used the *Telescopium* or Trunke-spectacle."

1620 SAMPAN

The English language has been enriched with words from the four corners of the globe. When *sampan*, from Chinese, *san pan*, "three boards," first appeared in print in English in 1620 ("… trym up a China sampan to goe with the fleete"), it was one more indication that English ships were sailing in the waters that lapped the shores of China and Japan. Most of the ships in the early 1600s sailed under the banner of the English East India Company, formed in London in September 1599 by a group of merchants hoping to cash in on the riches of the Far East. But the Dutch had beaten them to it and resented the intrusion of the English in the Spice Islands (the East Indies). Open warfare raged for several years, until the English decided to concentrate their efforts on India and the trade in calico, indigo, cotton, silk, saltpetre and spices, thus laying the foundation for British rule in India.

1621 METEOROLOGIST

During the Middle Ages, changes in the weather were often attributed directly to God and the mood He happened to be in on that particular day (violent storms, for example, were sure proof of His anger). With the more secular and humanistic influences of the Renaissance in the 1400s and 1500s, a more scientific approach to the weather gradually gained acceptance, and it is interesting to note that ancient Greek was used to create a word to describe the study of the weather. *Meteorological* (from the Greek *meteoros*, "high in the air," from the intensifier *mita* and *aeirein*, "to raise") first appeared in print in 1570, and *meteorology* in 1620. The fancy name for a weatherman, *meteorologist*, made its debut the following year, when Robert Burton wrote in *The Anatomy of Melancholy*, "Whirlewindes … and … stormes … our Meteorologists generally refer to natural causes."

And regardless of what causes it, there is precious little we can do to change the weather, as one forecaster realized when he remarked: "Whether the weather be hot or whether the weather be cold, I'll weather the weather whatever the weather, whether I like it or not."

1622 KEELHAUL

Recorded by the Dutch as early as 1560, the practice of keelhauling became popular with English sea captains in the 1600s as a means of enforcing discipline on the high seas. Coming from the Dutch *kielhalen*, the English verb *keelhaul* appeared in print as early as 1622 and is defined by the *OED* as follows: "To haul [a person] under the keel of a ship, either by lowering him on one side and hauling him across to the other side, or, in the case of smaller vessels, lowering him at the bow and drawing him along under the keel to the stern." If you could hold your breath long enough and the sharks didn't get you, you just might survive the ordeal. And if a keelhauling did not sufficiently chasten you, the captain had other tortures up his sleeve: a thrashing with a cat-o'-nine-tails in full view of the crew, a few days in the brig on a diet of bread and water, or a few hours in the crow's nest in the middle of a raging storm. If, after all that, you still did not behave yourself, you would probably be obliged to walk the plank.

1623 VESTIBULE

In 1623, this word appeared in print thusly: "Vestibule, the porch of a dore." In this instance, *vestibule* (from the Latin *vestibulum*, "forecourt") was being used to describe a feature of architecture popular in ancient Rome: an entrance-court or forecourt outside the front door. And that's how the word was used until 1730, when a chap named Bailey wrote, "A vestibule is also used for a Kind of little Anti-Chamber before the Entrance of an ordinary Apartment." In other words, it took one hundred and seven years for this word to move from outside the building to inside.

If you check the *OED*, you will also find the word *vestibulotomy*, a surgical term for the cutting or opening of the vestibule, or central cavity, of the inner ear. Home renovators could also use this term to describe the tearing down and removal of the vestibule of a house in order to make a larger entrance hall.

1624 Cockroach

In a letter written in Virginia in 1624, Captain John Smith described the cockroach as "a certaine India bug, called by the Spaniards a cacarootch, the which creeping into chests they eat and defile with their ill-sented dung." What John Smith was looking at was the American version of the cockroach, a pesky insect found throughout the world. It is highly probable that European cockroaches (which were known as beetles before 1624) arrived in America on board the *Mayflower* in 1620 and that the American variety found its way to Europe by the same means.

Most people regard cockroaches as objects of loathing and disgust, chiefly because they often emit a foul odour and infest kitchens to sponge off your food supply. But the cockroach is one of the most fascinating of all insects. It is the most primitive of all living winged insects, having been around without major change for three hundred and fifty million years. And the secret of its long lifespan as a species lies in its ability to adapt to its surroundings. In *Marvels & Mysteries of Our Animal World*, J.D. Ratcliff describes its eating habits: "[The cockroach] has been known to eat everything from orchid buds to shoes to the glue that holds cartons together. He sips beer, chews through gravy spots on neckties, nibbles at paint, relishes soap. He even eats his own cast-off skin and, if sufficiently hard-pressed, dines on the eggs of his own species … Without visible ill effects he can live about a month without any food or water, two months on water alone, and five months on dry food but no water."

1625 Onslaught

This word, a synonym for "fierce attack," appeared in a quotation from 1625: "I doe remember yet that anslaight, thou wast beaten, And fledst." The *OED* is uncertain as to whether this word comes from the Middle English word *slaught*, meaning "slaughter," or from the German *anschlag*, "a striking at." If a slaughter does take place, we often say that the ranks of the losing side have been decimated. This word comes from the ancient Romans, who disciplined their troops by killing every tenth man in a mutinous legion, a practice known as *decimation* (from the Latin *decimus*, meaning "tenth"). Today the word has completely reversed its meaning because, in an army that has been decimated, only about one-tenth of all the troops are still alive.

1626 PLACID

Sir Francis Bacon used this word in 1626: "It conduceth unto long life, and to the more placid motion of the spirits." You can find this word, from the Latin *placere*, "to please," on a map of New York state if you look in the heart of the Adirondacks for Lake Placid, site of the 1932 and 1980 Winter Olympics. And that's just one of a whole slew of place names in the Empire State with interesting etymologies. Manhattan and Harlem are reminiscent of the days when the Dutch ruled the roost along the Hudson River. New York City itself was named after the Duke of York, later to become King James II (1685–1688). Syracuse and Rome take you back to the Mediterranean of classical antiquity (the original Rome produced the word *romance* and the name for *Roumania*, a Roman province on the Black Sea). Avon, New York, comes from the Celtic word for "river" (and Stratford-on-Avon literally means Stratford on the river). Middlesex, in western New York state, comes from the Middle Saxons of England — who lived near the South Saxons (Sussex), the East Saxons (Essex), and the West Saxons (Wessex). Troy is near Albany, and Ithaca is in the Finger Lakes district. It was from another Troy that the Greek hero Ulysses departed around 1200 B.C., after ten years of warfare, to sail to his island home of Ithaca, a journey that took him another ten years. And close to the Hudson River, you will find

Kinderhook, an old Dutch town that, some etymologists believe, gave us the expression *OK* or *okay*, from a political club in the town that called itself "Old Kinderhook," or O.K. for short.

Many settlements in New York state were given names from classical literature in the early 1800s by a committee appointed by the state government. In an attempt to avoid controversy, the committee drew upon the respected works, writers and cities of ancient Greece and Rome.

1627 LANDFALL

This word (a noun) is defined by *Merriam-Webster's Collegiate Dictionary* as "a sighting or making of land after a voyage or flight; the land first sighted on a voyage or flight." The most famous landfall in history occurred on October 12, 1492, when a member of the crew of Christopher Columbus shouted, "Land ho!" Soon after that, the *Nina*, the *Pinta* and the *Santa Maria* dropped anchor and the men on board set foot on solid ground. Columbus had been fearing a mutiny as the ships sailed farther and farther away from Spain, whose Queen Isabella reportedly hocked her jewels to pay for the voyage. Columbus, it is said, deliberately minimized the distance travelled each day in his ship's log to avoid spooking an already nervous crew. He found land where he expected to find it because his notion of the size of the world was considerably smaller than it actually is. To his dying day he thought he had reached Asia and was unaware that he had stumbled upon a continent unknown to Europeans — *and* that beyond that continent lay an ocean even bigger than the Atlantic. Had he known the true size of the Earth, he might never have sailed.

1628 WIGWAM

A chap named Levett wrote from New England in 1628, "We built our wigwam, or house, in one hour's space." English settlers had been living in New England for only eight years (the first to arrive had come on the *Mayflower* in 1620), when Levett first used this word, borrowed from the Native Americans and variously spelled *wiggwamme, wigwang, wiggwham, whigwham, wigwaum* and *weekwam*. *Teepee* was the preferred term west of the Great Lakes.

1629 PALINDROME

Although William Shakespeare (1564–1616) no doubt noticed that certain English words are spelled the same way backward and forward, no one apparently thought to give this phenomenon a name until 1629, when the word *palindrome* entered the English language (from the Greek *palin*, "back," and *dromos*, "running"). Several palindromic words are common, everyday terms, including *Mom, Pop, Sis, level, kayak, radar* and *noon*. The only palindromic name of a language is Malayalam, which is spoken in southern India. The longest palindromic word in English is the nine-letter *redivider*, but the longest known palindromic word in any language is the nineteen-letter Finnish word for a soap salesman: *saippuakivikauppias*.

Well-known palindromic sentences include the words someone put in the mouth of Napoleon: "Able was I ere I saw Elba"; the tribute to the engineer who joined the Atlantic to the Pacific: "A man, a plan, a canal, Panama"; and the first words ever spoken in the Garden of Eden: "Madam, I'm Adam." Eve's reply to that remark is not on record, but my guess is she came up with a palindrome of her own: "Oho!"

1630 RATTLESNAKE

The earliest mention of *rattlesnake*, from Old English roots, dates back to 1630, when the first few English settlements were gaining a foothold along the Atlantic seaboard of North America. The first rattlesnake encountered was probably an eastern diamondback, a subspecies found between Florida and the Carolinas, which grows to more than eight feet in length. The western diamondback, slightly smaller in size, ranges from southern California throughout the southwest to Oklahoma, Arkansas and Missouri.

Also dating from 1630: *copulate, genuflect*

1631 STEWARDESS

An employee who supervised the domestic affairs of the household of his master or mistress was called, in Old English, *stigweard*, from *stig*, "house," and *weard*, "ward." The feminine version of the word that evolved into *stewardess* did not appear until 1631. By the mid-nineteenth century, *stewardess* had extended its meaning to include a female attendant on board ship who looked after female passengers. In the 1930s it extended itself again, this time to cover female attendants on board airplanes who looked after the passengers. (The word *hostess* was also used in this context). By the early 1970s both *stewardess* and *hostess* had acquired sexist overtones and ended up on the endangered-word list. The airlines decided to replace these two offending terms with the sexually nondeclarative *flight attendant* in order to eliminate reference to sex in job titles.

But *stewardess* and *hostess* are not the only words that are now *verboten* in the friendly skies. In his fascinating book *On Language*, William Safire mentions another: "Why is a stewardess (excuse the sexism — 'flight attendant') trained to say 'mint' when she offers you what most other people would call a Life Saver? Not because the airlines want to avoid plugging a commercial product. The reason 'Life Saver' is taboo is the same as the reason 'safety belts' are now called 'seat belts.' Airlinese is the language of reassurance, and they don't want anyone reaching for a piece of candy to get the notion that the pilot is preparing to ditch."

1632 Punch

In 1632, an Englishman named R. Addams wrote to one T. Colley, a merchant: "I hop you will keep a good house together and drinke punch by no allowanc." That is the first recorded use of *punch* in English as applied to a beverage. The other punch (to punch someone in the nose) is much older, and comes from Middle English *punchen*, "to punch." The *OED* says the origin of *punch* (the beverage) is uncertain but goes on to say that a fellow named Fryer travelled in western India from 1672 to 1681 and claimed that the word *punch* comes from the Hindi word *panch*, meaning "five," from the five ingredients used in punch at that time.

1633 PREREQUISITE

This word is the stock-in-trade of high school and college students who must be sure to select courses that serve as prerequisites for the more advanced classes they intend to take. When Thomas Adams used this word, which comes from the Latin *pre*, "before," and *requirere*, "to seek," in 1633, he wasn't filling out a course selection sheet, but he *was* thinking about education: "Knowledge is but a prerequisite to … obedience." If you look up *prerequisite* in the *Oxford American Dictionary*, you will find this note of caution: "Do not confuse prerequisite with perquisite." That shorter look-alike refers to a payment or privilege given to someone in addition to their wages or salary. *Perquisite* is often abbreviated to *perk* when referring to something a company or other organization will do for its more valued employees, perhaps including a company car, membership in a prestigious country club or a key to the executive washroom.

1634 SKUNK

With the steady westward advance of the American frontier from its first foothold at Jamestown, Virginia, in 1607, one animal after another was discovered and named — usually by adapting the Native American name to English. The skunk was no exception. The Native people called him *sikako*, which was streamlined to *skunk*. It isn't known whether the first European to encounter a skunk did so by seeing it or smelling it, but we do know that the *OED* gives credit to a W. Wood for first mentioning the animal in English in 1634: "The beasts of offence by Squunckes, Ferrets, Foxes."

1635 SEDAN

Originally, a sedan was a closed vehicle seating one person and carried on two poles by two bearers, one in front and one behind. The *OED* is at a loss to explain where the word itself comes from. In its unabridged edition of 1958, it has this to say: "The conjecture connecting the word with the name of Sedan, a town of N.E. France, has nothing to support it, and seems unlikely…. The [sedan] had long been in use in Italy [and] it is therefore natural to suppose that the word might be from some South Italian derivative of Italian *sede* (Latin: *sedes*) seat, *sedere*, to sit; but there seems to be no trustworthy evidence of the existence of Italian dialects of any form from which the English word could be derived."

Be that as it may, the word *sedan* first appeared in print in English in 1635, in a play by Richard Brome entitled *Sparagus Garden*: "Shee's now gone forth in one o' the new Hand-litters; what call yee it, a Sedan." With the invention of the automobile, the word *sedan* took on a new meaning: a closed car with four doors and a front and back seat.

1636 SHORTHAND

Shorthand has had a long and fascinating history going back at least as far as ancient Greece and Rome. The Greeks employed a method of shorthand to record speeches and poems recited at the Olympic Games and other national festivals. Roman reporters speeded things up by using the initial letters of longhand words, a practice that has bequeathed to us the streamlined A.D. (*Anno Domini*), N.B. (*nota bene*), and P.S. (*postscriptum*). Egyptian records include a contract drawn up in the year 155 to teach a boy shorthand. And in the fourth century, a Roman scholar, Decimus Magnus Ausonius, wrote a poem to a young reporter, describing him as "skilled in swift shorthand."

With the fall of Rome and the onset of the Dark Ages, shorthand virtually disappeared. Its modern revival probably began in the 1500s, when Timothy Bright, sometimes called the father of modern shorthand, wrote a book about it in 1588 and dedicated it to Queen Elizabeth, who granted to her "well-beloved subject, Tymothe Brighte, Doctor of Physike," a patent for a "shorte and new kynde of writing by character to the furtherance of good learning." But apparently, neither Bright nor Good Queen Bess used the word *shorthand* itself. The *OED* gives the credit for the first use of the word to the title page of Jeffrey Hudson's *New Yeeres Gift* (published in 1636): "With a Letter as it was penned in short-hand." Two hundred and one years later, in 1837, Sir Isaac Pitman published his first shorthand manual, and the Pitman system became the most widely used in the English-speaking world outside of the United States. In 1893 the first American edition of the Irish-born John Robert Gregg's manual was published in Boston, and the Gregg system became the most widely used in the United States.

1637 LAMBASTE

Beat, thrash and *lambaste* are fighting words. The quote from 1637 says, "Stand off a while and see how Ile lambaste him." In 1678 Edward Phillips wrote: "Otherwise they would be fin'd, and lambasted with a good Cudgel." And in 1837 a very pugnacious Thomas Haliburton wrote, "I am six foot six in my stockin' feet, by gum, and can lambaste any two of you in no time."

If this word is not to your liking, *Roget's Thesaurus* has a surfeit of synonyms ready for you: *strike, spank, beat, buffet, pommel, trounce, lash, flog, whip, cane, horsewhip* and *beat black and blue*. Most of these words stem from good old Anglo-Saxon roots, but the origin of *lambaste* remains a mystery. Not even the editors of the *OED* have discovered where it came from.

1638 FIREPROOF

The first use of this word in English has been credited to a chap named Mede who wrote in 1638, "… such as had departed out of this life not fully purged [of sin] … should not be found fire-proof at [Judgement] day." In other words, the flames of hell would swallow you up if you died before cleansing yourself of all wrongdoing.

Later uses of the word are more secular. A fellow named Fuller in 1642 wrote about fireproof brick, J. Badcock in 1823 wrote about how "to render Wood Fire-proof," and sometime during the nineteenth century (the *OED* doesn't know the exact year), a fellow named Moore wrote about "a grim old dandy, seen about with a fire-proof wig."

500 YEARS OF NEW WORDS

If you or anything you own is fireproof, then it is nonflammable — not inflammable, but nonflammable. These two terms are sometimes confused, but the *American Heritage Dictionary* spells out the difference: "Flammable and inflammable are alike in meaning and interchangeable in literal usage. One can speak of a flammable fluid or an inflammable one. Figuratively, one can refer to an inflammable nature or temperament, but not to a flammable one. Flammable [and here is the point worth noting] is especially appropriate in technical writing and where the term serves expressly as a warning, since it is less susceptible to confusion than inflammable, which is sometimes mistaken for non-flammable or non-combustible."

It's easy to see why the prefix *in-* causes confusion. In some words, such as *incompetent, inarticulate* and *indestructible*, it means "not." That being the case, you might think *inflammable* meant "not able to catch on fire." But the prefix *in-* also means "in" or "into," and in this sense it crops up in words such as *influx, inhale* and *ingress*. To this list we can add INFLAMMABLE, because that's what it means: able to burst into flame. Oil and gasoline trucks at one time had the word INFLAMMABLE printed in large block letters across the back, but today those same trucks, in an effort to avoid any possible doubt as to the explosive nature of the cargo they contain, use the word FLAMMABLE.

1639 PROPRIETOR

Although this word, from the Latin *proprius*, "one's own," is used today to refer to the owner of a business, it first entered the language in reference to the "Lords-proprietary," who were given grants of land in the New World in order to advance the process of English colonization. When the American Revolution broke out in 1776, there were thirteen English colonies along the Atlantic seaboard. Some, like New York, had been established by direct action of the English crown; others, such as Virginia and Massachusetts, were created through the efforts of a trading company chartered by the king, while still others were begun by individuals who came to be known as proprietors and who received land grants from the king of England in return for promising to settle the land with good English colonists. These varied methods of colonization stood in sharp contrast to the policy followed by the French crown. New France was controlled very closely by the government of France, at considerable expense to the royal treasury. The English kings, perhaps more parsimonious by nature when it came to colonial adventures, preferred to let others take the risks until the ventures began to pay off.

By the end of the 1700s, France had lost her empire in Canada (except for two little islands in the Gulf of St. Lawrence), while England had lost her empire along the Atlantic seaboard (now called the United States) but ended up with what France once had — Canada.

1640 Autograph

When *autograph*, from the Greek, *auto*, "self," and *graphein*, "to write," first appeared in print in English in 1640, it meant "that which is written in one's own handwriting." That use of the word was probably quite common in previous centuries, when most people were unable to read or write and had to dictate to a scribe whatever they wished to have written. The more familiar meaning (a person's own signature) first came into use around 1791.

The word *autograph* is of special significance to authors, who are always being asked to autograph copies of their books. When doing this, the author must take care to spell correctly the name of the person who has purchased the book. An American author was recently on a promotional tour across Australia and encountered many lineups of eager purchasers anxious for a signature. One woman suddenly became quite agitated and said, "No! No! Emma Chisit! Emma Chisit!" The store manager heard the commotion and came over to explain to the author that Emma Chisit was not the woman's name at all. It was simply her way of asking, in a thick Australian accent, for the price of the book ("How much is it?").

1641 APARTMENT

The earliest mention of *apartment* in the English language was in 1641 when, in his *Memoirs*, John Evelyn wrote, "Our new lodgings ... a very handsome apartment just over against the Hall-court." This word comes from the French *appartement*, "a suite of rooms," so called because they are set apart from the rest of the house or building.

The word *apartment* was sufficiently novel as late as 1890 to warrant being put in quotation marks (*Harper's Magazine*, January 1890): "Mr. and Mrs. Delancy Robinson reside in a cosy flat, or 'apartment,' as they prefer to call it, in New York City." And what, if any, is the difference between a flat and an apartment? On September 12, 1903, the *New York Evening Post* attempted to answer that linguistic sizzler: "The chief distinction between a flat and an apartment, according to the accepted definition, is that the apartment has an elevator."

1642 DEBAUCHERY

The verb form of this word (*debauch*), which came to the English language from France, appeared as early as 1595 and was used by John Florio in 1603 to convey his sense of boredom with it all: "My debauches or excesses transport me not much." John Milton was the first to use the noun, and he did so in 1642 when he wrote about "truanting and debauchery."

Students of the seamy side of history are fond of using the phrase "unbridled orgiastic debauchery" when discussing the atmosphere of moral depravity and licentiousness that ran rampant through Rome when the empire was at its height. All the salacious details of those wild nights of revelry were chronicled by Roman biographers who knew all and told all. The modern reader seeking more information is advised to wade through *The Twelve Caesars* by Suetonius, now available in paperback at your local bookstore.

1643 TURNSTILE

The next time you pay your fare for a subway ride and walk through the turnstile, you might reflect upon the fascinating history of this word and the apparatus it describes. In bygone centuries turnstiles — the word being a combination of Old English *tyrnan*, "to turn," and the Latin *stilus*, "post" or "pole" — were used on toll roads known as *turnpikes*. The *stilus*, or *pike*, was turned to allow people through after they had paid their fare. Today, motorists using turnpikes have to pay their toll at toll booths, some of which have large metal baskets into which the fare can be thrown if the driver has exact change.

The first major turnpike in the United States was built by the Lancaster Turnpike Company. It stretched from Philadelphia to Lancaster, Pennsylvania, a distance of sixty-two miles, and opened for business in 1795. Soon other companies were building them (one hundred and seventy-five companies were organized in New England alone between 1792 and 1810), hoping to make a fat profit. But turnpike stocks were practically worthless by 1825 because the money they brought in barely covered the costs of keeping up the roads. Many travellers preferred to use the bumpier secondary roads because they were free, and these penny-pinchers came to be known as *shunpikers*, a word you can find in the *OED*. Today, we call a cheap and stingy person a *piker*, likely a contraction of *shunpiker*.

1644 SEMICOLON

In 1644 a chap named Hodges distinguished between the comma and the semicolon: "At a comma, stop a little.... At a semi-colon, somewhat more." What Hodges did not bother to mention was that a much earlier form of punctuation took the form of an upside-down semicolon. It was called the point and tickle, and it flourished in England between the ninth and twelfth centuries. The point (.) was on the bottom; the tickle (') was on the top. On July 15, 1979, Father Leonard Boyle, a University of Toronto professor who specializes in ancient manuscripts and punctuation history, was interviewed by Stef Donev of the *Toronto Star* and had this to say: "The point and tickle developed when most reading was done aloud and the point signified a breathing space, but the tickle warned the reader not to change his tone of voice." And why did it die out? According to Donev, "as literacy spread and more and more people started reading to themselves, punctuation became more pointed and less ticklish."

In the early nineteenth century, an American businessman had his own unique solution to the ups and downs of punctuation. His name was Timothy Dexter and he published a book in 1802, *A Pickle for the Knowing*, which was totally lacking in punctuation of any kind — no commas, no periods, no semicolons, nothing! When he brought out a second edition, Dexter yielded somewhat to the cries of outrage from grammarians and schoolmarms by including lots of punctuation — all of which was lumped together in an appendix at the back of the book so that readers could "pepper and salt [the book] as they please."

1645 Backgammon

Backgammon literally means "back game" (from Old English *baec*, "back," and Middle English, *gamen*, "play"), because the pieces being moved across the board are often obliged to go back. The earliest mention of the game in English is dated at 1645, and by the end of that century it was widely popular in France and England. Backgammon probably grew out of Parcheesi, which it closely resembles, and likely has had a long history. Boards, dice and counters have been excavated at Babylon and Ur, with one board dating back to 3000 B.C. Whether this equipment was used for backgammon as we know it, or for some other parent game, is not known. One of the earliest references to backgammon was made by Plato when he wrote about *ludus duodecim scriptorum*, or the "twelve-lined game" (backgammon uses twelve lines or points on each side of the board). The game has been popular in the United States since the 1930s, when American players adopted a new rule about doubling and redoubling the stakes, thus speeding up the pace.

1646 Euthanasia

The word *euthanasia* literally means "a good death," from the Greek *eu*, "good," and *thanatos*, "death." Other words that share the same Greek prefix include *eulogy*, "words of praise"; *euphonious*, "having a pleasant sound"; *euphemism*, a gentle way of saying something unpleasant; *eugenics*, "breeding for the improvement of the species"; and *euphoria*, a feeling of well-being.

When Julius Caesar was once asked what kind of death he preferred, he replied: "A sudden one." He got what he wanted. With twenty-three stab wounds, it was certainly not a painless death, and therefore does not qualify as an example of euthanasia. When this word first appeared in print in 1646, it simply meant a gentle and painless death, such as dying in one's sleep. In Edmund Burke's *Correspondence* from 1768, we find this sentiment: "At her age, no friend could have hoped for your mother any thing but the Euthanasia." In recent years the term has been applied to proposed changes in the law that would permit putting painlessly to death those people suffering from incurable and very painful diseases.

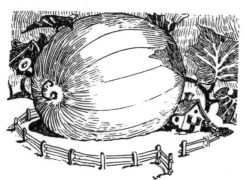

1647 PUMPKIN

First appearing in print in 1647 in a rather bizarre quotation ("He would come over to us, to helpe recruite our pumpkin-based brains"), the pumpkin is now almost as American as apple pie — especially at Hallowe'en, when the hollowed skins of pumpkins turn into jack-o'-lanterns to ward off evil spirits. Being native to America, the pumpkin replaced the turnip, which was used as the jack-o'-lantern in Scotland and by Scottish immigrants to America. Hallowe'en itself, known as All Saints' Eve during the Middle Ages, has a history going back to Celtic and Anglo-Saxon times, when October 31 marked the beginning of the new year as well as the onset of that half of the year that was darkest and gloomiest — hence the legions of ghosts, witches, goblins and demons of all kinds roaming about.

The word *pumpkin*, from the Greek, *pepon*, "a large melon," has over the years inspired the formation of several "nonce words" (words appearing in print only once), including *pumpkinish* (resembling a pumpkin), *pumpkinism* (pompous behaviour or language), *pumpkinity* (the nature or quality of a pumpkin, analogous to *divinity*), and *pumpkinification* (transformation into a pumpkin), something with which Cinderella was all too familiar.

1648 Submarine

The first recorded use in English of the word *submarine*, from Latin *sub mare*, "under the sea," dates back to 1648, when a chap named Bishop John Wilkins wrote a book called *Mathematical Magick*. In it he writes, "concerning the possibility of framing an Ark for submarine Navigations." In pondering how such a vessel would get around, he adds: "These submarine Navigators will want the usuall advantages of winds and tides for motion."

In 1670 the British scientist Sir Robert Boyle wrote a tract called *Submarine Regions*, in which he clarifies the meaning of this new word: "By the Apellation of Submarine Regions 'tis not to be supposed that the places so called are below the Bottom of the Sea, but only below the surface of it."

When was the world's first submarine constructed? According to the *Encyclopedia Americana*, "the first known practical submersible was a leather-covered, twelve-oared rowboat designed and built by Cornelis Drebbel, a Dutchman, in 1620. Drebbel's wooden boat was reinforced with iron against the water pressure at its operating depth of about fifteen feet (five and one-half meters). The boat is said to have operated on the Thames River from 1620 to 1624 and to have been able to remain submerged for several hours."

The first submarine built for war was the *Turtle*, designed by the American inventor David Bushnell and pressed into service in 1776. It was a wooden egg, seven feet deep and five and a half feet wide, operated by one very busy man who propelled it forward using one hand-cranked propeller and up or down via another. He had to steer by means of a tiller, take on ballast with a foot-operated valve, and pump it out again by hand, doing all this while peering through a tiny viewing port that was barely out of the water when the sub was floating on the surface (the periscope came later). The *Turtle* had a top speed of three miles per hour (depending on the stamina of the fellow inside) and could descend to a depth of twenty feet. It carried one hundred and fifty pounds of gunpowder in a detachable container, to be screwed onto the bottom of an enemy ship sitting at anchor and then detonated by a timer. It was sent into action against the flagship of a British squadron blockading the port of New York. Alas, the hull of the flagship was sheathed in copper and the explosive charge could not be attached. The *Turtle* was forced to beat an ignominious retreat.

1649 SERENADE

The year 1649 was a grim one for King Charles I of England. He had his head chopped off on January 30 of that year, after a trial conducted by Oliver Cromwell and the Roundheads, who had defeated the king in the English Civil War. More than three hundred years later, this bloodstained event was being used by English teachers to impress upon their students the importance of punctuation: "King Charles the First walked and talked ten minutes after he had his head chopped off." Supply the missing punctuation and you'll get a sentence that makes sense. (See page 227)

In that same year, the English poet Richard Lovelace used the word *serenade*, from the Italian *sereno*, "the open air," in the earliest example ever found by the editors of the *OED*: "Or the soft Serenades above In calme of Night, when Cats make Love." Seven years later, the English poet Abraham Cowley wrote disapprovingly of the quality of music floating up from below: "Foolish Prater, what do'st thou So early at my window do With thy tuneless Serenade?" And in 1843, in the novel *Hadley Cross*, English author Robert Smith Surtees included a sentence for all those slumberers rudely awakened in the middle of the night by feline courtship: "… I will finish wot I've left unsung, as the tom-cat said when the brick-bat cut short his serenade."

1650 TYRANNICIDE

The death of King Charles I of England on the executioner's block on January 30, 1649, prompted the birth of a new word the very next year, when Thomas Hobbes wrote, "Tyrannicide, that is, the killing of a Tyrant, [is] not onely Lawful, but also Laudable." Hobbes was using a word that traces its origin back to ancient Greek: *tyrannos*, a ruler who takes power by unconstitutional means. And that's all that the word *tyrant* meant back then: someone who seizes power wrongfully. Many of the tyrants of ancient Greece were actually quite popular (they had to be if they wanted to stay in power). By the ancient definition of *tyrant*, Adolf Hitler was not a tyrant at all because he became chancellor of Germany by perfectly legal means. What he did after he gained power, however, qualifies him as a modern-day tyrant.

1651 AUTOPSY

When this word first appeared in print in 1651, it simply meant a personal eyewitness or inspection, from the Greek *autos*, "self," and *opsis*, "sight." By 1678 it had acquired its modern meaning: the dissection of a dead body, usually in order to determine the cause of death. By 1895 it was joined in the dictionary by its livelier counterpart: *biopsy*, an examination of living tissue. And in 1900 *autopsy* was used as a verb by an English newspaper: "It was the first walrus that had been autopsied in London for many years."

On May 14, 1974, one of the most unusual autopsies of all time was performed at the Princess Margaret Hospital in Toronto, Canada, on a fifteen-year-old Egyptian boy named Nakht. This young lad had died more than three thousand years before in Egypt, and his well-preserved body was now to be cut open in the interests of medical science. Forty doctors and scientists from all over North America took part. After the linen wrappings were carefully removed, the chest and abdomen were cut open to permit a detailed examination of the internal organs. Nakht had suffered a ruptured spleen (perhaps the cause of death) and his lungs were darkened, possibly from the smoke of fires used for cooking. Traces of granite dust could also be found in the lungs, suggesting he may have spent some time in a granite quarry. The dry Egyptian climate had so completely dehydrated Nakht's body that by the time of his autopsy he weighed only eleven pounds.

1652 RECESSION

When this word first entered the English language, it meant a withdrawal or retirement, and this sense of the word still survives today, as when, for example, your dentist talks about gum recession (a medical condition giving rise to the expression "long in the tooth"). But the most widely used definition of *recession* today is the economic one: a mild economic slump. No one wants to use the word *depression* because of the memories it evokes of the Great Depression of the 1930s. And so linguists are faced with a problem: at what point does a recession become a depression? Here's one way of telling the two apart: when your neighbour is out of work, it's a recession. When *you're* out of work, it's a depression.

1653 ESCAPADE

The word *escapade* is based on the word *escape*, which comes to us from the Latin *es*, "out of," and *cappa*, "cape," because a thief in ancient Rome, when apprehended, might often try to slip out of his cape and make his getaway. *Escapade* was first used in English by Sir Thomas Urquhart in his 1653 translation of Rabelais: "I wish your bum-gut [may] fall out and make an escapade." The word has changed somewhat in meaning since then, now referring primarily to a lighthearted adventure.

The most famous escape in recent American history is the one engineered by Canadian ambassador Kenneth Taylor, who hid six American diplomats in the Canadian embassy in Tehran from November 4, 1979, until January 26, 1980. They were furnished with Canadian passports and, on the morning of January 26, boarded a plane for Frankfurt, West Germany, and then home to the United States. The American hostages who still remained in Teheran had another year of captivity ahead of them. In speaking of his role in helping the six who got away, Kenneth Taylor used a relatively new term in military circles. If he had been sending troops in small numbers behind enemy lines, he would have been helping them infiltrate enemy territory; but because he was helping them escape in small numbers from enemy territory, the word he coined was *exfiltrate*.

1654 RUM

This word of uncertain origin broke into print smack-dab in the middle of the Interregnum (from Latin, *inter*, "between," and *rex, regis*, "king"), that eleven-year period of English history between the reigns of King Charles I (who was beheaded in 1649) and King Charles II (who ascended the throne in 1660), during which the Puritans ruled England. Their strict moral code allowed for no drinking of intoxicating spirits, least of all the demon rum. But not all Englishmen were willing to live a dry life. One Puritan complained that on May Day in 1654, the very year in which *rum* first appeared in print: "much sin [was] committed by wicked meetings with fiddlers, drunkenness, ribaldry and the like…" Rum found its way to the shores of New England as well; in fact, the fortunes of many old New England families can be traced back to the early days of the rum trade, an immensely profitable business

that was part of the so-called triangular trade that linked New England with Africa and the West Indies. In his action-packed "unputdownable," *The American Pageant*, Thomas Bailey explains how it worked. "A skipper … would leave a New England port with a cargo of rum and sail to the Gold Coast of Africa. Bartering the fiery liquor with African chiefs for captured African slaves, he would proceed to the West Indies with his screaming and suffocating cargo sardined below deck. There he would exchange the survivors for molasses, which he would then carry to New England, where it was distilled into rum. The Yankee captain could then repeat the trip, making a handsome profit at each angle of the triangle."

1655 SIESTA

Siesta is based on the Spanish word for "sixth," because the Spaniards were accustomed to working for six hours, then taking a nap in the early afternoon when the heat of the midday sun was most intense. But did you know that the English word *noon* is based on the Latin word for "nine"? It goes back to the Middle Ages, when the monks in monasteries arose at dawn and worked for nine hours before stopping to eat. The eating time was known as the *nones*, from the Latin *nona* [*hora*], meaning "ninth hour," and was usually observed at midafternoon. As monasteries became wealthy and more comfortable, the monks began knocking off work earlier and earlier until the *nones* were eaten at midday — in other words, at noon.

1656 VENTRILOQUIST

In 1656, in the earliest known use of this word, Thomas Blount defines *ventriloquist* as "one that hath an evil spirit speaking in his belly, not moving his lips." Early practitioners of this art were believed to possess magical, even devilish, powers. The word comes from Latin *venter*, "belly," and *loqui*, "speak." In *Witchcraft*, published in 1718, Bishop Francis Hutchinson writes, "There are ... many [witches] that came from Words and Voices in their Stomach, which shall seem to come from others rather than the Person that speaks them. Such people are call'd Engastriloques, or Ventriloquists." In 1749 Charles Wesley claimed: "there was a compact ... between the ventriloquist and the exorcist."

By 1791 ventriloquism had come to the attention of the editors of the *Encyclopaedia Britannica*, who questioned the suitability of this word: "It is with no great propriety that ... their art [is called] *ventriloquism*, since they appear more frequently to speak ... from the roof or distant corners of the room, than from their own mouths or their own bellies." In his diary of January 12, 1826, Sir Walter Scott reveals an equally low opinion of the word: "Mathews ... confirms my idea of ventriloquism (which is an absurd word), as being merely the art of imitating sounds at a greater or a less distance." However, these critics did not come forward with a better word. Interestingly, ventriloquism is almost exclusively a phenomenon of English-speaking peoples.

1657 NURSEMAID

Merriam-Webster's Collegiate Dictionary defines this word as "a girl or woman who is regularly employed to look after children." The word *nurse* as a noun comes from Middle English in the thirteenth century, and can be traced back to the Anglo-French *nurice*, from Late Latin *nutricia*, from the Latin feminine form of *nutricius*, "nourishing." As a verb, *nurse* goes back to the fourteenth century and the Middle English *nurshen*, to suckle or nourish.

The word *maid* appears to be just as old, dating back to the thirteenth century for "an unmarried girl or woman especially when young; virgin" (Merriam-Webster). The word *virgin* also goes back to the thirteenth century and comes from Latin, the language spoken by the Romans, who worshipped Vesta, the goddess of the hearth. The vestal virgins were "consecrated to the Roman goddess Vesta and to the service of watching the sacred fire perpetually kept burning on her altar."

1658 LEXICOGRAPHER

Although several English-Latin dictionaries were compiled during the Middle Ages, the first strictly English dictionaries were not on the market until the mid-1500s. It would be another century before a fancy word came along to describe the people who perform this type of work. The earliest known example of *lexicographer* (a person who compiles dictionaries) in print dates from 1658, the year Oliver Cromwell died. The word itself comes from Greek *lexis*, "speech," and *graphein*, "to write."

The three most famous lexicographers in the English-speaking world are Samuel Johnson (1709–1784), Noah Webster (1758–1843) and James Murray (1837–1915). Johnson entered the field of lexicography in 1747, when Lord Chesterfield offered him an advance of £1,575 to write a dictionary of the English language. Supremely confident of his literary powers, Johnson readily accepted (he also needed the money) and boasted that he would finish the task in just three years. When his friends pointed out that forty French scholars had taken forty years to produce a French dictionary, Johnson declared that since a single Englishman was the equivalent of forty Frenchmen, he had nothing to worry about. The task actually took him not three years but eight, and proved to be well worth the time spent. Published in 1755 in two volumes with 41,000 definitions, *A Dictionary of the English Language* by Samuel Johnson became an immediate linguistic and commercial success.

Noah Webster was the American lexicographer *par excellence.* In addition to producing several editions of a dictionary that included for the first time the thousands of new words born in America, he also wrote the

Blue-back Speller, which sold an incredible one million copies a year for seventy years! The royalties from this little speller gave Webster a remarkable degree of financial independence.

He would need it. Although his first few dictionaries were financial successes, his final and most monumental one was not. Much of his own money went into it, and he was in financial difficulty when he approached his death bed in 1843. He was forced to surrender the rights to the publisher that was handling it — G. & C. Merriam of Springfield, Massachusetts. These arrangements were complete by 1847, and ever since then the dictionaries that are the direct descendants of the one compiled by Noah are known as Merriam-Webster dictionaries.

The last of the three famous lexicographers was James Murray, who was persuaded to take the editorship of the biggest lexicographical project in the history of the human race: the compiling and publishing of the *Oxford English Dictionary*. Years later, Murray would say that if he had known the enormity of the task that lay before him when he started, he would have turned the job down. Nevertheless, he stuck with it until he died in 1915. His first volume came out in 1884, while the last appeared in 1928, more than a decade after his death. The *OED* traces the history of every word in the English language.

1659 SIPHON

Although first used in print in 1659 ("A Syphon ... hath that end which is without the vessel longer than the other"), the principle this word describes was common knowledge at least as far back as the days of the ancient Romans, who used siphonic action to draw water from their aqueducts. During the gasoline shortages in the United States in the late 1970s, black-market entrepreneurs used siphonic action to drain fuel from the tanks of automobiles, and sales of key-locked gas caps sky-rocketed all over the country. But stolen gas was not the only hot item for sale. In those states that enacted odd-even licence plate fuel rationing (allowing motorists to buy gasoline only on odd-numbered days of the month if their licence plate ended in an odd number, and vice versa), some drivers woke up in the morning to find their cars had been stripped of their plates.

110

1660 Pendulum

The great Italian scientist Galileo first discovered the laws governing the pendulum by watching a lamp swing back and forth. His findings were used by the Dutch scientist Christian Huygens, who built the world's first pendulum clock in 1657. Three years later the word *pendulum*, from Latin *pendulus*, "hanging," began to appear in English writings. During one of his experiments, the British physicist Robert Boyle wrote: "We thought it not amiss to try if a Pendulum would swing faster, or continue swinging longer in Receiver."

Pendulum is also used in a figurative sense to describe persons or events that swing back and forth between extremes. In this sense, it is highly appropriate that the word *pendulum* should first appear in English in 1660, the year in which the English people stopped swinging between the extremes of king and Parliament. By insisting on the "divine right of kings" to rule, Charles I provoked a series of events that triggered the English Civil War and led finally to his beheading. For the next eleven years, England struggled along under a so-called Puritan parliament, which found itself increasingly unable to cope with the problems of government. Finally, in 1660, the son of Charles I was invited back from exile to become Charles II, provided he was willing to have certain restrictions imposed on his power. Parliament was now gaining the upper hand. Charles, having no wish to spend his whole life in exile, readily agreed and England once more had a monarchy.

1661 Barbecue

Some say that the word *barbecue* comes from the French *barbe à queue*, "from beard to tail," because the first animal to be barbecued was a goat. The editors of the *OED* have heard that story, too, and here is their comment: "The alleged French *barbe à queue* 'beard to tail' is an absurd conjecture suggested merely by the sound of the word." According to the *OED*, *barbecue* is a Native West Indian term that first appeared in English in 1661 in a book called *Jamaica View'd* by Edmund Hickeringill: "Some are slain, And their flesh forthwith Barbacu'd and eat." It was first used as a noun in 1697, when it was defined as: "a rude wooden framework, used in America for sleeping on, and supporting above a fire meat that is to be smoked or dried."

The backyard barbecue boom got under way in the 1950s, when a new generation of homeowners discovered the joys of outdoor cooking. That same new generation also discovered the joys of owning a new car, and old ones were junked so fast that new ways had to be invented for getting rid of them. One new way was the *carbecue*, defined by *The Barnhart Dictionary of New English* as "a device for disposing of a junked car by rotating it over a fire." In the January 2, 1968, issue of *The New York Times*, Robert Trumbull describes the carbecue [as] "a machine that turns an old automobile body into a solid lump of metal by pressure and heat." Just don't try it in your backyard.

1662 VANILLA

Although it is believed that vanilla was first imported into England from Mexico by the Spaniards around 1510, the word *vanilla* did not appear in print in English until 1662, when H. Stubbe wrote about the Native peoples of Mexico: "They added ... the Vaynillas [to the Chocolate] for the like ends, and to strengthen the brain." The word comes to us from Latin, through Spanish, from *vagina*, "sheath," because of the shape of the bean pods. The Native peoples had been using vanilla as a flavouring in chocolate and other delicacies long before the arrival of Europeans. Most of the world's vanilla now comes from Madagascar and other islands of the Indian Ocean, where it was introduced from Mexico shortly after the European discovery of America. Because of the high cost of vanilla extract, scientists have developed a number of substitutes, but none of these imitations has succeeded in reproducing the delicate flavour of pure vanilla.

1663 AMUCK

In *Pinto's Travels*, an account of a journey to the Far East published in 1663, a chap named Cogan wrote, "... all those which were able to bear arms should make themselves *Amoucos*, that is to say, men resolved either to dye, or vanquish." The more familiar version of this word appeared nine years later, when a chronicler named Marvell wrote: "Like a raging Indian ... he runs a mucke [as they cal it there] stabbing every man he meets." And one hundred years after that, Captain James Cook tried to offer an explanation for this bizarre behaviour, common among the early inhabitants of Malaysia, from whom we derive the word: "Jealousy of the women is the usual reason of these poor creatures running amock [or amuck]." Cook himself was on the receiving end of an outburst of anger when, in 1779 in the Sandwich Islands (now called Hawaii), he was clubbed to death after thrashing a Native for stealing a boat.

1664 Champagne

Champagne first appeared in English in 1664, and it inspired a number of intriguing variations in the years that followed. Lord Byron used it as a verb in a letter he wrote on April 9, 1814: "We clareted and champagned till two." In *Public Dinner*, a fellow named Hood used it as an adjective in 1845: "[You] hear rather plainish a sound that's champaignish." Another adjectival use appeared in 1882 in a magazine that alluded to the stimulating effects of this beverage: "That peculiar champagney feel of mountain air."

For this word we can thank the wineries in the Champagne region of northeastern France, where this sparkling white wine first became famous. The word itself is not the exclusive property of those wineries, but similar wines produced elsewhere and labelled champagne must show the place of origin.

After downing some champagne at the Toronto Press Club, Peter Marucci of the *Toronto Star* presented me with a magazine in which he appeared in a photograph proposing a toast with a glass of champagne in his hand. I asked him to sign his name below the photo and to add "something clever." Marucci rose to the challenge magnificently as he scrawled: "Forget the sham pain. Let's have some real pain!"

1665 Condom

A condom is a thin rubber covering worn by men during sexual intercourse as a protection against disease or pregnancy. Although contraceptives made of sheep intestines had long been in use in the Middle East, the word *condom* itself did not appear in print until 1665, when a chap named Contin or Condon or Condum (no one seems sure of the spelling) popularized a male contraceptive that he made from dried lamb intestines which he oiled to make flexible. Some claim he was a French physician; other accounts describe him as a London doctor at the court of Charles II; still others claim he was a colonel in Britain's Household troops. In any event, one of his first customers was the great lover Giacomo Casanova, who ordered twelve "English caps," as he was fond of calling them. Although the city of Condom in southwestern France apparently played no part in creating this new word, tourists like to send home postcards with the Condom postmark prominently displayed.

By the end of the 1700s, condoms were widely available, prompting Pope Leo XIII to issue a papal bull in 1826 denouncing the device because "it hindered the arrangement of providence." What Leo would have said about the birth-control pill is easy to imagine.

1666 PANDEMIC

In *Morbus Anglicus*, or *The Anatomy of Consumptions*, published in 1666, Gideon Harvey wrote, "Some [diseases] do more generally haunt a Country ... whence such diseases are termed Endemick or Pandemick." Gideon Harvey had every reason to be thinking of *pandemic*, a word that describes an epidemic that covers a wide area, from the Greek *pan*, "all," and *demos*, "a people." In the previous year, England had been struck with the plague that had periodically ravaged Europe since the Middle Ages. This time, Londoners were dying at the rate of seven thousand a week. Daniel Defoe, who lived through it and would later write *Robinson Crusoe*, recorded: "the face of London was now indeed strangely alter'd.... Sorrow and Sadness sat upon every Face.... London might be said to be all tears.... The shrieks of Women and Children at the Windows and Doors of their Houses, when their Nearest Relations were perhaps dying, or just dead, were so frequent to be heard, as we passed the Streets, that it was enough to pierce the stoutest Heart in the World, to hear them."

Another disaster struck London the following year: the Great Fire, which started in a bakery shop in Pudding Lane and raged for three days and nights before it could be extinguished. The light from the fire could be seen from forty miles away, and yet the destruction was a blessing in disguise, for the fire apparently burned away the last remnants of the dreaded plague.

1667 PANDEMONIUM

In his literary masterpiece, *Paradise Lost*, published in 1667, John Milton created the name Pandemonium for the capital of Hell, from the Greek *pan*, "all," and *daimon*, "demon." Over the years Milton's word lost its capital letter and became a synonym for uproar and bedlam. It's interesting to note that the year before Milton's book was published happened to be the year of the Great Fire of London. A classic case of pandemonium breaking out.

By the next year, Milton's book was on sale and London was busy rebuilding itself. The man most responsible for making the new London rise phoenixlike from the ashes of the old was Sir Christopher Wren, architect *par excellence*. He designed more than thirty new churches for the city, including the new St. Paul's Cathedral. When the great dome of St. Paul's was set in place, Wren stood back, looked up, and said, "It's awful!"

But he wasn't complaining. He meant it filled him with awe.

1668 PENIS

According to the dates in the latest *Merriam-Webster's Collegiate Dictionary* (published in 2003), the word *penis* popped up in the English language fourteen years before *vagina* (our main entry for 1682). Coming from the Latin *penis* (tail), this word appeared in the 1693 translation of *Blancard's Physiological Dictionary*: "Penis, the Yard, made up of two nervous Bodies, the Channel, Nut, Skin, and Fore-skin, & C." Today, most dictionaries define the penis simply as the organ with which a male copulates and urinates.

You will search in vain through the words of Shakespeare for any mention of the word *penis* because it apparently did not join the English language until fifty-two years after the Bard of Avon died (at age fifty-two!).

However, Shakespeare did make reference to the male organ of copulation and urination, not once but several times. He simply used other words. For example, one of Shakespeare's most endearing characters is

Falstaff, the portly sidekick of Prince Hal in *Henry IV, Part One and Two*. Shakespeare's fondness for wordplay is well known, and a classic example is the name *Falstaff* itself, which the Bard concocted as a synonym for *false staff* (i.e., "limp penis"). Apparently, Falstaff was not a big hit with the women, and his name reflects his lack of virility. If Shakespeare had intended to portray Falstaff as an irrepressible womanizer, he probably would have called him Tallstaff — or even Stiffstaff.

1669 PHOSPHORUS

Of the more than one hundred elements so far discovered, only ten were known to the people of ancient times: gold, silver, copper, iron, lead, tin, sulphur, mercury, carbon and antimony. Around 1250 a German named Albertus Magnus discovered arsenic, thereby earning for himself the distinction of being the first person in history to discover an element that was unknown before his time. Then along came Hennig Brand, an alchemist born in Hamburg around 1630, who began searching for the philosopher's stone in, of all things, urine. He never found what he was looking for, but in 1669 he did find something dramatic and mysterious: a white waxy substance that glowed in the dark. He called it *phosphorus*, from the Greek *phos* and *phoros*, meaning "light-bearing."

The word *Phosphorus* had been put into use — as a proper noun — as another name for the planet Venus at least forty years earlier, but Brand's discovery transformed it into a common noun. People often misspell it because the noun itself is *phosphorus*, but the adjective (for something containing or resembling phosphorus) is *phosphorous*.

News of Brand's discovery quickly spread through Germany and beyond. He refused to make public his method of producing phosphorus, but instead sold the secret to Johann Krafft of Dresden, who in turn tried at various times to sell it himself. In 1677 Krafft performed some phosphorus experiments before members of the Royal Society in England, and a few years later Robert Boyle, the famous British chemist, devised a method of producing the element. The *Encyclopaedia Britannica* describes the impact of Brand's discovery: "It is easy to understand the widespread interest that was aroused in the seventeenth century by the discovery of such a remarkable substance as phosphorus.

A substance which glowed in the dark and took fire spontaneously upon exposure to air was something startlingly new and mysterious. It is indeed notable that an element so difficult to isolate should have been discovered through the unguided fumbling of an alchemist."

What happened to Brand after his dramatic discovery is not known. He faded from the stage of history and died in obscurity. But we do know what phosphorus did to Brand's home city of Hamburg. Phosphorus was a key ingredient in the incendiary bombs the Allies dropped on Germany during the Second World War. As a result of this aerial bombardment, Hamburg was almost totally destroyed.

1670 NEWSPAPER

Although the story may be pure fiction, some claim that the word *news* is an acronym based on the initial letters of the four compass points — North, East, West and South — because any newspaper worth its weight in printer's ink collects news from the four corners of the globe. Most dictionaries give you a less glamorous etymology: *news* is simply the plural of *new*, which comes from the Middle English *newe*, meaning "new."

The growth of English newspapers coincided with the growth of English coffee houses, which began sprouting all over London in the latter half of the seventeenth century. The first newspapers were little more than newsletters circulated among the patrons of these coffee houses, who were attracted as much by the spirited political discussions as they were by the coffee. In his role as printer and publisher in Philadelphia, Benjamin Franklin greatly advanced the development of the newspaper in America, but it was Melville E. Stone of Chicago who, in 1876, popularized the daily newspaper that sold for a penny a copy. Stone was competing against nickel papers, but pennies were scarce in Chicago at that time because most larger items in stores were priced in nice round dollar figures.

In a stroke of marketing genius, Stone persuaded several Chicago merchants to drop their prices by a penny in order to attract impulse buyers into thinking a former two-dollar item now marked down to "only $1.99" was a real bargain. The merchants who tried it found that it worked. Stone travelled to Philadelphia to purchase several barrels of new pennies from the U.S. Mint and brought them back to the Windy City, where they went into circulation. Merchants could now make change on the marked-down items and the customers used their pennies to buy Stone's paper.

Stone himself soon became rich and famous. He later founded Associated Press and saw his *Chicago Daily News* turn into one of the most successful newspapers in the country. This book you are reading sells for $24.99 instead of $25.00, and for that you can give thanks to the entrepreneurial pizzazz of Melville E. Stone.

1671 CESSPOOL

If you look at the size of the sewers of ancient Rome, you might easily conclude that the Romans regarded the elimination of bodily wastes as the prime function of civilization. Huge aqueducts poured thousands of gallons of fresh water into the city daily, and the Cloaca Maxima, or Great Sewer, built in Rome by the Etruscans, is still carrying sewage today after twenty-five hundred years.

When the barbarians overran the western half of the Roman Empire in the fifth century, the great age of sewers and drains came to an end in western Europe. A new one would not dawn for more than a thousand years. Plumbing facilities in medieval castles often consisted of a stone slab out of which a hole had been carved for a toilet seat, below which a pipe angled outward to the castle wall, down the side of which slowly oozed the human effluvia before it slid into the waters of the moat far below. It has been said that you could smell many a medieval castle or town before you were close enough to see it.

But by the 1600s the living habits of Europeans were becoming more refined, and England was no exception. With the new wealth that England's overseas empire was bringing to her shores, more money was available for creature comforts. It is probably more than mere coincidence that the earliest recorded use of the word *cesspool* can be dated to 1671, just five years after the Great Fire of London. A new city arose from the ashes, with new churches, homes, places of business — and sanitary facilities. According to an Act of the Common Council of London dated October 27, 1671, "A Fall or Cestpool of convenient bigness shall be made ... to every Grate of the Common Sewer ... to receive the Sand or Gravel coming to the same, so to prevent the choaking thereof." Unfortunately, where the word itself came from remains a mystery.

1672 SERUM

Although we usually associate this word with the fluid that will protect you from a disease through inoculation, it was first used in 1672 to describe the greenish-yellow fluid that is left after blood has clotted: "That morning I let her bloud, taking away about ten ounces with a rotten Serum upon it." Bloodletting was a popular remedy back then. Doctors believed they were draining off the disease when they drained off a patient's blood. No wonder so many died.

But by the late nineteenth century, many diseased patients were surviving and recovering because of the serum, from the Latin word for "whey," taken from immunized animals and used as an antitoxin to protect people against certain bacterial diseases.

1673 SHOPLIFT

This word first appeared in English in 1673 as a noun: "The tenth is a Shoplift that carries a Bob, When he ranges the City the Shops for to rob." Seven years later the suffix -er had been added to it: "Towards Night these Houses are throng'd with People of all sorts.... Shoplifters, Foilers, Bulkers." Ninety years later still, the crime carried a stiff penalty: "A shop-lifter was once hang'd in England." And in 1881, in *Library* by A. Lang, we find a euphemism for the crime: "The papers call lady shop-lifters 'kleptomaniacs'."

Shoplifting today costs all of us millions of dollars a year. In an effort to combat the problem, a well-known drugstore chain decided to take a new approach: the names of all those people convicted of shoplifting were posted in full view in the store in which they committed the crime. Public disgrace apparently is a powerful deterrent: the incidence of shoplifting in that chain of stores was drastically reduced.

1674 ZEST

In 1674 Geoffrey Blount defined *zest* this way: "… the pill of an orange, or such like, squeezed into a glass of wine, to give it a relish." That meaning is now classified as rare or obsolete, the more popular definition today being illustrated by this quote from 1895: "The Greek people had an almost unrivalled zest for life." The former meaning belies the origins of the word, which comes to us from the Old French *zeste*, "lemon peel."

Ever wondered why the letter *Z* come at the end of the alphabet? Believe it or not, it wasn't always at the end. It comes from *zeta*, which was, and still is, the *sixth* letter of the Greek alphabet. When the Romans adopted the Greek alphabet, they had no words using zeta, so they dropped it. Later on, as the Roman Empire and Latin language expanded, the Romans discovered they needed the letter after all, and so they revived it and stuck it at the end of the alphabet. It has been there ever since.

1675 PLAYTHING

This word first appeared in Traherne's *Christian Ethics* in 1675: "Say he delighteth in armies and victories, and triumphs, and cornonations; these are great in respect of playthings; but all these are feeble and pusillanimous to a great soul." The word *plaything* has no sexist connotations; the same cannot be said for *playboy*, a word that joined the English language in a much later century. It is now the title of a magazine available on every newsstand in North America. But when the first issue of *Playboy* came out in 1953, publisher Hugh Hefner did not bother putting a date on it because he didn't know if there would be a second issue.

1676 BUNGALOW

The entry of this word from the Hindustani *bangla*, "of Bengal," into the English language in 1676 was yet another sign of the growing might of the British Empire. When Queen Elizabeth I granted a charter to the East India Company in December 1600, she took the first big step toward the establishment of British rule in India. Nearly seventy-six years later, the word *bungalow* was imported into England along with cargoes of tea, ivory and spices. The *OED* includes, as a subentry, the adjective *bungaloid*, "having the appearance or style of a bungalow, the one-storey houses especially popular in the warmer climates of the world, such as India." A Canadian wordsmith recently concocted the word *dungalow* to describe the one-storey houses in India constructed of cattle dung.

1677 WITTICISM

This word was coined by the English man of letters John Dryden, who took the word *witty*, from the Old English *witan*, "to know," and grafted it to *criticism*, ending up with *witticism*. Dryden himself was considered a literary trendsetter in the latter half of the seventeenth century, and he owed his long-running popularity in part to his ability to change his religious and political views with each change of English rule. His poetry sang the praises of such disparate leaders as Oliver Cromwell, Charles II and James II. Dryden was named poet laureate in 1670 and held numerous royal offices until he refused allegiance to King William III in 1688.

Incidentally, the French have a saying for that witty remark or witticism that you think of too late. They call it *l'esprit d'escalier*, "staircase wit," because you are usually descending the stairs from a party when you think of the brilliant remark you could have used a little while earlier. No English equivalent of this French expression exists in English, although speed-reading expert Joel Bonn of Montreal has come up with one he thinks should be snapped up by the editors of Funk & Wagnalls: *quiptoolate*. You can use it as a noun or a verb and the word says exactly what it means: a quip thought of too late to use.

1678 BARRACUDA

This infamous tropical fish first appeared in print in English (from the Spanish) in 1678, when Edward Phillips included it in the latest edition of his book *The New World of English Words*. It was about time: the English had been borrowing Spanish words for over a hundred years to describe the exotic new plants and animals of newly discovered lands and oceans.

Many of these Spanish words were brought back to England by the "sea dogs" from Plymouth, the seaport from which Francis Drake had sailed more than one hundred years earlier to attack Spanish treasure ships in the New World. To the Spaniards, Drake was the scum of the earth, a pirate whose vile deeds were costing them a fortune. He helped defeat the "invincible" Spanish Armada in 1588 and paved the way for the growth of English sea power in the New World. Today, England and Spain are at peace, a condition that is symbolized by the harmonious juxtaposition of two words — one English and one Spanish — on the nameplate of an automobile built by the Chrysler Corporation from 1965 to 1974: the Plymouth Barracuda.

1679 SKYLIGHT

Skylights with plastic bubble windows are now all the range in new or renovated houses, but the word itself is not new. It appeared in print as early as 1679, meaning "light from the sky" ("It being intended that a Skie-light shall fall through the Hollow Newel upon the Stairs"), and as early as 1690 for a small glass opening in a ceiling or roof to let light in. But the architectural feature itself is much older than the word. Wealthy Roman villas in the days of Julius Caesar were often built around a central courtyard that was open to the sky to admit light, fresh air, and rainwater that fell into a pool in the middle of the floor.

1680 BLOCKADE

A blockade is the closing off by enemy forces of a harbour, city, coast or country to trade and traffic, a popular military strategy since the dawn of history. No famous battle was raging when this word entered the English language, only a mere castle under siege.

It was Napoleon who showed the world just how big a blockade could be when he imposed his Continental System on the rest of Europe in 1807 in an attempt to force England into surrender. (No countries under his control were to trade with England.) But the English retaliated with their Orders-in-Council, by which the European coastline was placed under British blockade so that the lands conquered by Napoleon could not trade with any other parts of the world. European imports of coffee, tea and sugar dwindled to a trickle, and Europeans from the Baltic to the Mediterranean chafed and squirmed under the French yoke, looking for an opportunity to throw it off. It took the Battle of Waterloo to finish Napoleon, but the blockade as a strategy of war had a busy future.

When the American Civil War broke out in April 1861, the Union navy lost no time in blockading the coastline of the Confederacy in order to stop shipments of cotton to England, the proceeds from which the South was depending on to raise cash to pay for the war effort. Perhaps more than any other strategy, this Union blockade brought about the ultimate surrender of the Old South. And after the war, Rhett Butler asked Scarlett O'Hara for her hand in marriage. He was now a very wealthy man, having earned his fortune during the war as a blockade runner in the pages of Margaret Mitchell's best-seller, *Gone with the Wind.*

1681 PENNSYLVANIA

When Charles II returned from exile in Europe to claim the English throne in 1660, he did so with the help of many powerful families in England who wanted to see a return of the monarchy after eleven years of Puritan rule. One of these families was the Penn family, and they naturally expected to be rewarded for their assistance. The big payoff finally came in 1681, when Charles II granted a charter to William Penn, authorizing him to found a colony on the land now occupied by the Commonwealth of Pennsylvania (even today, it is not officially called a state). The name literally means "Penn's Woods," with the *sylvania* coming from the Latin root *sylvan*, meaning "woods."

How many other American states are named after people? There are, including Pennsylvania, eleven of them: Delaware was named after Lord De la Warr; Georgia was named after King George II of England; Louisiana was named for King Louis XIV of France; Maryland for Queen Henrietta Maria of England, consort of Charles I; New York after the Duke of York in England; North Carolina and South Carolina after Charles IX of France; Virginia after Queen Elizabeth I of England, popularly known as the "Virgin Queen"; Washington after George Washington; and West Virginia also after Elizabeth, because it used to be part of Virginia. We could also include Hawaii on the list because Captain James Cook, the first Englishman to discover them, called them the Sandwich Islands in honour of Lord Sandwich of England.

1682 VAGINA

The word *vagina* was first used in English by Thomas Gibson in 1682 ("It [the pelvis] has passages … for the neck of the Bladder, and in women for the vagina of the womb") and comes from the Latin *vagina*, meaning "sheath," a long and hollow container for holding a sword. The analogy between *sword* and *sheath* on the one hand and *penis* and *vagina* on the other was a natural one for people living in the seventeenth century, when swords were still the chief weapon of combat. The word *penis*, incidentally, appeared in print in 1668 (see page 115), fourteen years before *vagina*. And if you flip back to *vanilla*, the entry for 1662, you will discover that that word comes from the same Latin root as *vagina*.

1683 PIANO

In 1683 the word *piano* had nothing to do with the musical instrument that now sits in a corner of your living room. It was simply a musical notation instructing a musician to play softly and quietly, from the Latin *planus*, or "flat," which later came to mean "soft and low." The piano as a musical instrument was the invention of Cristofori, who called it a *pianoforte* (literally "soft and strong," from the Italian *piano*, "soft," and *forte*, "strong") to indicate the wide range of tone it could produce. The name was stream-lined to *piano*, and that's what it has been called ever since. When this new instrument appeared on the musical scene in the 1750s, the harpsichord was the supreme keyboard instrument. But the piano's ability to play its percussive notes at any volume, loud or soft, gave it an expressiveness vastly superior to the harpsichord's inflexible plucking. Piano sales rose sharply after the world's first public piano concert was given in London in 1767, and many of these handcrafted instruments were shipped to America. In 1771 a young man named Thomas Jefferson gave one of these pianos to his fiancée, Martha Wayles Skelton. And when Mozart and Haydn began playing the piano, the harpsichord was on its last legs.

1684 ACUPUNCTURE

Although *acupuncture* was introduced into North America only within the last few years, its first recorded use in the English language goes back to 1684, when it was mentioned as a possible cure for gout. But the practice itself is much older than that. It originated in China hundreds of years before the birth of Christ and has been used to treat a wide variety of diseases, including arthritis, convulsions, headaches, colic and lethargy. Practitioners of acupuncture claim that the inserted needles (the Latin root *acus* means "needle") relieve pressure on various nerves and thereby assist the brain in sending messages to diseased or injured parts of the body in order to effect a natural cure. The needles themselves are of various shapes and sizes and are inserted into one or more of 365 designated spots on the human body to cure illness or induce anesthesia.

Unfortunately, some of those needles have been inserted into American patients by American medical practitioners who apparently don't know what they are doing. According to Samuel Rosen in *The New York Times* (May 28, 1974), "Acupuncture anesthesia does indeed work.... Unfortunately, acupuncture has become an American fad instead of the subject of serious experimental research. Acupuncture in America has become transformed into 'quackupuncture.'"

1685 REFUGEE

On October 31, 1517, a German monk named Martin Luther nailed to the door of the church in Wittenburg a list of ninety-five grievances, or protests, that he was lodging against the Roman Catholic Church. That act triggered a chain of events that came to be known as the Protestant Reformation, and for the next two centuries Catholics and Protestants all across Europe killed each other in the name of God. One of the worst examples of religious butchery took place on August 24, 1572, in Paris, when Catholics killed so many Protestants (known as Huguenots) that the Seine turned red with blood. Known as the St. Bartholomew's Day Massacre, it quickly spread to the provinces until an estimated ten thousand Huguenots had been killed. In 1598 Henry IV of France tried his best to end the bloodshed by announcing the Edict of Nantes, which gave the French Protestants legal recognition.

That status lasted almost a full century. Then, in 1685, the Sun King, Louis XIV, revoked the Edict of Nantes, not because the Huguenots were causing trouble but because Louis considered it a personal insult that so many of his subjects followed a religion that differed from his own. Rather than wait for another massacre, thousands of Huguenots left France and moved to England, where they were known as *refugies* or *refugees*, from Latin *fugere*, "to flee." The new word caught on and has been in our language ever since.

1686 SAUCEPAN

The earliest known use of this word in print goes back to an issue of the London *Gazette* in 1686, in which mention is made of "two Silver Porringers [shallow cups or bowls with a handle], one Silver Sawcepan." In 1729 Jonathan Swift uses the word in his advice on what to do when dinner guests complain about the butter: "If you have a Silver Sauce-pan, and the Butter smells of Smoak, lay the Fault upon the Coals." And in 1861, in *Paul Foster's Daughter*, the mention of this word points out the need for more elbow grease: "Do you call that saucepan lid clean? — because I don't."

The *sauce* in *saucepan* comes from the French word *sauce*, which in turn comes from the Latin *salarium*, "salt," one of the chief ingredients of a good sauce. And because many Roman soldiers were paid in salt, that Latin root gives us our word *salary*. And now you know where the expression "to be worth one's salt" comes from.

1687 MADHOUSE

When this word first appeared in print in 1687, it was two separate words: "He was severely reprimanded, and told he was fitter for a mad house." In the title of an Act of Parliament passed in 1774, during the reign of George III, the two words had merged into one: "An Act for regulating Madhouses." King George himself was supposed to have been a prime candidate for such an institution. One day, while riding in his carriage, he is said to have jumped out and addressed an oak tree as the king of Prussia. For the last two decades of his long reign (1760–1820), the running of the country was left in the hands of those who still had their wits together.

One of the most famous of all lunatic asylums was St. Mary's of Bethlehem, founded as a priory in London in 1242 and turned into a hospital for the insane in 1402. The name was shortened to Bedlam, which became a synonym for "lunatic asylum" and now covers any scene of great uproar.

1688 Pigtail

When this word first appeared in print in 1688, it referred to a strip of tobacco twisted into a thin rope or roll (because of its resemblance to a pig's tail). It was not until 1752 that it acquired the definition it has today: a plait of hair hanging down from the back of the head. This hair-style was very popular with English soldiers and sailors in the latter part of the eighteenth century — although Hollywood star Clark Gable in 1935 had reason to wish it were not. He had been cast by MGM to play Fletcher Christian in *Mutiny on the Bounty*, a role that required him to wear knee breeches and a pigtail. The prospect terrified him because he thought his image as a virile male star would suffer permanent damage. He need not have worried: he turned in one of the best performances of his career, and *Mutiny on the Bounty* — with its plethora of pigtails — won an Oscar for the best film of 1935.

1689 Woodchuck

"How much wood could a woodchuck chuck if a woodchuck could chuck wood?" That popular nursery-school tongue-twister pays tribute to a stocky, short-legged, furry rodent whose name entered the English language in 1689, probably from the Native American word *wecyeka*.

The woodchuck, indigenous to northern and eastern North America, is also known as the groundhog, and it is by that name that this furry little fellow has become part of American folklore. They say that if he comes out of his burrow on February 2 and sees his shadow he will go back underground, and that means the rest of us will have to suffer through six more weeks of winter.

1690 BILLION

John Locke is probably the only writer, living or dead, who has introduced not one, not two, three, four, or five, but *eight* new words into the English language in a single sentence! In his classic book *On Human Understanding*, published in 1690 after seventeen years of research, you can find this passage "… to show how much distinct names conduce to our well reckoning, let us see all these following figures in one continued line: — Nonillions Octillions Septillions Sextillions Quintillions Quadrillions Trillions Billions Millions." Only the last word in that list had been seen in print before. When Locke used the word *billion*, he was probably using it the way the British use it today — to refer to a million million. Americans, however, perhaps because they are in a bigger hurry to get to a billion, use it to mean a thousand million.

1691 SQUIRM

Although this word has probably been part of spoken English since Anglo-Saxon times, no record of its use in print has been found before 1691, when it showed up as an entry in John Ray's *A Collection of English Words*: "To Squirm, to move very nimbly about, after the manner of an Eel. It is spoken of an Eel." In 1890 the English biologist Thomas Huxley (who coined the word *agnostic* in 1869 — see page 237) found *squirm* to be the perfect word to describe the movements of newborn infants: "These poor little mortals … have not even the capacity to do anything but squirm and squall." Today, *squirm* not only means to wriggle and writhe but also to feel embarrassed, like the young lad who squirmed and fidgeted under the stern gaze of the headmaster.

1692 Protectorate

This is one of those words that was coined after the fact — in this case, thirty-three years after the fact. *Protectorate* in 1692 specifically meant that period of English history from 1653 to 1659, when Oliver and then Richard Cromwell held the title of Lord Protector of England. Since then, the word has broadened its meaning to describe a small or weak country under the protection and partial control of a larger one. For example, with the Platt Amendment of 1901 after the Spanish-American War in 1898, the United States government established a protectorate over Cuba that lasted until the Good Neighbor Policy introduced by Franklin Roosevelt in 1934.

Protectorate is based on the word *protect* (from the Latin, *pro*, "in front of," and *tegere*, "to cover"), and one of its synonyms is *defend*, a word with an interesting background. It comes from the Latin *de*, "from," and *fendere*, "to beat off." In the seventeenth century, ships had old pieces of iron cable called *defenders* hanging from the sides to protect or defend them from damage in collisions. The twentieth century has shortened the word to *fender*, the part of a car that defends the driver and passengers by fending off other vehicles. *Defend* first meant an act of defence, as in "fending off a blow," and now we have fences that fend off any neighbours who try to invade our privacy.

1693 Tragus

This word first appeared around 1693 and refers to "the prominence in front of the external opening of the outer ear." It comes from the Greek *tragos*, "a part of the ear, literally, goat," (Merriam-Webster) and probably not one person in a hundred can name that part of the body.

1694 Snicker

Laughter has been called the nectar of the gods. That nectar has flowed down upon the human race in great big gobs of hilarity, if *Roget's Thesaurus* is any indication. Inside that treasure chest of synonyms and antonyms, you will find nearly a dozen different ways to laugh: *giggle, titter, snicker, crow, cheer, chuckle, shout, guffaw, roar* and *split one's sides*. But there is one word that is missing, perhaps because it was coined after Roget compiled his thesaurus: *chortle.* It was invented by Lewis Carroll, author of *Alice in Wonderland,* and it covers that special kind of laugh that is a cross between a chuckle and a snort.

Snicker, by the way, first got into circulation in 1694, when Pierre Antoine Motteux translated Rabelais: "While he said this, the Maidens began to snicker at his Elbow, grinning, giggling, and twittering among themselves."

1695 DENIM

This word takes its name from *serge de Nimes,* a strong cotton twill cloth used for making clothes that was manufactured in Nimes, a city in the southwest of France. Edward Hatton is credited with first mentioning the new word in English when, in 1695, he wrote in *Merchant's Magazine* about "serge Denims that cost 6 1. each."

Levi Strauss of San Francisco was the American pioneer of the modern denims, or blue jeans. He patented his line of denim clothes (riveted at the stress points) in the 1860s, and they proved to be a big success with ranchers, miners, railway workers and other frontier folk of the Old West. *Levis* is still a trademark in the United Sates, although many people treat it as a generic term by dropping the capital letter — for example, Jack Kerouac in *On the Road* (1957): "Dean was wearing washed-out tight levis and T-shirt."

By an interesting coincidence, the words *denim* and *jeans* both trace their origin back to European cities. Denim, as mentioned already, is from Nimes in France; *jeans* comes from the Italian city of Genoa (known as Genes in Old French), the place where jean material was first manufactured. It crossed the Atlantic in 1492 because that's what Columbus used for the sails of his ships.

1696 PEPPERMINT

It is surprising that this word did not show up in print long before 1696. The peppermint is native to Europe, the British Isles and North America, and it produces an oil that is used in medicine, in candy as a flavouring, and in the manufacture of soaps and perfumes. First mentioned by the Englishman John Ray in 1696 ("Pepper-mint [was] found by Dr. Eales in Hartfordshire"), the plant must have grown wild under one or more other names until some unknown genius discovered its value. A member of the mint family, peppermint, from the Sanskrit *pippall,* "berry," is probably the most popular of all flavourings used in candy; about sixty times as much peppermint is used as wintergreen, and four times as much as spearmint.

1697 Avocado

With the discovery of the New World by Europeans, thousands of new words crossed the Atlantic to be added to Spanish, Portuguese, Italian, French, Dutch and English. The new words that reached Britannia's shores often came via Spanish, especially those terms originating in the Spanish colonial possessions in Central and South America. Such a word was *avocado,* a Spanish word loosely adapted from the Native Mexican word *ahuacatl,* meaning "testicle," because of the shape of the fruit.

By an interesting coincidence, *avocado* is also the Spansh word for an "advocate," or lawyer, a term derived from the Latin *advocare,* "to speak for (one's client in court)." And when the lawyer's client steps forward to testify, he is literally swearing by his organs of reproduction, because the words *testify* and *testicles* come from the Latin root *testis,* meaning "a witness" (the presence of testicles bears witness to one's manhood). In other words, the person in court testifies by his testicles that he is telling the truth.

1698 Maharajah

This word first entered the English language in 1698, when John Fryer used it in *A New Account of East India and Persia.* It comes from two Sanskrit words: *maha,* "great," and *raja,* "prince," and was used by the inhabitants of India itself to describe any very powerful and wealthy ruling prince. The India of 1698 was largely a land of mystery to the English, whose chief contact with the large subcontinent at that time was through the East India Company, chartered by Queen Elizabeth I in the year 1600. By the end of that century, the company was doing a brisk business in Bombay, Madras and Calcutta and was casting covetous glances at the riches of the interior. In order to protect its trade, the officers of the company allied themselves with Native troops and princes, who often managed to embroil the British in their own squabbles with neighbouring tribes and rulers. But direct British rule in India did not begin to take root until the latter half of the eighteenth century, and that was when a new synonym for *maharajah* managed to elbow its way into the English language: *panjandrum.* You'll find the story behind that word on page 170.

1699 CHOPSTICKS

In the record of his voyages to the Far East, published in 1699, William Dampier was the first Englishman we know of to use the term *chopsticks* in print: "At their ordinary eating they use two small round sticks about the length and bigness of a Tobacco-pipe. They hold them both in the right hand, one between the fore-finger and thumb; the other between the middle-finger and fore-finger…. They are called by the English seamen Chopsticks."

Nearly two hundred years later, *chop suey* joined the English language. It happened in 1896 when Li Hung-Chang, the Chinese ambassador to the United States, arrived in New York and received a tumultuous welcome from the public and many American statesmen, including President Cleveland. The day after he arrived, Chang treated his hosts to a lavish dinner and ordered his personal chef to come up with something that would appeal to both Chinese and American tastes. The chef rose to the challenge and concocted a main course that he dubbed *chop suey* (Chinese for "odds and ends"). It was an instant success. Newspapers all across the country published the recipe, restaurants began serving it, and word of this new dish eventually reached China itself, where chop suey is now served much as it was for the gala New York banquet of August 29, 1896.

The 1700s

In 1712 the English inventor Thomas Newcomen devised a steam pump for pumping water out of coal mines. Because it was so inefficient, it had to be close to the source of the coal that powered it in order to be economically viable. Fifty-seven years later, James Watt built the first truly efficient steam engine, and thus triggered off the Industrial Revolution.

Newcomen and Watt were only two of a whole army of eighteenth-century English inventors who tinkered and experimented with a wide range of labour-saving devices. In 1701, an Oxford graduate named Jethro Tull constructed a seed drill that, when drawn behind a horse, would dig the furrow, plant the seed and cover it with soil — all in one operation. The seeds were planted in straight, neat rows and, after the crops began to grow, the soil could be made more productive by frequent hoeing, something that had been impossible when seeds were scattered by hand. With Tull's drill, farmers discovered that a smaller supply of seed would produce more grain per acre. Later in the same century, James Hargreaves invented the spinning jenny, which greatly accelerated the spinning of wool or cotton into yarn. Edmund Cartwright invented the power loom, Abraham Darby began smelting iron with coke, Henry Cort introduced mill-rolled iron, John Wilkinson improved the cannon-borer, and Joseph Bramah, in 1778, began to manufacture the modern water closet.

The new words that entered English in the eighteenth century reflected this burst of inventiveness: *piston, propeller, orrery, stopwatch, scalpel, trombone, Fahrenheit, dentist, oxygen, parachute, uranium, nitrogen, chromium* and *waterbed.* Other new words reflected the fact that English ships and sailors were now doing business with India, the Orient and Australia, as witness *ketchup, serendipity, seersucker, jungle, Polynesia, kangaroo* and *platypus*. Native American words continued to cross the Atlantic, including *totem, warpath, cougar* and *succotash*. Africa contributed, among other words, *albino* and *chimpanzee*. And the French Revolution passed along *guillotine* and *terrorist*.

But who was keeping track of all these new words? Only a few lexicographers here and there. Then, in 1747, Lord Chesterfield approached the English man of letters Dr. Samuel Johnson to propose that he compile a bigger-than-ever-before dictionary of the English language. Johnson accepted the challenge with great enthusiasm and set to work. Both he and Chesterfield knew there would be a good market for such a book. The English middle class was rapidly rising in power and influence, hence there was a growing demand for dictionaries that could be used as verbal etiquette books laying down the law on what was acceptable in language and what was not — an indispensable guide for anyone aspiring to a higher social station.

When Johnson began work on his dictionary, he hoped he could freeze the English language with the publication of his book, which came out in 1755. But before he finished, he realized that English always had been, and probably always would be, a living and changing tongue, completely unfreezable. However, Johnson did help to nail down one part of the English language: the spelling. Before Johnson's day, you could spell any given word one of several ways without worrying whether it was right or wrong. In fact, in Shakespeare's time, a man who knew only one way to spell a word was considered not to be very educated. Johnson's spellings quickly became standard and, except for the Americanization of some words by Noah Webster (*color, labor, traveler, center* and so forth), words are spelled much the same way today.

Although Johnson's *Dictionary of the English Language* contains much new material not previously published in dictionary form, he relied extensively on the work of previous lexicographers. As to who wrote the first English-language dictionary, that honour has been claimed for two works: Richard Huloet's *Abcedarium Anglico-Latinum pro Tyrunculis,* published in 1552 with twenty-six thousand words, and Robert Cawdrey's *Table Alphabeticall,* published in 1604 with twenty-five hundred entries of "hard usuall English Wordes." Johnson included some forty thousand words in his dictionary, although he took pains to omit any and all vulgar terms, believing that linguistic crudities had no place in a work such as his. He was guided in his choice of words by using those employed by the literate Londoners of his time and those found in well-respected literary works of the previous two centuries.

Two features of Johnson's dictionary guaranteed its success: its elegantly written definitions and its lavish use of quotations from literature to illustrate the use of each word in its natural habitat. Johnson included a history of the English language, some rules of grammar, notes on the origins of many of the words, and, although he supplied no pronunciation, he did indicate which syllable in a word should be stressed. His definitions sometimes revealed his sense of humour (a dictionary-maker, he wrote, is "a harmless drudge") and his personal prejudices ("oats — a grain which in England is generally given to horses, but in Scotland supports the people"), but on the whole his dictionary was, and continues to be, regarded as a sound work of linguistic scholarship.

On December 13, 1784, Samuel Johnson died of pneumonia at the age of seventy-five. More new words have been added to the English language in the two centuries since his death than in the preceding thousand years. If he came back to life today, he would probably head for the dictionary section of the nearest bookstore to catch up on what he had been missing.

1700 SKINFLINT

In early use, a flint was any hard stone, especially a piece of flint-stone struck with iron or steel to produce a spark. If you were so greedy and stingy that you would "skin" a piece of flint, you were called a *skinflint*, a word that entered the English language in 1700 as a synonym for *miser*. *Roget's Thesaurus* does not skimp on syllables when listing the synonyms for *skinflinty*: *parsimonious, penurious, stingy, miserly, niggardly, sparing, grudging, illiberal, ungenerous, mercenary, venal, covetous, avaricious, greedy, grasping* and *rapacious*.

Exactly two hundred years after skinflint joined the English language, *tightwad* made its debut. Breaking into print in 1900, this word refers to anyone who is stingy enough — or careful enough — to keep a tight grip on the wad of money in his or her pocket or purse.

1701 SUBSELLIUM

Some years produce more new words than others. If you browse through the *OED* you will find a number of quotations illustrating the meaning and usage of each entry. The first quotation listed is the earliest one ever found, and either the exact year is indicated or the initials M.E. (Middle English) or O.E. (Old English) are used. There are lots of entries for, say, the year 1611 because it was in that year that the King James Version of the Bible was published. But there are lean pickings for 1701; no huge literary work that might have flooded our language with new words came out that year, and we have to settle for the relatively obscure word you see listed above. *Subsellium*, however, is not a total loss, if we concentrate first on the prefix *sub*, meaning "under." The word *suburbs* literally means "under or below the city" (*urbs* is the Latin word for "city") and can be traced back to the famous Seven Hills of Rome, on which that great city was built. The outskirts of the city were below (*sub*) the level of the city itself. *Sella* is Latin for "seat," thus *subsellium*, or "below seat," the word for a seat in an amphitheatre — where each successive row is below the last. And on the subject of "below" or "under," there is the famous line that every student of Latin knows by heart: *Semper ubi sub ubi*. That's what Julius Caesar might have said to his legionnaires just before they crossed the snow-capped Alps to invade Gaul. A loose translation: "Always wear underwear."

1702 VENEER

A veneer, from the French *fournir*, "to furnish," is a thin strip of fancy wood used in cabinetmaking and other woodwork as an elegant or highly polished outer layer, over top of cheaper woods. It first appeared in English in 1702 in the London *Gazette*: "A Large Parcel of French Walnutt-Tree Venears will be exposed to Sale ... on Thursday." Four years later, the suffix *-ing* was added: "Veneering, a sort of in-laid Work among Joyners, Cabinet-makers, & C." As the use of this word spread, writers began using it to describe the thin coating of respectability that conceals our bestial proclivities. A chap named Farrar had this in mind when, in 1874, he wrote about "a savage barbarian with a thin veneer of corrupt and superficial civilization."

1703 BAMBOOZLE

"Sham Proofs, that they propos'd to bamboozle me with." That sentence appears in a book by Colley Cibber, published in 1703 and bearing the intriguing title, *She Wou'd, and She Wou'd Not*. No earlier use of the word *bamboozle* has ever been found. No one knows where it came from, but it likely originated in slang, without any linguistic ancestry.

Some new words are welcomed into the English language most heartily, while others have to fight for a foothold in the dictionary. *Bamboozle* falls into the latter category. It was stoutly resisted by language purists of that day who despaired of the "continual corruption of our English tongue" by slang terms such as *banter, put, kidney, sham, mob, bubble* and *bully*. And yet, over and over again, the slang of yesterday becomes the standard English of today.

1704 PISTON

What caused the decline and fall of the Roman Empire? That may seem like a strange question to ask here, but there is good reason to ask it. Among the many causes for Rome's decline and fall put forth by those who study history, one of the most fascinating is the theory offered by Claire Patterson, a California geophysicist: Rome fell because of, or at least partly because of, a decline in silver production beginning around the year 200. The Roman supply of coins relied heavily on silver, which came from mines in the vicinity of the Mediterranean. But these mines were becoming so deep that they were filling with water, and the Romans never devised an adequate means of pumping it out. The result: silver production declined, silver became scarce, silver coins began to be debased with cheaper alloys, prices began climbing (inflation!), and the economy gradually slid backward from coinage to barter. An empire may have fallen for want of a good piston to pump the water out of the mines.

(The word *piston* comes to us from the Latin *pistare*, "to pound," as you might do with a *pestle*.)

Ironically enough, the Romans had pistons right under their noses. Philo of Byzantium, Ctesibius of Alexandria, and Hero of Alexandria all devised piston pumps sometime between 200 B.C. and 200 A.D., but the world had to wait until 1550 or thereabouts before the piston was applied to a machine that would do useful work. And what did those sixteenth-century pistons do? They pumped water out of mines!

But the name *piston* did not appear in print in English until 1704, when John Harris used it in his *Lexicon Technicum*: "Each time the Piston or Sucker of the Pump is drawn back, the Air in the Receiver must expand it self so as in some measure to fill up the Cavity of the Pump left vacant by the Piston, as well as the Receiver it self." Eight years later, Thomas Newcomen would use a piston in the first working steam engine of modern times — and the stage was set for the Industrial Revolution.

1705 Ad Lib

When *ad lib* first appeared in English, it was a notation in music that told you to play with freedom (as opposed to *obbligato*, an Italian term that says you must play in a certain way, as, for example, including an accompaniment without which the performance would be incomplete). Over the years, *ad lib* extended its meaning to speakers who added extemporaneous remarks to what they were saying, or who might deliver an entire speech "ad lib." The Latin root *libitum* means "desire," and this is the root Sigmund Freud had in mind when he used the term *libido*, the emotional energy produced by basic biological drives, especially the sex drive.

1706 Obituary

In the sixth edition of Edward Phillips's *New World of English Words*, published in 1706, *obituary* makes its debut and is defined as "a Calendar, or Register-Book, in which the Friars in a Monastery enter'd the Obits, or Obitual Days of their Founders and Benefactors." The word comes from the Latin *obitus*, which means to fall or die. The word has shifted somewhat in meaning since 1706, and is normally used today in reference to the death column in a newspaper. The death notices in your local paper usually appear alongside the birth and marriages notices (and isn't it odd that people always get born, married, and die in alphabetical order?). Reporters assigned to cover births, marriages and deaths are often fond of telling their friends they are working on "hatches, matches and dispatches."

1707 ARMISTICE

The most famous armistice of modern history went into effect on the eleventh hour of the eleventh day of the eleventh month of 1918, when World War I officially came to an end. On that day each year ever since, a dwindling number of war veterans gather at cenotaphs and cemeteries to pay tribute to their fallen but not forgotten comrades. And forty days after each November 11, you come to a day that is etymologically linked to the word *armistice*. December 21 is the date of the winter solstice, the shortest day of the year for those who live in the Northern Hemisphere (for Australians, the shortest day is June 21). The longest day is known as the summer solstice. The two words, *armistice* and *solstice*, are based on the same Latin root, *sistere*, "to cause to stop." An armistice causes the use of arms — from *arma*, Latin for "weapons" — to stop, and the solstice marks the point at which the sun — *sol* in Latin — in its daily journey across the sky, stops sinking lower or rising higher with each passing day, and changes direction to signal the start of a new season. In the tropics one season is very much like another because the sun never sinks very low in the sky. The boundaries of the tropics are determined by how far north or south the sun shines directly overhead throughout the year. The sun appears to move back and forth between the Tropic of Cancer and the Tropic of Capricorn. And the word *tropics*, surprisingly enough, has nothing to do with heat, even though the highest temperatures in the world are in that area. Tropics comes from the Greek *tropos*, "to turn," because the overhead sun turns back and forth each year between the northern and southern limits of the tropics.

1708 Camera

No one was taking photographs back in 1708, and so that use of the word *camera* did not appear until the mid-nineteenth century. In 1708 a camera was simply "a vaulted or arched Building, an Upper-Chamber or Gallery," from the Latin word for room, *camera*. Although it is listed here for that year, there were two terms in use before 1708 that employed the word *camera*. There was the *camera obscura* and the *camera lucida*, which the *Encyclopaedia Britannica* defines as "two simple optical devices used by artists, scientists and others to aid them in drawing, viewing or demonstrating an object by projecting an image of it onto a suitable screen." The modern photographic camera developed from the camera obscura, and there were two Frenchmen who stand out in its development: Joseph Niepce and Louis Daguerre. Niepce has the honour of taking the first photograph of all time in 1822. But the technique he employed was far from perfect, and further work had to be done. The big breakthrough came in 1839, when Louis Daguere demonstrated the secret of taking lifelike photographs. He used a light sensitive silver-coated metallic plate and developed his pictures (known as *daguerreotypes*) with a mercury vapour. The shutterbug age had arrived.

1709 Veinstone

A veinstone is a vein of metallic ore running through the earth between other layers of rock or soil. The word first appeared in print in 1709 in *The Natural History of Westmoreland and Cumberland*, in which Thomas Robinson wrote about "the appearance of several Veins of Spar, Soil, and Veinstone breaking out upon the Surface." In addition to the vein itself, *veinstone* (or *vein-stone*) is also used to describe the layers of rock that surround a vein containing metallic ore.

The word *vein* comes from the Latin *vena*, meaning "vein," and the veins of the human body are the blood vessels that carry impure blood back to the lungs and heart, where it is purified and pumped back through the body. The blood vessels that carry the pure blood are called *arteries*, from the Greek root *arteria*, meaning "windpipe," because the ancient Greeks thought these tubes carried air instead of blood.

1710 CHIT-CHAT

Book titles today are often short and snappy, especially for those written by Arthur Hailey (*Airport, Hotel, Wheels, Overland*, etc.). The fashion in book titles in the 1700s favoured something longer and perhaps more informative. In 1710 Samuel Palmer published his *Moral Essays on Some of the Most Curious English, Scotch, and Foreign Proverbs*. Amid the words of wisdom contained therein you will find this sentence: "'Tis the custom of foolish people … in their chit chat to be always biting people's reputation behind their back."

Things haven't changed much from that day to this.

1711 KETCHUP

In 1711 in *An Account of the Trade in India*, Charles Lockyer writes, "Soy comes in Tubbs from Jappan, and the best Ketchup from Tonquin." Ketchup is usually made from tomatoes, and a reading of the above quote could give you the erroneous idea that tomatoes are indigenous to the Far East. They are not. They originated in the Western Hemisphere and were cultivated by the Native peoples before the first Europeans arrived. The first recorded mention of the tomato by a European dates from 1554, and over the next two hundred years this juicy, red fruit was carried around the globe to be planted and eaten. Italians began growing it in the 1550s and were probably the first Europeans to eat it.

Strangely enough, there is no record of the tomato being cultivated by white men in North America until after the signing of the Declaration of Independence. Thomas Jefferson grew some in 1781. A French refugee from the Caribbean allegedly introduced it in Philadelphia in 1789, and an Italian painter brought some to Salem, Massachusetts, in 1802.

It was only a matter of time before someone discovered how to convert tomatoes into ketchup. But why the word *ketchup* for the sauce from tomatoes? It comes from the Malay word *kechap*, which in turn comes from *ke-tsiap*, the Chinese word for pickled fish sauce. Apparently the first batch of ketchup must have had the same spicy tang as pickled fish sauce.

1712 ZIGZAG

When this word, which is possibly based on the shape of the letter *Z*, first showed up in English, it was spelled *zic-zac*, as this quote from 1712 illustrates: "42 Steps of Grass laid in Zic-Zac." In 1728 Alexander Pope used the spelling we find familiar today: "Nonsense precipitate, like running Lead, That slipp'd thro' Cracks and Zig-zags of the Head." If you look up *zigzag* in the *OED*, you will find it in the final volume (V–Z), but you will also find twelve pages of *Z* words following it. The last entry is *zymurgy* ("the practice or art of fermentation, as in winemaking, brewing, distilling, etc."), although if you check the *Webster Universal Dictionary* you can find an entry even lower in the alphabet: *zyxomma* ("a dragon-fly with large eyes and narrow head, found in India").

It is highly unlikely that words are ever deliberately coined to come last in the dictionary, but names in telephone books are a different story. A Mr. Turner living in Toronto, Canada, took on the name of I. Zzzup to get the last listing in the Toronto telephone book. When the phone book came out, he discovered he had been out-zeed (or out-zedded) by Shannon Zzzyk ("I'm sorry…") and by Zzzzoom Toys and Games ("… that number is no longer in service.")

For what it was worth, Mr. Turner/Zzzup got the last working number in the book.

1713 ORRERY

Around 1700 an Englishman named George Graham invented a model of the sun, moon, Earth and other planets which, when cranked, would cause these heavenly bodies to rotate around a tabletop in the same manner in which they rotate through their orbits in space. Graham's contraption contained only six planets — Mercury, Venus, Earth, Mars,

Jupiter and Saturn — because the three outermost ones had not yet been discovered. In 1713 John Rowley, an instrument maker, constructed one of these devices for Charles Boyle, the Scottish Earl of Orrery, and according to Richard Steele, decided to name it in his honour: "Mr. John Rowley … calls his Machine the Orrery, in Gratitude to the Nobelman of that Title." These orreries appeared on the market at a time when popular interest in the heavens was growing with every passing year, spurred on by the discoveries made possible through the telescope and the work of such scientists as Sir Isaac Newton. But not everyone rushed out to buy an orrery, and the scientific community regarded them as little more than a fancy piece of furniture, with Sir John F. W. Herschel writing in 1833 about "those very childish toys called orreries." Herschel was the son of Sir William Herschel, the German-born English astronomer who, in 1781, made the earliest orreries obsolete by discovering a new planet in the solar system, which he named Uranus.

1714 Connoisseur

Because France is so close to England, ever since the Norman Conquest thousands of French words have crossed the English Channel to Shakespeare's "scepter'd isle." *Connoisseur*, as far as we can tell, made the crossing in 1714, but it made an earlier overland crossing hundreds of years before that when it wended its way through the Alps from Italy to France. *Connoisseur* is based on the French verb *connaitre*, "to know," which comes from the Latin *cognoscere*, "to perceive" or become acquainted with. The original meaning is still preserved today because a connoisseur not only knows a particular subject — music, painting, sculpture, food, wine and so forth — but is often a well-informed critic in many of these areas — that is, a member of the *cognoscenti*.

Some people try to pass themselves off as connoisseurs of great art when they really have no idea what it's all about. The English man of letters Oscar Wilde (1856–1900) found one of these phonies on a journey through the western United States in the late nineteenth century: "So infinitesimal did I find the knowledge of Art, west of the Rocky Mountains, that an art patron — one who in his day had been a miner — actually sued the railroad company for damages because the plaster cast of

Venus de Milo, which he had imported from Paris, had been delivered minus the arms. And, what is more surprising still, he gained his case and the damages."

1715 WHISKEY

The first example of this word in English acknowledges the intoxicating powers of this spiritous liquor: "Whiskie shall put our brains in rage." Those words appeared in 1715 in James Maidment's *Book of Scottish Pasquils*, but the beverage itself is much older than that. No one knows when whiskey was first distilled in the British Isles (the land of its origin), although the earliest reference to it can be found in the Scottish exchequer rolls of 1494: "Eight bolls of malt to Friar John Cor wherewith to make aquavitae." The Latin term *aquavita* means "water of life," and when the Scots and Irish (the first people to make this beverage) translated the Latin into Celtic, they came up with *uisgebeatha*, which was gradually shortened and anglicized into *whiskey*.

The whiskey business came to America in the seventeenth century and took root in western Pennsylvania, where an outcropping of limestone supplied the clear spring water necessary for the distillation process. When the U.S. Congress imposed an excise tax on whiskey in 1791, the farmers and distillers of western Pennsylvania were outraged. The result was the Whiskey Rebellion of 1794, which was quickly put down but which prompted some Pennsylvanians to move further west to escape the reach of the federal tax collectors. Many of these migrants simply followed the outcroppings of limestone across Ohio, into Indiana, and down into Kentucky, a move that enabled them to stay in the same business.

Incidentally, for modern trade purposes, the Irish and American product is spelled *whiskey*, whereas the Scottish and Canadian distillers use the shorter *whisky*.

1716 SCHOONER

A schooner is a sailing ship with two or more masts. Where does the word come from? The *OED* offers its readers this possibility: "The story commonly told respecting the origin of the word is as follows. When the first schooner was being launched (at Gloucester, Massachusetts, about

1713), a bystander exclaimed 'Oh, how she scoons!' The builder, Capt. Andrew Robinson, replied, 'A schooner let her be!'"

1717 SHAY

In his diary on September 20, 1717, S. Sewall wrote, "The Govenour went through Charleston … carrying Madam [Mrs.] Paul Dudley in his shay." Charleston, South Carolina, is a long way from the soaring spires of Gothic cathedrals that dot the landscape of Europe, but believe it or not, there is a definite linguistic connection between the governor's little horse-drawn carriage and those magnificent European monuments of stone and glass. The word cathedral comes to us from the Greek *kathedra*, meaning "seat" or "chair," and because the bishop occupied the principal church in a diocese, such churches came to be called cathedrals. Following another path, the Greek root *kathedra* passed through Latin and into Old French in the form of *chaiere*, which changed to *chaire* in modern French, and meant "pulpit" or "professional chair," as in the sentence, "He occupied the chair of Classical Studies at Oxford." Another meaning developed from *chaire* in the French word *chaise*, which has come into English as *chaise longue*, or "long chair." But in addition to this, *chaise* can also mean *post chaise*, or "travelling carriage." And somewhere along the line an Englishman, ignorant of French, thought *chaise* was the plural form meaning "carriages" and so came up with the word *shay* to serve as the singular. The mistake has never been corrected, and the word *shay* has been in the English language to this very day.

1718 SYPHILIS

The two most common forms of venereal disease are syphilis and gonorrhea. They may have entered the bodies of English men and women around the same time in history, but they didn't enter the English language at the same time. According to the *OED*, the first mention of *gonorrhea* in English dates back to 1526. *Syphilis* did not appear in English for nearly another two hundred years — until 1718.

But if we date *syphilis* from its first appearance in Italian, we end up back in 1530, and in this sense *syphilis* is almost as old as *gonorrhea*. It was in 1530 that Girolamo Fracastoro, an Italian physician from Verona, wrote a widely published medical poem, "Syphilis sive morbus gallicus" ("Syphilis, or the French disease"). The poem tells the story of Syphilis, a shepherd boy who blasphemed against the Greek god Apollo and was stricken with the disease as punishment.

The name Syphilis probably comes from the Greek *suphilos*, "lover of pigs." (Incidentally, Fracastoro was not the only one to refer to syphilis as "the French disease." The British still describe it as "the French welcome," thus maintaining an old tradition of blaming other countries for things you despise and deplore in your own. In what must be one of the most insulting ethnic slurs of all time, we find that the word *buggery* can be traced back to the Medieval Latin *Bulgarus*, a Bulgarian, because the Eastern Orthodox Bulgarians were regarded as heretics by the Roman Catholic Church and therefore guilty of unnatural practices.)

For a long time, the terms *syphilis, gonorrhea* and *venereal disease* were considered unfit to be used in mixed company. During a debate in the New York State Legislature in 1937 on a bill dealing with the control of syphilis, State Senator John McNaboe bitterly denounced the bill on the grounds that widespread use of the word *syphilis* would "corrupt the innocence of children, and would create a shudder in every decent woman and man." We can easily imagine McNaboe's hypothetical reaction to the Valentine's Day card given to a schoolteacher in Ohio by a little boy in her second-grade class: "Dear Teacher: Have a happy VD."

1719 APHRODISIAC

The earliest mention of *aphrodisiac,* a drug or food that stimulates or intensifies sexual desire, in the *OED* is 1719; the earliest mention of *syphilis* is 1718. Logic would dictate that the sequence be reversed.

Aphrodisiac is based on Aphrodite, the Greek goddess of love, who has donated not one but two words to the English language: *aphrodisiac* and, because she was known to the Romans as Venus, *venereal disease.* Venus was married to Vulcan, the Roman god of fire and metallurgy who has given us the word *volcano.* We don't know if Venus gave any disease to her husband, but we do know she had a red-hot love affair with Mars, the Roman god of war, while she was still married to Vulcan. For this reason, Vulcan came to be known as the special patron of cuckolds.

1720 Corkscrew

The earliest example of *corkscrew* in print takes us back to a rhyming sentence written by a chap named Amherst in 1720: "This hand a corkscrew did contain, and that a bottle of champaigne." When Charles Dickens wrote *The Pickwick Papers* in 1837, he used this noun as a verb: "Mr. Bantam corkscrewed his way through the crowd." Fifteen years later, Dickens used the word again, this time in a context sounding very much like extortion: "… from what Small has dropped, and from what we have corkscrewed out of him."

Most corkscrews are employed for the removal of corks from bottles of wine, but at least one corkscrew was designed with another purpose in mind. U.S. Patent #560,351 was issued for a corkscrew device which, its inventor claimed, could put dimples on your cheeks.

1721 Stultiloquence

Although this word, which means foolish or senseless talk (a contraction of *stultified eloquence*), is seldom heard nowadays, the two separate Latin roots that make it up are alive and well and flourishing in English. *Stultified* (or *stultify*) is based on the Latin *stultus*, "foolish," and *facere*, "to make." Eloquence is based on the Latin *loqui*, "to speak," and this root has sprouted many English branches, including *loquacious, eloquent, somniloquent, elocution, soliloquy*, and *circumlocution*. For people who like to talk, *Roget's Thesaurus* has lots of synonyms for *loquacious: talkative, garrulous, declamatory, fluent, voluble* and *effusive*. Unfortunately, they don't mention the one that is my favourite: *bombasticate* — to speak with great bombast.

But what about those people at the other extreme — the strong, silent types? Roget gives us *taciturn, laconic, concise, sententious, reserved* and *reticent*. Of all of these, *laconic* is the only one you can find on a map. It comes from Laconia, an area in southern Greece where the tight-lipped ancient Spartans lived. Because they were obsessed with maintaining a military state, the Spartans paid scant attention to literature or the arts. So sparing were they in the use of words that the name of their homeland entered the English language as a synonym for "terse." When Philip of Macedonia, so the story goes, was storming the gates of Sparta, he sent a message to the Spartan king inside: "If we capture your city, we will burn it to the ground." The king answered with a single word: "If."

1722 TERRA COTTA

Terra cotta (which in Italian means "cooked earth") is hardened, ceramic clay used by Mediterranean peoples for pottery, statues and building construction. I never see the word without thinking of Carlo Lerici, a retired Italian millionaire who, nearly single-handedly, brought an ancient civilization back to life. The story begins in 1956, when Lerici began looking for a tombstone for himself and his wife to symbolize their long and happy life together. He found what he was looking for in a museum in Rome: a terra cotta sarcophagus on which the semi-recumbent figures of a man and a woman had been fashioned in an attitude of exquisite serenity. It was well over twenty-five hundred years old and had been made by the Etruscans, a strange and mysterious people who had lived in Tuscany and Latium before the dawn of Roman history. Lerici made arrangements with the museum to have a bronze replica made, and he dropped in daily to oversee the work. While there, he browsed through what was the largest collection of Etruscan artefacts in the world and became completely captivated by these enigmatic people. One day he noticed a wall chart showing a cross-section of a typical dig for Etruscan relics, and that's when he had his brainstorm: why not use his vast experience in mining and geophysics to drill for relics the way he used to drill for oil?

Soon Lerici was flying over Tuscany, taking photos of likely looking sites. Then he began drilling into the earth in hopes of breaking through the ceiling of a beehive tomb of a sort the Etruscans were known to have built all through the area. If his target turned out to be a tomb, Lerici lowered his periscope (which had a light at its tip) and had a look inside. If it looked promising, he took photos and studied them before deciding whether or not to dig. This was a necessary step because Lerici found so many tombs that he could not possibly excavate them all.

By the late 1960s Lerici had located more than eight thousand Etruscan tombs, sixty of which were outstanding in the extent of artefacts and wall paintings they contained. Thanks to Lerici, the Etruscans have now been brought out of history's shadows into the light of modern knowledge. They were the ones who nurtured the Romans in their early years, teaching them how to drain swamps and build sewers and walls, as well as the dubious art of how to predict the future by studying the flight of birds and the entrails of animals. The Etruscans were to the Romans what the British were to the Americans before 1776.

Little did the unknown Etruscan who built that terra cotta sarcophagus realize that his handiwork would be the instrument through which the memory of his people would be perpetuated in the world of today.

1723 MISWEND

Miswend is a verb meaning to lead or go astray, from Middle English, *mis*, "wrong," and Old English, *wendan*, "to turn."

This is another word you don't see much of anymore, mainly because we have found other words to describe people who are led or who go astray. Maybe you've had someone give you a "bum steer" or "lead you down the garden path." If you wend your way through something, whether it be a forest or a library, you are following a winding course, and if you were travelling on foot through Anglo-Saxon England, you would probably have to make a lot of twists and turns before you reached your destination. The highways, byways and pathways followed the natural shape of the land, and if there was a hill in your way, you probably wended your way around it.

1724 TROMBONE

This instrument, which takes its name from *tromba*, the Italian word for "trumpet," first appeared in the early eighteenth century. It was a good century for a new musical instrument to make its debut; the eighteenth century was the age in which the art of music-making came into its own. A more specific system of musical notation, replacing the old scores with their cryptic instructions and heavy demands for improvisation, opened wide the field for musical amateurs, many of whom played as well as the professionals. Because every single note to be played was shown, along with instructions on how to play it (loud, soft, and so on), even a child could play an instrument — and many did, including a seven-year-old Mozart at the harpsichord.

Orchestras also underwent great changes in the eighteenth century. The old Baroque orchestra — which stressed a clear distinction in the sound produced by each instrument — was giving way to the new symphony orchestra, which did what its name (from the Greek *sun*, "together," and *phone*, "sound") implies: it blended all its instruments into a single, glorious voice. A typical eighteenth-century orchestra included flutes, violins, violoncellos, violas, oboes, clarinets, bassoons, double basses, horns, drums and trumpets. Some even had trombones.

1725 GALANTINE

Derived from the Latin *gelatus*, past participle of *gelare*, to congeal or freeze, galantine is "a cold dish consisting of boned meat or fish that has been stuffed, poached, and covered with aspic" (Merriam-Webster). The earliest recorded appearance of this word in English has been dated to 1725, during the reign of George I (1714–1727). He became king after the death of Queen Anne. And because he came from the German House of Hanover, he reached England without knowing how to speak English.

1726 YAHOO

"Whether we read it, as children do, for the story or as historians, for the political allusions, or as men of the world, for the satire and philosophy, we have to acknowledge that it is one of the wonderful and unique books of the world's literature."

So wrote Edmund Gosse in *The History of English Literature* about a book written by Jonathan Swift and published in 1726: *Gulliver's Travels*. At least, that's what we call it today. Back in the eighteenth century, long book titles were all the rage, and what we now identify with a mere two words carried a real mouthful (amounting to twenty-one words) on the title page: *Travels into Several Remote Nations of the World, by Lemuel Gulliver, first a Surgeon, and then a Captain of several ships.*

Gulliver's adventures begin when he is shipwrecked on the coast of Lilliput and finds himself in a country inhabited by pygmies. Then he is thrown among the people of Brobdingnag, giants of enormous size who have donated the word *brobdingnagian*, "gigantic," to the English language. His third adventure takes him to Laputa, a land ruled by quacks and knaves. On his fourth and last voyage, he visits the land of the Houyhnhnms, where horses have the ability to reason and rule over a race of savage brutes in human form called Yahoos. Two hundred and fifty-four years after *Gulliver's Travels* came out, the *Oxford American Dictionary* was published, and it bears witness to the fact that Swift's word lives on. The fourteenth entry on page 808 is "ya-hoo (yah-hoo) *n.* a coarse or brutish person."

And today, Yahoo! is the well-known name of a widely used Internet search engine and portal.

1727 AUDITORIUM

The 1727 edition of *Chamber's Encyclopedia* carries this entry: "Auditory, Auditorium … was that part of the church where the *audients* stood to hear, and be instructed." The word comes to us from the common Latin root, *audire*, "to hear," as in *audio* or *audience*. By the 1800s the word *auditorium* was also used for the reception room of a monastery, since the monks who lived there would be under a vow of silence and normally would not talk, but only listen. Today the auditorium is usually the largest room in a school, larger even than the gymnasium. In order to reduce costs in school construction, many school boards are telling their architects to design a single large room with fold-up seats that can serve as both auditorium and gymnasium. These dual-purpose rooms are called *gymnatoriums* (or, as a purist would insist, *gymnatoria*), formed by a contraction of *auditorium* and *gymnasium*. But anyone familiar with ancient Greek and Latin roots might look at that sign on the door and think some wild in-the-flesh orgies were going on inside. The Greek root *gymna* means "naked," because many ancient Greek athletes competed in the nude. And the suffix *orium* means "place where" — hence *gymnatorium*, a place where activities are conducted in the nude.

1728 SALOON

In 1728 *Chamber's Encyclopedia* defined the word *saloon*, from the French *salon*, thusly: "A very lofty, spacious Hall, vaulted at Top, and sometimes comprehending two Stories, or Ranges, of Windows…" Several other definitions are listed in the *OED*, including: "a large cabin in a passenger-boat for the common use of passengers … a railway car furnished as a drawing room … a place where intoxicating liquors are sold and consumed."

That last definition is the one most widely used today, and it first appeared in print in 1884, when the *New York Herald* reported "[two men] demanded drinks in the saloon [on] Myrtle Avenue [in] Brooklyn." When the women's temperance movement got into full swing in the late nineteenth century, saloon smashing became an occupational hazard for the proprietors of such establishments; without warning, an army of axe-wielding women would descend upon the local "den of iniquity" and destroy everything in sight. One of the leaders of this movement was Carry A. Nation (1846–1911), whose photograph can be seen on page 874 of the *American Heritage Dictionary*. In the photo she is holding the hatchet she used to smash bottles and furnishings in saloons.

1729 MERRY-GO-ROUND

The *Daily Post* of August 23, 1729, carries this invitation: "Here's the merry-go-rounds; Come, who rides?" The first ones must have been man-powered or horse-powered, because in 1729 the steam engine was still in its infancy. Today's merry-go-rounds are powered either by electricity or the internal-combustion engine.

Two additional uses for this word have cropped up since 1729. By adding the suffix -*er* to the end, you get *merry-go-rounder* — "a cause of astonishment." In 1838 Charles Dickens wrote in *Oliver Twist*: "Oh, my eye! Here's a merry-go-rounder! — Tommy Chitling's in love!" The other new meaning first appeared in 1963 to describe a train of coal hoppers running perpetually on a circular route between consignor and consignee. The big advantage of such an arrangement is efficiency. In *Spotlight on Trains*, published in 1972, a chap named Levy reports: "British Rail came up with the idea of the 'merry-go-round' train … a long train of coal hoppers running in a circular route between the coal mine and the power station."

1730 BASEMENT

The city of Venice is slowly sinking beneath the waters of the Adriatic Sea. Similarly, the word *basement* has been sinking into the earth ever since it first appeared more than two hundred and fifty years ago. When one Mr. Gordon wrote in 1730, "There is a small Basement … under the lower Pilasters," he was referring to the lower level of a building that may or may not have been below ground level. Since then, the word *basement* has sunk into the earth until it has become synonymous with *cellar*, a word that first appeared in print in 1225.

Your dictionary, by the way, will probably tell you that *basement* and *cellar* are synonyms, but your real estate agent will tell you otherwise. If you're shopping around for a house and find one with a cellar, all you'll get is a hole in the ground. The word *basement* has more class, especially if you stick the word "finished" in front of it. If you're selling a house that has only a cellar and you want to get the best possible price, borrow a few bottles of champagne from your well-heeled friends and turn that hole in the ground into a wine cellar.

1731 ULTIMATUM

Under the Treaty of Utrecht of 1713, Spain granted to England the exclusive right to supply Spanish colonies in America with African slaves, and the privilege of sending one ship a year to trade at Veracruz, a busy Spanish port in Mexico. That arrangement harboured the seeds of the next war between England and Spain, because English smugglers persisted in supplying the Spanish colonies with far more goods — and far more often — than the treaty allowed. Spain retaliated by intercepting British ships in the Spanish West Indies and seizing contraband goods. British sailors and sea captains who were caught redhanded were often punished severely, while tales of Spanish cruelty drifted back to England and stimulated the demand for another war.

It was in this climate of impending hostilities that the word *ultimatum*, from Latin *ultimus*, "last," first appeared in English, in the January 1731 issue of *Gentleman's Magazine*. "There are privately handed about here Copies of the *Ultimatum* [or last Proposals] of the Allies of Seville, as transmitted hither from Paris." Actual war between England and Spain would not break out for another eight years, but the tension kept building. In 1738 a Captain Jenkins appeared before the House of Commons in London and told the members that, in 1731, he had been sailing home from Jamaica when the Spanish intercepted him, plundered his cargo and then tied him to the mast and cut off both his ears. Jenkins held up before the House an ear, carefully preserved in a bottle, to help substantiate his story (he was wearing a hat and wig throughout his speech). War finally broke out in October 1739, and the conflict has often been called the War of Jenkins' Ear.

1732 SUPERCILIARY

Superciliary is an adjective that means pertaining to the eyebrows. It comes from the Latin *super*, "above," and *cilium*, "eyelid." In *The Anatomy of Human Bones*, published in 1732, Alexander Munro wrote, "The Foramina, or Holes … of the frontal Bone [are] … one in each superciliary Ridge."

The noun on which this adjective is based is *supercilium*, a fancy word for "eyebrow" that appeared in print as early as 1563. But there is another adjective relating to this noun which is apparently older than the noun itself. *Supercilious* goes back as far as 1529 and is used to describe those people with a haughty and disdainful air. In other words, people who are so stuck up they raise their eyebrows at the mere sight of you.

1733 STICK-IN-THE-MUD

Today a stick-in-the-mud is an old-fashioned, stubborn or unprogressive person. The original stick-in-the-mud hit the pages of the Glasgow *Evening*

Post on November 15, 1733: "George Fluster, alias Stick in the Mud, has made himself an Evidence, and impeached the above two persons." It took four words to describe George's alias, but today it takes only one, as the component parts are strung together with hyphens. If George was guilty of being old-fashioned, the *Evening Post* reporter could have called him *antediluvian*, a word that has been part of our language since 1646. It is based on the Latin prefix *ante*, meaning "before," and *diluvium*, "flood," to describe those people who are so old-fashioned that they must have been around before the flood that carried away Noah and his ark.

1734 VAMPIRE

Stories of corpses that rise from the grave at night to feed on the blood of the living have been part of the folklore of eastern Europe for several centuries. One such creature that haunted eighteenth-century Belgrade was put out of action in 1732: "It leaned to one side, the skin was fresh and ruddy, the nails grown long and evilly crooked, the mouth slobbered with blood from its last night's repast. Accordingly a stake was driven through the chest of the vampire who uttered a terrible screech whilst blood poured in quantities from the wound. Then it was burned to ashes."

Two years later, the word *vampire*, from the Serbian *vampir*, reached England in the account of the travels of three English gentlemen who had journeyed through eastern Europe: "These vampires are supposed to be the Bodies of deceased Persons, animated by evil Spirits, which come out of the Graves, in the Night-time, suck the Blood of many of the Living, and thereby destroy them."

Vampire became a household word after the 1897 publication of *Dracula*, the story of a Transylvanian vampire written by Bram Stoker, an Irish novelist. Stoker's book is loosely based on the life of Vlad Tepes, a fifteenth-century ruler of Walachia who impaled his enemies on wooden stakes. Dracula quickly became a best-seller, was produced as a play in 1927, and was first filmed in 1931.

Vampire legends may have gotten their start from premature burials, which in the absence of proper medical knowledge were apparently quite common before the twentieth century. Vampirologist Montague Summers claims that as recently as 1900 in the United States, an average of one burial a week was premature, and in *Buried Alive*, published in 1895, Dr. Franz Hartmann reports seven hundred cases in his own neighbourhood (the doctor, by the way, was an occultist, which may help to explain how he came by this information). The truth of some of these burials was undoubtedly unearthed by grave robbers who would be the horrified witnesses of corpses contorted and bloodied in the throes of death while trying in vain to escape the confines of their subterranean prisons.

A few lucky ones were rescued in time. Summers tells the story of Zaretto, a certain villager who became drunk, then was drenched in a downpour, and who fell asleep with his wet clothes on: "He was seized with horrible convulsions; toward eleven o'clock, he went into a state of coma: he became cold and his breathing stopped. At last he was dead.... At eight o'clock next morning, he was taken away to be buried." By a stroke of good luck, the bouncing of the hearse over the rocky road that led to the cemetery jolted Zaretto out of his drunken stupor and thus postponed his inevitable departure from this life.

1735 CIGAR

Tobacco first reached England from the Spanish West Indies around 1565, and those English who could afford it quickly adopted the smoking habit. Because the cigar and cigarette were as yet unheard of, Englishmen smoked their tobacco in pipes.

In 1735 the English caught their first whiff of cigar smoke in John Cockburn's *Journey over Land*: "These Gentlemen (3 Friars at Nicaragua) gave us some Seegars to smoke.... These are leaves of Tobacco rolled up in such Manner that they serve both for a Pipe and Tobacco itself ... they know no other way (of smoking) here, for there is no such Thing as a Tobacco-Pipe through out New Spain." The word *seegar*, eventually to become the present *cigar*, probably came from the Mayan word *sik'ar*, to smoke.

There were at least seven different spellings for *cigar* back then: *see-gar, cegar, seguar, sagar, segar, cigarre* and, of course, *cigar*. Cigarettes did not appear until the early nineteenth century. That word was coined in France shortly after the Napoleonic Wars and began popping up in England by 1842.

1736 THESAURUS

The word *thesaurus,* Greek for "treasure house," as a synonym for "storehouse or treasury of knowledge," has been kicking around in the English language ever since 1736. But the man who made thesaurus a household word was an English scholar, physician and word lover named Peter Mark Roget, who published his first edition of *Roget's Thesaurus* in 1852, when he was seventy-three years old. It was an instant success and, before his death at the age of ninety in 1869, Roget had the pleasure of supervising no fewer than twenty-five new editions and printings. In his introduction to the Cardinal edition of *Roget's Pocket Thesaurus*, I.A. Richards explains, with a minimum of synonyms, what the book is all about: "A thesaurus is the opposite of a dictionary. You turn to it when you have the meaning already but don't yet have the word. It may be on the tip of your tongue, but what it is you don't yet know…"

The words that fill the bill must be words that other people know and use (otherwise you end up talking to yourself), and the editors of *Roget's Thesaurus* must keep pace with the words that fall in or out of fashion in our rapidly changing language. When Roget's first edition appeared in 1852, the word *sinner* was given a big spread, but the word *sex* was nowhere to be found. In the latest edition, *sinner* has been dropped but *sex* is in — presumably to stay.

1737 STOPWATCH

In a book entitled *Farriery Improved,* published in 1737, author Henry Bracken provides this sentence fragment: "Provided he is truly try'd by a stop watch." Because the word *farriery* meant the practice of shoeing horses or treating diseased horses, Bracken was probably alluding to some chap who could shoe horses faster than anyone else (or claimed to be able to). Such a person was known as a farrier (from Old French *ferrier*, "blacksmith," from the Latin *ferrum*, "iron"). Bracken is the first English writer we know of who used the word *stopwatch*, although, as you can see from the above quotation, it was two words in 1737 instead of one. Over the years, a hyphen was inserted between the two words (stop-watch) until finally that too disappeared.

The two most popular terms today for timepieces are *clock* and *watch*. The word *clock* goes back to the Middle Ages, when clocks were installed in clock-towers in medieval towns and cities. The word itself comes from the French *cloche*, "bell," because these early clocks had bells or chimes to sound out the time. Later on, when watches first appeared in the pocket, and later on the wrist, there were no bells to tell you what hour it was because the watch was too small. You had to watch the watch to see what time it was — hence the term.

1738 CHIMPANZEE

Credit for the first mention of *chimpanzee*, a West African name, in English goes to the September 1738 issue of *London Magazine*: "A most surprising creature is brought over in the *Speaker*, just arrived from Carolina, that was taken in a wood at Guinea. She is the Female of the Creature which the Angolans called Chimpanze…" The date for the entry of this word into English shows how slowly Africa was yielding her secrets to Europeans. Bartholomeu Dias rounded the Cape of Good Hope in 1487, but the source of the Nile River was not determined until the British explorers John Speke and James Grant visited Lake Victoria in 1862, three hundred and seventy-five years after Dias sailed past the future site of Cape Town. The Sahara Desert had long separated Europe and North Africa from the tropical lands to the south (the word *Sahara*, incidentally, means "desert"), and the absence of any large indentations of water such as Europe enjoys discouraged detailed exploration of the interior. Add to that dense jungles, intense heat, exotic diseases, hostile natives and deadly wild beasts, and you see why Africa was for so long called the Dark Continent.

1739 VAUDEVILLE

There are two possible origins for the term *vaudeville*: it may have come from *voix de ville*, "street songs," or from the *chansons* (songs) of the valley of Vire, *vaux de Vire*, in northwestern France. It was in that region that the Compagnons Galloix, a literary association, composed popular drinking songs from as early as the fifteenth century. By the mid-eighteenth century the term had been corrupted to *vaudeville* to describe a stage entertainment consisting of several unrelated acts.

In the United States, such performances were called "varieties," a term that stuck until the late nineteenth century, when *vaudeville* began to replace it. But not everyone liked the new word. Tony Pastor, who opened his first theatre on the Bowery in New York City in 1865 and who has been called the father of vaudeville, scorned the new term as "sissified" and persisted in calling his shows "varieties." His shows boasted a rapid-fire array of quick and dazzling acts featuring song, dance, magic, wild animals, acrobats, jugglers, mimics and comics. The idea spread, and by 1900 *vaudeville* was part of America's vocabulary and the theatrical form flourished unchecked for the first three decades of the twentieth century, nurturing to stardom such names as Ray Bolger, Fanny Brice, Eddie Cantor, George Burns and Gracie Allen, Jack Benny, Bert Lahr, Will Rogers, Al Jolson and the Marx Brothers. By the 1930s the vaudeville scene was getting stiff competition from radio, the movies and, after World War II, television. Yet much of the entertainment generated by these newer media owes a great debt to the vaudeville performers, many of whom made the transition from stage to movies and television. The variety shows that play to packed houses today in Miami Beach, the Catskills and Las Vegas fulfil the same role that vaudeville carried out in its heyday, and if you think it's all old hat, just remember Al Jolson's favourite line: "You ain't heard nuthin' yet!"

1740 MALARIA

In a letter he wrote in 1740, Sir Robert Walpole made mention of "a horrid thing called the mal'aria, that comes to Rome every summer and kills one." Because people at that time believed the disease was caused by the atmospheric exhalations of marshy or swampy regions, it was given the name *malaria*, which means "bad air" in Italian. The name was new, but the disease was not. The Greek physician Hippocrates described it in the fifth century B.C., and a malaria epidemic was recorded in America as early as 1493.

But it was not until early in the twentieth century that the true cause of the disease was discovered: people contracted malaria from the bite of a mosquito. William Gorgas, an American physician, found a cure for both malaria and yellow fever, thus removing the chief obstacle that blocked the construction of the Panama Canal (earlier attempts to build it had been frustrated by the prevalence of malaria in the region). The canal opened for traffic in 1914.

1741 FLOCCI-NAUCI-NIHILI-PILI-FICATION

This word is one of the longest entries in the *OED* and is often part of the vocabulary of high school and university students who pride themselves on having a gargantuan supply of big words at their fingertips. The word itself means the action of estimating as worthless, and comes from a bunch of Latin roots — *flocci, nauci, nihili* and *pili* — all of which mean "little" or "nothing." It first appeared in the letters of William Shenstone in 1741 ("I loved him for nothing so much as his flocci-nauci-nihili-pili-fication of money"), although it is not known if Shenstone actually coined it. It can be found in the Latin grammar book used at Eton in the eighteenth century, and Sir Walter Scott used the word in one of his works.

Also in 1741: *onanism*

1742 SCALPEL

The scalpel is a surgical instrument for making incisions in the body. The word comes from Latin *scalpere*, "to cut," and first appeared in the book *Medical Essays and Observations*, published by a medical society in Edinburgh in 1742. Medical science in the eighteenth century was a precarious business — especially in the branch we now call surgery. Surgeons had no special training, were not even considered doctors, and usually started their careers as barbers. The *Encyclopedia*, a multi-volume French repository of knowledge which first appeared in 1751, warned its readers to undergo surgery only as a last resort. No anesthetics or antiseptics were available, and many of the surgeon's tools more closely resembled what you would expect a carpenter to own. An illustration in the *Encyclopedia* shows how to use a long, tubular instrument to probe for a stone that was lodged in the bladder — just keep probing until you bump it loose and out it comes! The patient might die of shock, but the bladder would be back to normal.

George Washington died on December 14, 1799, but he might have lived long enough to see the arrival of the 1800s had not the doctors attending him in his final illness seen fit to engage in the often-fatal practice of bloodletting. Only one doctor — a young one — who was called in to assist objected to the practice, saying that it would weaken rather than strengthen the former president. But he was outvoted, and Washington died soon after.

1743 INFLUENZA

Influenza, also called the flu, is a viral disease producing fever, muscular aches and inflammation of the lungs. The word first appeared in English in 1743 in an issue of the *London Magazine*, which reported on "news from Rome of a contagious Distemper raging there, call'd the Influenza." The epidemic spread from Italy to the rest of Europe, including England, and thousands died. It broke out several times over the next century and a half and carried countless victims to the grave until modern medicine brought it more or less under control.

The word *influenza* itself comes from the Italian word for "influence," because the disease was believed to be caused by the astrological influence of the stars and planets. The Italian root goes back to the Latin *in*, "in," and *fluere*, "to flow," because of the way the germs flow through your body. Other words sharing the same root are *affluence, effluence, confluence* and *superfluous*. There is apparently no evidence to support the notion that *influenza* was coined one morning when a chap woke up in bed with a bad case of "enza" and said to his wife: "I'm sick, and it's all your fault. You left the bedroom window open all night and in flew enza."

1744 ESKIMO

In *An Account of the Countries Adjoining to Hudson's Bay*, Arthur Dobbs wrote in 1744 about "the East Main … [where] the Nodway or Eskimaux Indians live." Dobbs thus gets credit for first using the word *Eskimo* — or *Eskimaux* — in English. The word comes via French from a Native North American term meaning "eaters of raw flesh," and is, like the word *Indian*, a misnomer because the Eskimos cook their fish and game. Some of that wild game has found its way into the Holy Scripture; when the Bible was translated into the Eskimo tongue, Jesus Christ was described not as "the lamb of God" but as "God's seal-pup."

As modern civilization penetrates the Arctic, the old way of life of the Eskimos is disappearing. And along with it is disappearing the word *Eskimo* itself. With the settlement of land claims that has accompanied the exploration for oil and gas in the Arctic, the Native peoples of the far north have gained a new political awareness, and a desire to no longer be identified by a name that was not of their choosing. These people call themselves the Inuit, a Native term that means "the people."

1745 STASIS

This word can be found in the 1980 edition of *Webster's New Collegiate Dictionary* with the following definitions: "1. a slowing or stoppage of the normal flow of body fluids … 2. a state of static balance or equilibrium: STAGNATION." The word itself comes from the Greek *stasis*, "a standing or stopping," and first appeared in English in 1745 in *A Medicinal Dictionary* by Robert James.

When the Romans conquered the Greeks in the second century B.C., they added hundreds of Greek words to Latin, including *stasis*, which takes many forms (*sta-*, *stit*, *-sist*, *stet*, *status* and *stead*) in many words, but all have the original meaning: to stand. If you *assist* someone, you are standing by with help. If you have lots of *stamina*, you can withstand long periods of physical exertion. If you phone someone long *distance*, you are talking to a person who is standing far from you. If you *desist* in a course of action, you are stopping. If you *persist*, you are standing with it or seeing it through. If you are someone's *constant* companion, you are standing with (*con-*) them. The word *circumstances* refers to things that are happening (or standing) around (*circum-*) you. An *obstacle* is something that stands in your way. If you are *obstinate*, you are refusing to budge from your position. If you *resist* temptation, you are standing up to it, often again (*re-*) and again. Depending on your *status*, people know where you stand on the ladder of success. If you believe in *standards*, you believe people must at some point make a stand. A *stage* is a platform for actors to stand on. And if you deliver babies for a living, you are called an *obstetrician* because you stand facing (*ob-*) the mother giving birth.

1746 SPRY

Spry (which possibly comes from the Swedish *sprygg*, "brisk and active") is a synonym for "nimble," "agile" and "alert" and is often applied to elderly people who are full of pep. *Spry* had its debut (as far as we know) in *Exmoor Courtship*, a book written in an English dialect and published in 1746: "A comely prey vitty Vella vor anny keendest Theng." That probably translates as: "A handsome, spry, witty fellow game for anything." Elsewhere in the same book we learn "there's net a spreyer Vella in Challcomb."

1747 SLEEPWALKER

First mentioned in 1747 in *The Gentleman's Magazine*, the word *sleepwalker* has a fancy synonym based on two Latin roots: *somnus*, "sleep," and *ambulare*, "to walk." The synonym is *somnambulist* — and if you talk in your sleep, you are a *somniloquist* (from the Latin *loqui*, "to speak").

There should be a word for people who can sleep anywhere, anytime, and a word for people who don't like to sleep at all. Of the former, Napoleon and Winston Churchill were prime examples, able to catnap for a few minutes here and there during the day and then wake up fully refreshed. Thomas Edison thought sleeping was a waste of time and rarely spent more than three or four hours in bed each night. He figured our standard eight-hour sleep was "a heritage from our cave days" and hoped that his new electric lights would liberate mankind from this barbaric nighttime habit.

1748 MAGNOLIA

The name *magnolia* covers about eighty species of trees and shrubs that are native to America from the eastern United States to Venezuela and native to Asia from the Himalayas to Japan, Indonesia and the Philippines. Magnolias are highly prized for their large and fragrant white, yellow, pink or purple flowers and now adorn gardens throughout the world. They were named in 1748 in honour of Pierre Magnol, a French botanist who was born in 1638 and died in 1715. Indeed, hundreds of freshly discovered plants and animals were named during the eighteenth century by Europeans caught up in the new spirit of scientific inquiry that was sweeping across Europe. The Swedish naturalist Carl von Linneaus (1707–1778) spent the better part of his life classifying plants and animals in a scientific framework of genera and species and establishing guidelines for naming them. So thorough and logical are the guidelines he established that they are still used in the life sciences today.

1749 DUMBWAITER

If you consult Volume Three of the *OED*, you will find that the earliest instance in print of *dumbwaiter*, the mobile tray or shelf that holds food and drink, was in 1755, a full six years after the date you see at the top of this entry. The 1755 dumbwaiter cropped up in *The Memoirs of Captain Peter Drake*: "As soon as Supper was over, Glasses and a Bottle of Burgundy with a Flask of Champaign, was laid on the Table, with a Supply of those Wines on a Dumbwaiter."

If you then consult Volume One of the latest *OED* Supplement (A–G), published in 1972, you will find an earlier example of *dumbwaiter*, this one taken from John Cleland's book *Fanny Hill: The Memoirs of a Woman of Pleasure*: "A bottle of Burgundy, with the other necessaries were set on a dumb-waiter." It's easy to understand why this earlier use did not appear in the original *OED*, the last volume of which was published in 1928. *Fanny Hill*, first published in 1749, was one of the raciest books of all time. Cleland, its author, had been bailed out of debtors' prison by a twenty-eight-year-old printer named Ralph Griffiths for promising to write a salacious novel. Salacious it was, with no fewer than thirty acts of copulation and perversion (although, thanks to a plethora of euphemisms, not a single four-letter word). Fanny herself was a young lass of great beauty and intelligence whose boudoir acrobatics earned for the printer about £10,000, but for the author only twenty guineas. Cleland incurred the displeasure of the Privy Council, but, thanks to the intervention of Lord Granville, escaped punishment and even got a pension of £100 a year for promising not to write any more dirty books.

Fanny Hill went underground and remained there for two hundred years. Book censor Anthony Comstock called it "the most obscene book ever written." Then, in 1963, the New York publishing house of G.P. Putnam's Sons decided to test censorship by publishing the book openly. They were taken to court and they won, then lost on appeal, only to win again in New York's Court of Appeals by a vote of four to three. Now everyone can get their hands on Fanny Hill.

1750 ETIQUETTE

The word *etiquette*, borrowed from French, made its debut in the English language in 1750, when Lord Chesterfield wrote in a letter on March 19 of that year: "Without hesitation kiss his [the Pope's] slipper or whatever else the etiquette of that court requires." Not everyone in the eighteenth century was as confident as Lord Chesterfield in what the rules of etiquette demanded. A chap named Sterne recorded some doubts in 1768: "I was not altogether sure of my etiquette, whether I ought to have wrote or no." By the mid-nineteenth century, some people were getting fed up with all the rules. Robertson lamented in 1851 that "man is ... a slave ... to etiquette." But that could not have been said of Miss Braddon, who wrote in 1876, "After tea ... the bondage of etiquette was loosened."

It is entirely fitting that *etiquette* first appeared in our language in 1750, the middle year of a century during which a refinement of manners became an obsession in certain social circles. In fact, as Morton M. Hunt points out in his fascinating book *The Natural History of Love*, "Sometimes ... the overly civilized observance of politeness threatened to halt all normal human activities: the Duc de Coislin once saw a departing guest as far as his carriage, which was required; the guest, also as required, saw the Duc back to his own suite; but Coislin, the politest man of his time, then insisted … upon seeing his guest back to the carriage again, and the guest, seeing no other way to end the process, finally rushed out ahead of the Duc and managed to lock him in. Coislin, not to be outdone, leaped out the window and met him at the carriage. Having sprained his thumb in the leap, he then got it set by a surgeon, contested with the surgeon for the honour of opening the door for him, and sprained it again."

1751 BEGONIA

Begonia, which first entered English in 1751, was given its name by the eighteenth-century French botanist Charles Plumier in honour of Michel Begon, governor of Santo Domingo and an ardent promoter of botany. *Begonia* therefore is an eponym — a word based on someone's name. Begonias have plenty of company in the world of flowers because many others were named the same way. The magnolia was named after Pierre Magnol, the famous French botanist. The boysenberry was developed by and named after Rudolph Boysen, a twentieth-century American horticulturalist. The poinsetta was also named after an American: Joel Poinsett (1799–1851) of South Carolina, who, as American minister to Mexico, brought the plant back to the United States. The zinnia is named for Johann Gottfried Zinn (1727–1759), a German botanist and physician who lived in Gottengen. The fuchsia was named in honour of Leonhard Fuchs (1501–1566), a German botanist. The Douglas fir bears the name of its white discoverer (the Native Americans had found it much earlier), a Scottish botanist named David Douglas (1798–1834). The giant sequoia or redwood tree of California was given its name in 1847 in honour of Sequoyah, a Cherokee Indian who created a written alphabet for the hitherto-only-spoken Cherokee language.

There are many more, but let us finish with the most appropriate one of all: the gardenia. It was named after a botanist of Charleston, South Carolina, who lived from 1730 to 1791. His name? The very flowery Alexander Garden.

1752 Dentist

Back in the early Middle Ages, most dental work was performed by monks and other members of the Roman Catholic Church. Then, in 1131, in a fit of squeamishness, a church council at Rheims decreed that henceforth all members of the clergy were forbidden to practise surgery of any kind. For the next several centuries, dentistry was in the hands of barbers, whose red-and-white-striped poles attested to the fact that more blood than hair ended up on the floor.

With the growth of modern science in the eighteenth century, things began to improve. The French led the way, and were using the word *dentiste*, from the Latin, *dens*, "teeth," several decades before the English took note of it. The *Edinburgh Chronicle* (September 15, 1759) has been given credit for helping to introduce the new word into our language: "*Dentist* figures it now in our newspapers, and may do well enough for a French puffer; but we fancy Rutter [probably a local dental surgeon] is content with being called a tooth-drawer." Twelve years later the English physician John Hunter published his outstanding book, *The Natural History of the Teeth and Practical Treatise on the Disease of the Teeth*. Dentistry in England was quickly becoming respectable.

1753 Fahrenheit

Before temperature was measured with instruments, it was measured merely with words: hot, cold, warm, cool and "just right." Galileo made the first attempt to measure temperature accurately with his thermoscope, constructed in the early 1600s. Other scientists soon tackled the problem and produced a variety of thermometers. The one most Americans are familiar with is the Fahrenheit thermometer, developed in 1724 by Gabriel Daniel Fahrenheit (1686–1736), a German physicist living in Holland. Fahrenheit used the temperature of the human body as his fixed reference point, setting it somewhat arbitrarily at 96 degrees, an easily divisible number. Then he calculated the freezing point of water at 32 degrees and the boiling point at 212 degrees. First coming to the attention of the English in 1753, the Fahrenheit scale has been in use in the United States since the eighteenth century, but Canada, like much of the rest of the world, has switched to the Celsius scale, developed in 1742 by Anders Celsius and using zero degrees for the freezing point of water and 100 for the boiling point. To convert from Fahrenheit to Celsius, subtract 32 from the Fahrenheit reading, then divide the remainder by 1.8.

Both Fahrenheit and Celsius thermometers use mercury, the only metal that is liquid at room temperature. Prolonged breathing of the fumes causes erethism, a disorder characterized by nervousness and irritability. Because the felt hat makers in "merrie olde Englande" used mercury to work the wool, many of them succumbed to the disease, including the Mad Hatter in Lewis Carroll's *Alice in Wonderland*.

Also in 1753: *papier-mâché, alfresco*

1754 SERENDIPITY

Horace Walpole, the fourth Earl of Orford (1717–1797), was an English politician and author who lived in "a little Gothic castle" in Twickenham, where he kept a printing press on which he printed several of his own works. In a letter written to a friend on January 28, 1754, he tells of a new word he coined: *serendipity*, the ability to make fortunate discoveries by accident. He based his word on the title of a fairy tale, *The Three Princes of Serendip* (an ancient name for Ceylon), because the princes "were always making discoveries, by accidents and sagacity, of things they were not in quest of."

The most outstanding example of a serendipitous discovery took place in 1492, when Christopher Columbus stepped ashore on the Caribbean island of San Salvador. Seeking a westerly water route to the riches of the Orient, he was convinced that he was standing on an island just off the coast of Asia. When he died in 1506, he still believed he had reached the Far East. The following year, the name "America" was given to the vast new continent upon which Columbus had so serendipitously stumbled.

Also in 1755: *extravaganza*

1755 PANJANDRUM

English playwright Samuel Foote (1720–1777) had a friend, Charles Macklin, who was fond of boasting that he could remember and repeat anything after hearing it only once. Foote decided to put Macklin's memory to the test by composing and reciting a nonsense verse and then asking him to repeat it: "So she went into the garden to cut a cabbage leaf to make an apple pie; and at the same time a great she-bear, coming up the street, pops its head into the shop. 'What! no soap?' So he died, and she very imprudently married the barber; and there were present the Picninnies, and the Joblillies, and the Garyalies, and the grand Panjandrum himself, with the little round button at top, and they all fell to playing the game of catch as catch can, till the gunpowder ran out at the heels of their boots."

Did Macklin pass the test? Neither the *OED* nor *Bartlett's Familiar Quotations* supplies the answer. Of one thing we can be sure: the rest of the world has long forgotten all of Foote's nonsense verse except for one word: *panjandrum*, a pompous official, the word often being applied humorously to someone with an inflated sense of their own importance.

Also in 1755: *warpath, ski*

1756 PUMPERNICKEL

The first example of this word in English also provides us with a good description of what it is. A chap named Nugent wrote, in *A Grand Tour of Germany*, which was published in 1756: "Their bread is of the very coarsest kind, ill baked, and as black as a coal, for they never sift

their flour. The people … call it Pompernickel." What Nugent neglected to mention was what this word means in German. Because this bread was popular with German peasants, the Germans living in towns and cities called it "pompernickel," a German term meaning "a big, stupid fellow."

But the bread we eat with our friends has given us a word whose etymology is far less insulting. When good friends gather to break bread, they are each other's companions, a word that comes our way through the French *compaignon*, from Latin *com*, "with," and *panis*, "bread."

1757 KAYAK

This word is a palindrome because it can be spelled the same way forward and backward. The same cannot be said of *canoe* or *dugout*, two early conveyances on the water dating back several centuries. *Kayak* comes from the Inuit *qayaq*, and is propelled by a double-ended paddle. Its entry into English reflects the explorations by Europeans into the far north of North America.

1758 OCTOPUS

Derived from the Greek *oktopous*, these eight-legged animals have starred in several Hollywood horror movies, often sharing the spotlight with giant squids, such as the one that tried to wreak havoc on Captain Nemo's *Nautilus* in Walt Disney's adaptation of Jules Verne's classic *20,000 Leagues Under the Sea*.

The Greek-rooted prefix *octo-* ("eight") shows up in many other everyday words in modern English, including *octagon, octahedron, octameter, octane, octant, octapeptide, octave, octavo, octillion, octodecillion, octogenarian, octoploid, octoped, octosyllabic, octothorpe* and the month of *October*.

But why *October*? It's the tenth month in our calendar, not the eighth. What's going on here?

Back in Roman times, the new year began on March 1. And that's when the seventh month was September (*septem* = "seven"), the eighth was October (*octo* = "eight"), the ninth was November (*novem* = "nine"), and the tenth was December (*decem* = "ten").

Then the Romans decided to add two new months at the beginning: January and February (see page 305 for Farch). The other ten months were then pushed two months back. And that's why our tenth month, October, contains the number eight.

Also in 1758: *duvet*

1759 OUTSET

This word has been traced back to 1759, and is a synonym for "beginning" or "start." The first three letters (*out*) date back to before the twelfth century and perhaps come from the Sanskrit *ud* (meaning "up" or "out"). The other three letters (*set*) also date back to before the twelfth century, and come from the Old English *sittan* ("to sit").

Open any modern dictionary and you'll find that *outset* has plenty of familiar company on the same page. Here are a few: *outback, outboard, out-box, outbreak, outburst, outcast, outcrop, outdance* (a Sherkism!), *out-distance, outdo, outdoors, outfit, outflow, outgoing, outline, outlook, out-number, out-of-body, outport, outpost, output, outrage, outreach, outride, out-rigger, outside, outskirt, outspend* and *outstanding*. You can probably think of dozens more without even looking in a dictionary.

1760 Totem

In 1760 a chap named Henry recorded this sentence in the journal of his travels in North America: "To these are added his badge, called in the Algonquin tongue, a totem, and which is in the nature of an armorial bearing." The totem usually consisted of the likeness of an animal, as this quote from 1887 illustrates: "Twelve of these replaced their totems opposite my signature; each totem consisting of the rude representation of a bear, a deer, an otter, a rat, or some other wild animal." *Totem pole* was added to our language in the late eighteenth century, when English explorers such as George Vancouver and Captain James Cook visited the Native peoples of the northwestern part of North America, who were fond of carving totem poles and mounting them outside their homes.

Totem is just one of dozens of words the English language has borrowed from the Natives of North America, others being *wigwam, tomahawk, moose, squaw* and *toboggan*. The authors of *Learning to Write* ask — and answer — a question that may be on your mind right now: "Why are so many of these new words nouns? The Englishman coming to Australia or Africa [or America] and happening upon some strange animal or plant was at a loss for a name for it. It was simpler and more natural to accept the Native word than to try to coin one of his own. The purist who thinks that the names for all new objects should be coined out of [one's] native language would find himself in difficulty with bamboo or spaghetti or alligator."

Also in 1760: *metric, précis*

1761 GRAVEYARD

You would think this word would date back much earlier than 1761, particularly when you consider that the word *grave* goes back to Old English, which flourished from the sixth to the eleventh centuries after Christ. *Graveclothes* (the clothes in which the corpse is buried) dates back to 1535, and *gravedigger* to 1593, but the popularity of *cemetery* (from the 1400s) and *burial place* (from 1633) made it possible for the English-speaking people to get by for more than a thousand years without a single graveyard in their vocabulary — at least as far as we know.

The fancy ancient word for a cemetery or graveyard is *necropolis*, literally "a city of the dead." The ancient Egyptians had special communities set aside for the preparation of corpses for burial, especially those of the royal family, who had the privilege of being mummified. The job of working in one of these places was passed down from father to son, and those who lived there were known by an Egyptian word meaning "those who carry the odour of death with them."

In the late nineteenth century, grave robbing became a lucrative business as medical schools paid good money for corpses suitable for research. Legislation to stamp out this ghoulish practice followed on the heels of the discovery, in 1878, that the cadaver lying in the dissecting room of the Ohio Medical College was none other than John Scott Harrison, the only American to be the son of one president (William Henry Harrison) and the father of another (Benjamin Harrison).

1762 SANDWICH

According to *The People's Almanac* by David Wallechinsky and Irving Wallace, "at 5 a.m. on August 6, 1762, John Montagu, 4th Earl of Sandwich, looked up from the gaming table and decided that he was hungry. The earl, an inveterate gambler in the midst of one of his famous round-the-clock sessions, wouldn't dare leave his cards for a meal and ordered his man to bring him some cold, thick-sliced roast beef between two pieces of toasted bread. Thus the first sandwich as we know it today was born."

The Earl of Sandwich received an additional honour when Captain James Cook named the beautiful Sandwich Islands (now Hawaii) after him, an honour no doubt prompted by the fact that Sandwich was in charge of the British Admiralty at the time and had outfitted all of Cook's ships.

The earl's private life was filled with unbridled orgiastic debauchery. In addition to his notorious promiscuity, he took a mistress only sixteen years of age who proceeded to bear him five children over a twenty-year period. The scandals that surrounded him eventually got the best of him, and he died full of bitterness at age seventy-four in 1792. Although the term *sandwich* was in use by then, it had not yet received official recognition by dictionary publishers. Thus, Sandwich died without realizing how the English language would immortalize him.

1763 AHEM

Ahem is the official spelling for the sound made in clearing the throat in order to attract attention to the speaker, probably coined on the basis of onomatopoeia. The *OED* credits Charles Johnstone with being the first writer to use *ahem*, in his book *The Reverie, or a Flight to the Paradise of Fools*: "Hem! Ahem! In the first place, said he, clearing his voice…"

Other words cut from the same cloth would include *atchoo*, *harrumph* and *oops*. *Atchoo* first appeared in 1873 for the sound of sneezing, and *harrumph* in 1936 for a coughlike expression of disapproval. As for *oops*, it appears in practically every major dictionary except the biggest one of all: the *OED*. And yet the very lexicographers who are, at this moment, working on the next edition of the *OED*, probably say "Oops!" as often as you or I. If you were to phone them right now, catch them unawares, and ask them why they have never included it, they might say: "Oops! We forgot to put it in."

Also in 1763: *orgasm*

1764 RUMPUS

The English author Samuel Foote ushered this word into the English language in 1764 when he wrote, "Oh, Major! such a riot and rumpus."

No one knows where Foote got this word, but it is certainly here to stay. In recent years it has functioned as an adjective in the phrase *rumpus room*, a room in a house (usually in the basement) set aside for children to play in. Such a room is also called a *recreation room*, or *rec room* for short. Some parents, watching how quickly their children can make a mess of things, think the term *wreck room* would be more accurate. And when the children grow up and move away, no more rumpus room and no more wreck room. That space in the basement can then be used by the parents to entertain their family and friends. Put to that use, it is called the *family room* or the *recreation room* (where a good party will help you to "re-create" yourself after a hard week's work).

With the popularity of recreation rooms, where does that leave the living room? More dead than alive. The living room is now, in many homes, simply a room for storing fancy furniture. It used to be called the *parlour* in Victorian times because people went there to talk (and *parlour* comes from the French *parler*, "to talk"). Before Queen Victoria, it was called the *drawing room* because the men retired to it after dinner and drew the sliding wooden doors across before lighting up their cigars. Now it's just the room you pass on the way to the family room. One quite indignant woman wrote to "Dear Abby" to complain about this trend: "Whenever we visit these friends of ours, we always end up in the basement. Just who are the extra special friends they're saving their living room for?"

1765 FIGUREHEAD

Merriam-Webster defines *figurehead* as "1) the figure on a ship's bow, 2) a head or chief in name only."

How do you pronounce *figure*? Some people say "fig-ur" and some say "fig-yer." According to Merriam-Webster, both are worthy of being listed.

A full-figured woman is one who is buxom and has a relatively small waist and rounded hips. The term "full-figured" derives from the number eight because of the shape of a full-figured woman. And some of these women have been carved on the bow of a ship.

1766 POLYNESIA

A chap named J. Callander gets the credit for introducing the word *Polynesia* into English in his book, *Terra Australis Cognita*, published in 1766 and based on an earlier but unacknowledged work: "We call the third division *Polynesia*, being composed of all those islands which are found dispersed in the vast Pacific Ocean." *Polynesia* is Greek for "many islands" (*polus*, "many," and *nesos*, "island"). Two other names on today's map of the Pacific bear mentioning here: *Indonesia*, a modern nation that occupies the islands of the former Dutch East Indies (hence the name *Indonesia*, meaning "islands of the Indies"); and *Micronesia*, a fairly recent coinage to describe the tiny islands of the western Pacific and including the Caroline, Marshall and Kiribati Islands.

Taking the Greek root for *island*, the Pulitzer Prize–winning author James A. Michener has coined the word *nesomania* to describe what he calls "an ingratiating disease that has afflicted me for most of my life. I am truly mad about islands." His favourite is a Polynesian island in the South Pacific near Tahiti called Bora Bora. "The most beautiful island in the world," enthuses Michener, "more musical than its name, more perfect than the reef that encircles its volcanic remnants." And what does Bora Bora offer the visitor? Breathtaking landscape and seascape, balmy weather, friendly island people (only twenty-five hundred, most of whom live in thatched huts), tropical plants in great profusion (including breadfruit, Captain Bligh's precious cargo on the *Bounty*), and much more — all on an island only four miles long and two and a half miles wide. Its ancient volcanic craters and ridges reach nearly half a mile into the sky, affording vistas of unparalleled beauty.

Equally important is what Bora Bora does not offer: traffic jams, souvenir stands, franchised fast-food outlets, high-rise buildings (by law, no building can be taller than the tallest palm tree), television and newspapers. Don't be fooled by the long slender tubes mounted on posts along the road-ways. They're not for newspapers or mail but for loaves of French bread delivered fresh every morning. Mmmmmmmm. No wonder Michener contracted nesomania.

1767 BROADCAST

Arthur Young wins the prize for getting this word into print before anyone else. In his *Farmer's Letters to the People of England*, published in 1767, he writes: "The sowing is either in the broad-cast mode, or by drilling." The "drilling" is in reference to the seed drill, invented around 1701 by an Oxford graduate named Jethro Tull (now more famous as the namesake for a long-lived progressive rock group), who tackled and solved the problem of how to hoe and weed a field if the seeds had been scattered by hand. With Tull's seed drill hitched behind a horse, the farmer could dig the furrow, plant the seed and cover it up in one operation. By planting the seeds in rows instead of broadcasting them by hand, the ground could be hoed and weeded while the crops were growing, thus producing more grain per acre while using less seed.

It was not until 1921 that *broadcast* assumed its more modern meaning: to transmit signals from a radio station. The letter *B*, for either *broadcast* or *broadcasting*, can be found in the names of all three commercial U.S. television networks — ABC, NBC and CBS — as well as in the name of the public PBS network and, north of the border, in CBC. The word is appropriate in this sense because television and radio stations have traditionally struggled to capture the widest possible audience, but in recent years a counterpart, *narrowcasting*, has shot to prominence. *Narrowcasting* describes the practice of airing specialized programming in hopes of capturing a specific, or narrowly defined, segment of the viewing or listening public.

Also in 1767: *boutique*

1768 BOULEVARD

Boulevard first appeared in English in 1768 as an import from France, where Paris was already famous for its boulevards, but not nearly as renowned as it would be by the 1850s, when the modernization of Paris made that city synonymous with boulevards. French Emperor Napoleon III had come to power in a coup d'état on December 2, 1851, and was determined, for a variety of reasons, to transform the face of his capital. According to *A Survey of European Civilization* by Ferguson and Bruun:

"To make Paris a more beautiful capital for the Second Empire, and to provide work for the unemployed, Napoleon had the city modernized under the direction of his able friend Baron Haussmann. At enormous expense beautiful boulevards and broad squares replaced many of the city's ancient and crooked streets. The program of reconstruction made Paris the most elegant and spacious capital in Europe, but it also made the task of the troops easier in case of insurrection. Broad boulevards are less convenient to barricade than narrow lanes, and crowds in open squares are defenceless before gunfire or cavalry."

As with many similar schemes of urban renewal, the denizens of the slums had their humble homes pulled down to make way for progress. An 1864 issue of *Saturday Review* tells us that expropriation in Paris was not a pleasant experience: "The boulevardizing of Paris has ... caused great misery to the poor."

Also in 1768: *larva, letdown*

1769 CABOOSE

This word, from a Dutch shipping term, *kombuis*, is used today for the last car on a freight train, equipped for the use of the crew. But in the late eighteenth century a caboose was a small kitchen on the deck of a ship. It was sometimes a dangerous place to be, as Duncan points out in his *Mariner's Chronicle* from 1805: "A sea broke ... and swept away the caboose and all its utensils from the deck." And a chap named Farrar wrote in 1879, "The caboose and utensils must long ago have been washed overboard."

Also in 1769: *mynah* (bird)

1770 KANGAROO

We can pinpoint the entry of *kangaroo* into the English language down to the exact day: June 24, 1770. That's when the English explorer Captain James Cook entered the word in his ship's log after seeing one of these creatures and asking one of the natives what it was called. The fellow he asked didn't know the name either and so answered by saying "Kangaroo," an Australian Aboriginal term meaning "I don't know."

In more recent times, English has been dubiously enriched with the term *kangaroo court*, a label given to any court characterized by dishonesty and incompetence, so called because the irregular proceedings resemble the apparently random leaping of a kangaroo.

Also in 1770: *fandango*

1771 Nosing

The rounded edge of a bench or step came to be called the *nosing* because it sticks out like a nose and has a similar shape. The word *nose* itself goes back to the Anglo-Saxon days of Old English, whereas *noseless* ("having no nose") first appeared in the late Middle Ages. The word was probably applied to prostitutes, since it was a common practice back then to cut off the nose of a woman convicted of prostitution.

Ever since I received the following letter from Jocelyn Classey of Toronto, the word *nose* has been a useful aid in teaching my students about the strange quirks of the English language:

> Dear Mr. Sherk:
>
> Surely a pressing need is for a pronoun meaning he or she and here I have failed. I've tried *hesh* but people think you mean "Shut up!"; *heesh* is just about as awkward as the original, and *they* won't do because it's plural. Your students might enjoy the problem presented by: "Everyone in the room was blowing his nose." (No females present?)
> "… his or her nose." (ugh!)
> "… their nose." (a nose belonging to more than one person?)
> "… their noses." (more than one nose per person?)

Also in 1771: *avalanche*

1772 Grackle

Merriam-Webster supplies two definitions for *grackle*: "any of a genus of large American blackbirds having iridescent black plumage," and "any of various Asian starlings (as the hill mynahs)."

When you think of blackbirds, you might also think of the raven (another black bird). And that bird might remind you of Edgar Alan Poe's poetic masterpiece "The Raven," which begins thusly:

> Once upon a midnight dreary, while I pondered weak and weary
> Over many a quaint and curious volume of forgotten lore,
> While I nodded, nearly napping, suddenly there came a tapping,
> As of some one gently rapping, rapping at my chamber door.
> "'Tis some visitor," I muttered, "tapping at my chamber door —
> "Only this and nothing more."

> Ah, distinctly I remember it was in the bleak December
> And each separate dying ember wrought its ghost upon the floor...

1773 GALLICIZE

Once more we open Merriam-Webster, which offers this definition of *gallicize*: "to cause to conform to a French mode or idiom."

It is no accident that this word popped up in English when it did (in 1773). The French king, Louis XIV (who died in 1715), constructed the magnificent royal palace and gardens at Versailles to symbolize the power of the French nation and culture throughout Europe. Louis XIV was known as the Sun King because his enormous ego demanded that France be the most powerful nation on the continent, with all the lesser nations revolving around it in the same way the planets in our solar system revolve around the sun.

But Louis's interminable wars squandered lives and money, and when his funeral cortege rolled through the streets of Paris in 1715, many French citizens could be seen spitting on his coffin.

However, French culture, and particularly the dazzling court life at Versailles, continued to set the trends throughout Europe during the reign of Louis XV (1715–1774) and beyond. The French language for quite some time was the international language of diplomacy, much as English is today.

If you lived in England in 1773 and "gallicized" your daily life, you were probably aping the lifestyle of the French nobles living at Versailles.

1774 COUGAR

You can plot the westward tide of English settlement in America simply by reading the *OED*, listing the names of all animals indigenous to North America, and noting the year in which they first entered the English language. *Alligator* and *crocodile* came in via Spanish in the mid-1500s because Spanish explorers and settlers penetrated Florida and the Caribbean long before the English. The first permanent English settlement in North America was established at Jamestown, Virginia, in 1607 and, within the following few years, hundreds of Native words for animals and manmade things found their way into the vocabulary of the English — *skunk, moccasin, powwow, tobacco* and many more.

Cougar (another Native word) entered the English language on the eve of the American Revolution. Its earliest recorded appearance dates back to 1774 in a book entitled *Natural History* by Oliver Goldsmith: "There is an animal of America, which is usually called the red tiger, but Mr. Buffon calls it the cougar." Three years later the word *puma* (another name for the cougar) appeared in *The History of America* by William Robertson: "The Puma and Jaguar, [America's] fiercest beasts of prey, which Europeans have inaccurately denominated lions and tigers, possess neither the undaunted courage of the former, nor the ravenous cruelty of the latter."

At that time the cougar or puma (also called the mountain lion) ranged across North America from the Atlantic to the Pacific. But with the westward flow of settlement, the cougar was eliminated from the eastern half of the United States and is found today only in the lands in and around the Rocky Mountains.

1775 Nymphomaniac

According to the *OED*, the word *nymphomaniac* first appeared in print in 1775 as a description of a woman with a morbid and uncontrollable sexual desire. The word itself is made up of two Greek roots: *nymphe*, "bride," and *mania*, "madness," possibly from the notion that a bride on her honeymoon may fall into a frenzy of sexual excitement. The Greek root *nymphe* also means "nymph," a young and fair goddess of ancient Greek mythology who dwelt in a wood, grove, fountain, river or similar setting of natural beauty.

Most people today know the meaning of the word *nymphomaniac*, but how many know the word that describes the same degree of sexual passion in the human male? The word, which first entered English in 1657, is *satyriasis*, from the Greek *satyr*, defined by the *Webster Universal Dictionary* as "a woodland deity in Greek mythology, represented with long-pointed ears, flat nose, short horns, and a hair-clad man's body, with the legs and hoofs of a goat, fond of sensual enjoyment." Over the years *satyriasis* acquired a synonym, *satyromania*, perhaps to make it rhyme with *nymphomania*.

1776 Jungle

In the early summer of 1776, Thomas Jefferson was composing the Declaration of Independence. In that same year, an English author named Nathaniel Halhed wrote, "Land Waste for Five Years ... is called Jungle." Halhed's use of the word *jungle* is the earliest known in English. It comes from a Hindi word meaning "desert," "wasteland" or "forest." In 1783 Edmund Burke wrote about a land "almost throughout a dreary desert, covered with rushes, and briers, and jungles full of wild beasts."

By the mid-nineteenth century, *jungle* was used to describe any land, particularly tropical, which was overgrown with dense, tangled vegetation. Its figurative use became more popular, with Thomas Carlyle writing about "a world-wide jungle of red tape" and modern life giving rise to the *asphalt jungle*, the *concrete jungle* and the *blackboard jungle*.

Also in 1776: *killjoy, bovine*

1777 ALBINO

The *American Heritage Dictionary* defines *albino* as "an organism lacking normal pigmentation, such as a person having abnormally pale skin, very light hair, and lacking normal eye coloring, or an animal having white hair or fur and red eyes." The word comes from the Latin *albus*, "white," and was first used in English in 1777 in William Robertson's book *The History of America*: "The former are called Albinos by the Portuguese." Robertson is referring to native Africans who have white skin instead of black, and these were first called "albinos" by the Portuguese who were engaged in the slave trade. Albinism is an inherited condition, with some people being part albino and others completely albino. The frequency of complete albinism in humans is roughly the same for all racial groups: about one in twenty thousand.

1778 POMPANO

This word comes originally from the Latin *pampinus*, by way of the American Spanish *pampano* to give us the word *pompano*, defined by Merriam-Webster as "1) a carangid food fish of the Western Atlantic and Gulf of Mexico; *broadly*: any of several related fishes, 2) a small bluish or greenish butterfish of the Pacific coast of North America."

Immediately preceding this word in the dictionary is *pompadour* (1756), named after the hairstyle popularized by the Marquise de Pompadour.

1779 DEADLOCK

In 1779 the Irish-born English playwright Richard Sheridan created a famous comedy for the stage entitled *The Critic*, with the subtitle *A Tragedy Rehearsed*. The three principal characters are an author named Fretful Plagiary, a critic named Dangle, and a windbag promoter named Puffs, all of whom help to satirize the contemporary theatre scene. In the play, Sheridan introduced a term that apparently no author had ever used before: "I have them all at a dead lock! for every one of them is afraid to let go first."

Sheridan's new term consisted of two words instead of one, but by the time a chap named Hawthorne used it in his *French and Italian Journal* (1858), the two words were linked by a hyphen: "In Newgate Street, there was such a number of market-carts, that we almost came to a dead-lock with some of them." Today the word is written with no space and no hyphen: just plain *deadlock*. And when it applies to traffic jams, we have a new term that very likely developed directly out of *deadlock*. See page 302 for *gridlock*.

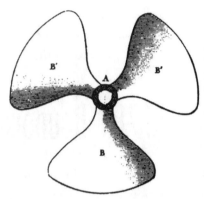

1780 PROPELLER

In 1780 the British government issued Patent #1252, "a grant unto William Bache of Birmingham, for his new invented instrument or machine which he calls by the name of a Propeller." Bache's invention was actually a turbine water wheel used to drive, or *propel,* machinery. The more familiar meaning of *propeller,* the revolving device with blades providing motion for ships or aircraft, from the Latin *pellere,* "to drive," appeared in 1809. In that year Robert Fulton obtained for his steamboat a U.S. patent, which said: "The successful construction of steam boats depends on their parts being well proportioned, whether wheels or any other propellers be used."

But having a propeller on a steamboat was no guarantee that the boat would keep moving. The *London Daily News* of April 22, 1870, reported that "the *City of Brussels* left New York on the 28th March, and lost her propeller three days afterwards." Sometimes a propeller would simply fall off, and sometimes a blade would hit something and become bent or broken.

Shortly after the end of World War I, a Canadian boatbuilder named William Johnson began building boats with a disappearing propeller. The boats were about eighteen feet in length, made of cypress, and powered by a one-cylinder, two-stroke engine mounted under a seat in the middle of the boat. The propeller and shaft protruded below the middle of the keel at an angle facing the back of the boat. Just in front of the propeller was a curved strip of metal called a "skeg," which shoved the propeller and shaft up inside a housing in the hull whenever the boat crunched over a rock. This ingenious device meant that you could pilot your boat through reefs and shoals without breaking the blades off your propeller.

William Johnson built hundreds of these boats at his Port Carling, Ontario, factory and exported many of them to the United States and several other foreign countries. These boats were finally forced off the market by the growing popularity of outboard motor boats (which were much faster) and fibreglass hulls, which required far less maintenance. However, the disappearing propeller boats (called "dispros" or "dippies" by the people who own them) have not disappeared. Many of them are now being restored with tender loving care by antique boat enthusiasts who are putting them back in the water.

1781 BOUDOIR

When English poet William Hayley wrote a poem in 1781 called *The Triumphs of Temper*, he imported a new word from French into English: "As the French boudoir to the Gothic tower,/Such is the peer, whom fashion much admires,/Compar'd in person to his ancient sires." Two new variations on that word arose in the years that followed: *boudoiresque*, describing matters pertaining to the boudoir, and *boudoirize*, a verb meaning "to frequent the boudoir."

The boudoir — from the French *bouder*, "to pout or sulk" — of a lady of elegance in the eighteenth century was an elaborate chamber in which milady could pamper and preen herself before sallying forth on a sparkling round of social engagements. It epitomized a lifestyle coveted by many women of the time, including those of England. In *The Age of Enlightenment*, Peter Gay affords us a glimpse of what that life was like, from the boudoir to the salon: "Private life for a woman of French society [in the eighteenth century] was an elaborate ceremonial from the moment she awoke until the small hours of each day. Her toilette was a public affair at which friends, lovers, hairdressers, husbands, abbés and others gathered to exchange new rumours, or to give old rumours new sparkle by a graceful turn of phrase. Marriage scarcely interfered with a woman's freedom to amuse herself; 'a husband who would wish to have sole possession of his wife,' Montesquieu said, 'would be regarded as a disturber of public happiness.' … Imitation of the aristocratic Frenchwoman's exquisite manners soon became the hopeless goal of all of fashionable Europe."

Also in 1781: *capitalist, farceur*

1782 POLYSYLLABIC

This adjective applies to a word having more than one — and usually several — syllables, and has been dated as far back as 1782. The noun form of this word (*polysyllable* — in itself a polysyllabic word) appeared as early as 1570.

Some people pride themselves on having a polysyllabic vocabulary in the hope of impressing others with their command of big words. A *sesquipedalian* word is one having several syllables, and it dates back to 1656. The Latin prefix *sesqui-* means "one and a half," while *ped* means "foot" — translated literally, then, it describes a word a foot and a half long.

The author of this dictionary coined the term *sesquilingual* in 1975 to describe people who know one language and part of another, a term that probably applies to the majority of Canadians, who know English and a smattering of French, or vice versa. The Latin prefix *sesqui-* is sufficiently unfamiliar to most people that if you describe yourself as sesquilingual, they'll often think you speak six languages instead of one and a half.

Getting back to *polysyllabic*, its opposite is *monosyllabic*, "having one syllable." In the 1930s, Winston Churchill was one of the highest-paid authors in the English-speaking world. When he became prime minister of the United Kingdom on May 10, 1940, he delivered a statement that demonstrates the power of monosyllabic words: "I have nothing to offer but blood, toil, tears, and sweat."

1783 SILHOUETTE

First mentioned in English in 1783, a quotation from 1806 tells us that neither this new word, nor the art form it describes, was yet fully accepted: "Whenever they send me their silhouettes, or what do they call them, I chuck them out the window." The word *silhouette* is an eponym because it is based on the name of Etienne de Silhouette, who was appointed controller-general of France in 1759. He soon became unpopular when he proposed a land tax on the estates of the nobles and a cut in government pensions. Although etymologists are not certain why his name came to be applied to a particular style of portraiture, here is the most plausible guess: in attempting to bring French finances in line with reality, Silhouette tried a number of cost-cutting schemes, and because the portraiture that now bears his name is the cheapest form of that art, his name was affixed to it.

1784 AMATEUR

In 1784 an issue of *European Magazine* carried this line, "The President will be left with his train of feeble Amateurs." Used in this way, the word *amateur* meant someone who loves or is fond of something or who has a taste for something, hence the origin of the word in the Latin verb *amare*, "to love." *Amateur* later acquired the more familiar meaning, a person who pursues a subject as a pastime and not as a professional. By 1803 this new term was in sufficiently wide circulation to merit mention in the *Rees Encyclopedia*: "Amateur, in the Arts, is a foreign term introduced and now passing current amongst us, to denote a person understanding, and loving or practising the polite arts of painting, sculpture, or architecture, without any regard to pecuniary advantage."

Also in 1784: *flywheel, lollipop*

1785 PARACHUTE

They say that necessity is the mother of invention, and this certainly holds true for the parachute. The first balloon flight in history took place in 1783 from the courtyard at Versailles, when the Montgolfier brothers sent up a hot-air balloon with a duck and a rooster on board. The flight lasted eight minutes and was witnessed by Louis XVI and Benjamin Franklin. One month later, the two brothers engineered the first manned balloon flight as Louis's historian, Jean Pilatre de Rozier, was hoisted aloft on a five-minute flight that carried him to an altitude of eighty feet.

The balloon craze was soon under way, and it quickly became apparent that there were risks in travelling aloft. Two English balloonists set out from Dover early in 1785 to cross the English Channel. While over the water, they lost so much altitude they threw nearly everything overboard, including most of the clothes they wore. They finally landed — nearly naked — in the woods near Calais. In June of that same year, the now-famous Pilatre de Rozier decided to conquer the English Channel the other way — from France to England. He didn't make it. His balloon burst into flames at three thousand feet, giving him the unenviable honour of being history's first fatality of flight.

It's too bad de Rozier wasn't carrying a parachute. According to the *OED*, they were available by 1785, the year de Rozier fell to his death.

It seems only fitting that the country that gave us ballooning should also give us the word parachute, from *parer*, "to make ready," and *chute*, "a fall."

Also in 1786: *dumbbell*

1786 CUISINE

When Hannah More wrote about French cuisine in 1786, she was perhaps the first English writer to use the word *cuisine* in an English sentence. It's easy to see why this French word (which comes from Late Latin *coquina*, "kitchen") entered the English language when it did. France in the eighteenth century was the trendsetter of Europe, thanks in no small part to the glittering court life created at Versailles by Louis XIV. French kings and aristocrats set the pace for fashion in clothes, art, architecture, music, furniture and food. The Duc de Montausier, for example, began the practice of placing silver forks at every table setting — an unheard-of luxury in an age when it was customary to bring your own fork when invited out to dinner. In noble French kitchens, it was the age of the sauce, and French cooks needed at least a hundred sauces in their repertoires if they expected to impress their blue-blooded employers. Cooking was a serious business. One cook, Vatel by name, committed suicide when fish for the king's dinner failed to arrive on time. Many French noblemen in pre-revolutionary France drove themselves to the brink of bankruptcy in a frantic attempt to outdo one another in staging lavish feasts of exotic dishes.

Some of these same nobles died in the bloodbath of the French Revolution — and this unwittingly gave a big boost to French cuisine in general and French restaurants in particular. In 1765 Paris had only one "restaurant" and it served only soups. To be sure, there were inns and hotels, but they catered mainly to travellers and they usually offered a one-course meal with no selection. By 1794 Paris had five hundred restaurants offering the finest food the world could provide, all to be chosen from long and elaborate menus. Many of these eating establishments were opened by the cooks of aristocrats who needed new employment after their noble masters were guillotined or exiled.

The French Revolution enhanced the food business in another way as well. In 1795 Napoleon announced he would award a prize of 12,000 francs (an enormous sum in those days) to anyone who could invent a way to preserve food supplies for an army on the march. An obscure French cook, Nicholas Appert, began experimenting in the tiny kitchen of his modest home. Frequent explosions could be heard as bits of glass and chunks of food came flying out his kitchen windows, but gradually his hard work began to pay off. In front of his neighbours, he ate a five-year-old jar of pâté without getting sick, and they were duly impressed. Finally, after fifteen years of work, Appert collected the prize money. He had perfected the art of food preservation by sealing the food in airtight cans, and thus gave birth to the modern canning industry.

Also in 1787: *millionaire*

1787 CORDUROY

In *The Academy of Horsemanship*, G. Gambado wrote in 1787: "Nothing but a pair of corduroys between him and the Horse's back." That is the earliest example of *corduroy* in English that the editors of the *OED* have found. And where does corduroy come from? Most people assume the word to be of French origin, but the *OED* thinks otherwise: "No such name has ever been used in French; on the contrary, among a list of articles manufactured at Sens in 1807, Millin de Grandmaison ... enumerates 'etoffes de cotton, futaines, kings-cordes', evidently from English. Wolstenholme's Patent of 1776 mentions nearly every thing of the fustian kind except corduroy, which yet was well known in 1790. Duroy occurs with serge and drugget as a coarse woollen fabric manufactured in Somersetshire in the eighteenth century, but it has no apparent connection with corduroy. A possible source has been pointed out in the English surname Corderoy."

By 1830 *corduroy* was being used as an adjective to describe a type of road popular in North America and constructed of logs laid transversely across the direction of travel. These corduroy roads kept you out of the mud, but not everyone appreciated them, as Catharine Parr Traill bore witness in *The Backwoods of Canada* in 1836: "Over these abominable corduroys the vehicle jolts, jumping from log to log."

1788 Stevedore

A stevedore is a dockside worker who loads and unloads ships. The word comes from the Spanish *estibador*, from *estivar*, "to stow or pack," and first appeared in English in a publication called *The Massachusetts Spy* in 1788. But where did the root *estivar* come from? We can trace it back to the Latin *stipare* — to compress, stuff, or pack.

And this is how many words of Latin or Greek origin entered the English language: by passing through another language first. If you look at the estimated one million words that now make up the English language, you will find that many of the foreign words we have borrowed from other languages can be traced directly or indirectly back to Latin or Greek. However, a small but fascinating number of words have been acquired directly from lands other than ancient Greece or Rome. For example, *alchemy* comes from Arabia, *buoy* from Holland, *canoe* from the West Indies, *caviar* from Turkey, *coyote* from Mexico, *geyser* from Iceland, *jubilee* from Palestine, *mammoth* from Russia, *mugwump* from Native American, *puttee* from India, and *waltz* from Germany. Such is the kaleidoscopic nature of the English language.

Also in 1788: *oxygen*

1789 Choreography

The definition in Merriam-Webster that reflects most usage is this one: "the composition and arrangement of dances especially for ballet." Also included is this definition: "something resembling choreography (a snail-paced choreography of delicate high diplomacy — Wolfgang Saxon)."

And now for the question everyone is asking these days: What part of your body should not be moving when you're dancing? Your bowels, of course.

Also in 1789: *ammonia, libertarian*

1790 CENTENARIAN

Someone who is one hundred years old or older is a centenarian. The Queen Mother made it. Bob Hope made it. Colonel Sam McLaughlin, father of General Motors of Canada, made it. They all hit the age of one hundred while standing still.

One woman was swarmed by reporters on her hundredth birthday, asking her to say something befitting the occasion. Her reply: "My goodness, if you make this big a fuss when I turn 100, I can't imagine what you'll do when I turn 200."

1791 WATERBED

When *waterbed* first appeared in print in 1791, it had nothing to do with sleeping. It simply referred to a layer or stratum of the earth through which water can percolate. In 1853 the term acquired its more modern meaning of a bed with a water-filled mattress. The first of these waterbeds were used in hospitals, particularly for patients suffering from bedsores. The modern waterbeds you now find in people's homes did not hit the mass market until the late 1960s or early 1970s. If you buy the king-sized version, you'll have two hundred gallons sloshing around underneath you, a far cry from the days when ancient Persians slept on goatskins filled with water.

Whenever the conversation gets around to waterbeds, there is always one question that inevitably pops up, and writer Claire Gerus tackles it head-on: "How is sex in a waterbed? It's all a matter of synchronizing your movements with that of the bed. One veteran likens it to 'choreographing a difficult ballet,' while another admits that although waterbeds are excellent for sleeping, he moves to his regular bed for lovemaking. Everyone agrees that it takes some getting used to. But, points out Andre

Kocsis (co-founder of Halcyon Waterbeds), 'There's more to sex than a waterbed.' One can't argue with that."

Also in 1791: *pemmican*

1792 OFFSET

This word has plenty of company in the *off-* section of the dictionary. Merriam-Webster lists no fewer than eighty, ranging from *offal* (fourteenth century), through *off-key* (1927 — "Is there a piano player in the house?"), to *off-white*.

As a word, *offset* can be traced back to circa 1555 as a noun (also an adjective or adverb). It's the verb use that takes us back to 1792: "to place over against something; to serve as a counterbalance for (his speed offset his opponent's greater weight)."

1793 GUILLOTINE

When the French Revolution broke out in 1789, a French physician named Dr. Joseph Guillotin suggested the use of a heavy blade sliding up and down in a wooden framework as a quick and painless way of executing people. Such an instrument had been in use before in Italy. The good doctor, far from inventing it, merely recommended its use in France as well.

By 1793 the word *guillotine* appeared in English as a noun, and as a verb the following year, to describe the bloodletting of the Reign of Terror. Guillotin himself was dismayed to discover that his name was applied to the device. Members of his family were equally dismayed and went to court seeking legal assistance in getting the name of the instrument changed. The judge, obviously a realist in linguistic matters, said it would be far easier for the Guillotins to change their name.

Contrary to popular opinion, Guillotin himself did not die by the blade that carries his name. He lived to 1814, just one year short of Napoleon's defeat at Waterloo.

Also in 1793: *spikelet*

1794 SKYSCRAPER

When *skyscraper* first appeared in print, it was a nautical term for a triangular sail mounted high above the deck of a sailing ship ("Four vessels hove in sight ... with ... royals and skyscrapers set."). It acquired several other definitions before picking up the one it has today. By 1826 a skyscraper was a very tall horse: "The huntsmen were all abroad ... trotting ... down the road, on great nine-hand sky-scrapers." By 1857 it was a very tall man: "I say, old skyscraper, is it cold up there?" It was later applied to the rider of a very tall bicycle popular in the 1890s: "Riders of the ordinary [cycle] ... are few and far between, and are often derisively styled 'skyscrapers.'" And it was even used in 1841 for an exaggerated story or "tall" tale: "My yarn won't come so well after your sky-scrapers of love."

By the 1880s a skyscraper was also a very tall building. The city of Chicago claims the honour of building the world's first skyscraper, the Home Insurance Company Building at LaSalle and Adams streets, construction of which began on May 1, 1884. Boasting a steel frame overlaid with marble and granite, it soared ten storeys high and opened for business in the fall of 1885. The city of Boston, however, claims the honour of first applying the word *skyscraper* to a tall building. The first of these buildings in Boston was built near the harbour, which was filled with sailing ships that sported skyscraper sails at the top of their masts. The word was simply transferred from the ships to the building.

Also in 1794: *accountability*

1795 TERRORIST

This term, from the Latin *terrere*, "to frighten," was first applied to the Jacobins and others like them who organized the Reign of Terror in the wake of the French Revolution. The guillotine (see page 193) was the chief instrument of execution for those found guilty of plotting against the new republican government, and among its victims were Louis XVI and his Austrian wife, Marie Antoinette. The flow of blood was at its greatest from the summer of 1793 (Louis and his wife had been dispatched the previous January) until the summer of 1794, during which time an estimated forty thousand persons lost their lives. But the popular notion that French aristocrats were the chief recipients of the guillotine blade simply is not true. In *A History of the Modern World*, R.R. Palmer and Joel Colton set the record straight: "The Terror showed no respect for, or interest in, the class origins of its victims. About eight per cent were nobles, but the nobles as a class were not molested unless suspected of political agitation. Fourteen per cent of the victims were classifiable as bourgeois, mainly of the rebellious southern cities. Six per cent were clergy, while no less than seventy per cent were of the peasant and labouring classes."

The terror struck fear in the hearts of French citizens from the English Channel to the Riviera. Butchery in the name of politics became the order of the day as one atrocity followed another. And not all victims were beheaded: at Nantes, for example, two thousand hapless souls were loaded onto barges and deliberately drowned.

1796 PAPERHANGER

Merriam-Webster supplies two definitions: "1) one that applies wallpaper, 2) slang: one who passes worthless checks."

If you fit the second definition and you're doing it in Canada, you are passing worthless *cheques*, because British spelling is still often used north of the Canada–U.S. border. To test the worth of a cheque, some people drop it on the floor to see if it bounces.

Many people today make their purchases with a debit card or credit card. Either way, it's a plastic card that can be used to scrape ice and snow off the windows of your car in the dead of winter.

And if your card is lost or stolen, you can call the police: "Help! I've been deplasticated!"

1797 URANIUM

Of the nine planets in our solar system, you can see only five in the night-time sky without the aid of a telescope: Mercury, Venus, Mars, Jupiter and Saturn (you can see a sixth planet, Earth, if you look at the ground beneath your feet). When the Italian astronomer Galileo constructed a telescope in 1609 and aimed it at the sky, he discovered four moons circling Jupiter and a set of rings surrounding Saturn, but he found no new planets. That honour went to the German-born British astronomer William Herschel, who discovered the planet Uranus in 1781. The name for the new planet was taken from the Greek god of the sky, Ouranos, who was the father of Cronos (known to the Romans as Saturn) and the grandfather of Zeus (known to the Romans as Jupiter).

Herschel's discovery took the scientific world by storm because Uranus was the first new planet to be discovered since primitive man first gazed upward at the sky. Eight years later, in 1789, the German chemist Martin Klaproth was conducting some experiments with a heavy, black mineral called pitchblende, in which he found evidence of a strange new metal. Because there was a new planet in the sky and now a new metal on Earth, Klaproth named the metal after the planet and called it "uranium." This new word officially entered the English language in 1797, when it appeared in the third edition of the *Encyclopaedia Britannica*.

1798 WOMBAT

Merriam-Webster describes these little animals as follows: "any of several stocky burrowing Australian marsupials … resembling small bears." The word derives from the Australian aboriginal language of the Port Jackson area.

The *Oxford World Encyclopedia* (2001) goes into more detail: "Either of two species of large, rodentlike marsupial mammals of SE Australia and Tasmania. Both species are herbivorous, primarily nocturnal, and live in extensive burrows. The common wombat (*Vombatus ursinus*) has coarse, black hair and small ears. The hairy-nosed wombat (*Lasioshinus latifrons*) has finer, gray fur and large ears. Length: to 3.9 ft. (1.2 m)."

It should be mentioned here that the wombat, without realizing it, plays a significant role in the Australian economy. Many tourist brochures include photos of the wombat to lure visitors to Australia. See also *kangaroo* (page 179) and *duck-billed platypus* (immediately below).

1799 Duck-billed Platypus

In 1788 the British established their first permanent foothold in Australia — a penal colony at Port Jackson, the site of present-day Sydney. Nine years later, in 1797, Lieutenant Colonel David Collins wrote a letter to his scientific colleagues in far-off London in which he described a strange creature he had found near the Hawkesbury River in New South Wales. After telling about the webbed feet and beaverlike tail of the furry little fellow, Collins added: "But the most extraordinary circumstance observed in its structure was its having, instead of the mouth of an animal, the upper and lower mandibles of a duck.... Its webbed feet enabled it to swim, while on shore its long sharp claws were employed in burrowing. Nature thus provided for its double or amphibian character."

This exotic creature was given its name in 1799 by Dr. George Shaw of England, who was the lucky recipient of a dried platypus skin. The name *platypus* is based on Greek for "flat foot": *platus pous*. A few years later the British Museum received a pair of pickled specimens sent in a cask of spirits by Governor James Hunter of New South Wales. By this time the scientific community in Europe was agog over this new discovery, with many skeptics claiming the animal was nothing more than a monstrous hoax. How could a mammal lay eggs and then suckle its young? Unheard of!

The controversy raged for nearly a century. Finally, in 1884, the British Museum dispatched Dr. W. H. Caldwell, a Cambridge zoologist, to Australia to try to find a platypus egg, if any existed. After searching high and low, he found not one, but two. He also confirmed reports of a similar creature, the spiny anteater, also alleged to lay eggs and suckle its young. The anteater and the platypus share a zoological classification known as *monotremes*. Caldwell excitedly cabled his colleagues in London: MONOTREMES OVIPAROUS.

But it would be many more years before the outside world would see a platypus in the living flesh. The first live specimen to be seen outside Australia was exhibited by the New York Zoological Park in 1922.

Also in 1799: *sexual intercourse*

The 1800s

In 1807 Robert Fulton sent his first steamboat chuffing up the Hudson River. In 1896 Henry Ford took his first car for a spin through the streets of Detroit. Between those two dates the English language expanded so rapidly with new words that dictionary publishers were hard pressed to keep pace. The British by now had planted colonies in all parts of the world and could boast of having an empire "on which the sun never set." Borrowing freely from whatever foreign languages lay at hand, the English-speaking peoples picked up *aardvark* from South Africa, *vodka* from Russia, *pajamas* from the Middle East, *yoga* and *cashmere* from India, *boomerang* from Australia, *cancan* from France, *hamburger* from Germany, *marathon* from ancient Greece, and many, many more.

By now, far more people were reading than ever before, partly because of the boom in Bible reading spawned by the religious revival that swept the British Isles in the early nineteenth century. When the demand for Bibles was at its height, a hundred thousand goats a year were slaughtered in England to supply the leather for Bible covers. (One goatskin covered ten Bibles, which translates into a million Bibles a year.) Many children first learned to read from the family Bible, and then, if lucky enough, they would be sent off to the local Sunday school for more learning. In 1870 the British government passed the Education Act, establishing a nationwide system of state-supported elementary schools. By 1880, with more than three million pupils attending these new schools, more words, both new and old, came within the reach of far more people than ever before.

Medicine was another rapidly growing field, one that was finding new cures for old diseases to say nothing of new diseases looking for even newer cures. In the pages ahead, you will read the stories behind such words as *bronchitis, ambulance, morgue, morphine, chloroform, sanatorium, claustrophobia, contraceptive* and *kleptomania*. You will even find the word *atchoo*, which first appeared in print in 1873, for the sound of someone sneezing. *Gesundheit*, however, did not show up until 1914.

The little pleasures and refinements of everyday living continued to multiply as Father Time wended his way thorough the nineteenth century. Along the way he would encounter *cafeteria, cigarette, goatee, saxophone, badminton, piccolo, xylophone, massage, brunch* and *fedora*.

The biggest flood of new words in the nineteenth century came from science and its many applications to everyday life. While Napoleon was waging war against the rest of Europe, chemists were discovering *potassium, magnesium* and *aluminum*. In the generation after Waterloo, the industrial output of England had made London the financial capital of the world, and to celebrate the promise of material abundance for everyone, Queen Victoria's husband, Prince Albert, sponsored the great Exhibition of 1851 in the specially constructed Crystal Palace in Hyde Park. Thirteen thousand exhibits were seen by more than six million visitors.

Meanwhile, a revolution was taking place in the fields of transportation and communication. George Stephenson, a colliery worker with a flair for engineering, built the Stockton-Darlington Railway in 1825 and persuaded the somewhat reluctant owners to use his newfangled steam locomotive to haul the truckloads of coal. They were glad they did, for Stephenson's little engine replaced forty teams of horses and cut the price of coal in Stockton by half. Five years later, Britain's first major rail line, between Manchester and Liverpool, opened for business. Fanny Kemble, a famous actress of the day, was one of the first customers, and she wrote an account of her first ride: "We were introduced to the little engine which was to drag us along the rails…. This snorting little animal, which I felt rather inclined to pat, was then harnessed to our carriage…. [The engine] set off at its utmost speed, thirty-five miles an hour, swifter than a bird flies…. My spirits rose to the true champagne-height, and I never enjoyed anything so much…. [My mother, however,] was frightened to death, and intent upon nothing but devising means of escaping from a situation which appeared to her to threaten with instant annihilation herself and all her travelling companions."

Not everyone shared Fanny's mother's "locomotiphobia"; by 1850, the six thousand miles of British railways were carrying seventy million passengers a year. The trains by that time were also carrying a lot of mail, ever since Parliament in 1840 introduced penny postage. In 1850 an underwater telegraph cable was laid between England and France, stirring some visionaries to dream of the day when a telegraph cable could be laid across the North Atlantic to connect Britain with North America. After several failures, that job was finished in 1866. Four years later, another cable bridged the gap between Britain and India, and a third cable was later laid between British Columbia and Australia.

The latter half of the nineteenth century brought wonders undreamt of by Napoleon and the others who had had their heyday when the century was young. Kerosene came on the market in 1854. The first oil well in North America was drilled in 1859. Gasoline was identified by name in 1865. The bicycle came along, also vinyl, dynamite, the typewriter, the telephone, pasteurized milk, the Bessemer method of manufacturing steel, phonographs, gramophones, Kodak cameras, diesel engines, and — wonder of wonders — gasoline-powered horseless carriages. So many new inventions were made so quickly that people simply couldn't keep pace with the task of dreaming up enough new words to label all the moving parts. And so an all-purpose noun came along in 1886 for all those mechanical parts whose names escape you. Just call each one a "gadget."

As the nineteenth century drew to a close, nearly everyone was expecting even greater wonders to come along in the twentieth. And if they were expecting an even heavier avalanche of new words, the twentieth century would certainly not disappoint them.

1800 PAJAMAS

Before the word *pajamas* came along, the English slept in nightgowns, street clothes and birthday suits. *Pajamas* made its debut in English in the year 1800 in reference to "Tippoo Sultaun's wardrobe ... [of] pajamahs or drawers." The Persian word is singular, but the English added an *s* to make it analogous to *breeches*, *drawers* and *trousers*. Variant spellings through the nineteenth century include *pigammahs, peijammahs, piejamahs, pajamas* and *pyjamas*. The last two are considered correct today (*pajamas* is chiefly American whereas *pyjamas* is British) — to which you can add the short forms *peejays* or *jammies*. And while most people think of *pajamas* as a noun, you can use it as an adjective as well, as shown by this quote from 1883: "Ten pyjamahed and betowelled unfortunates are standing … outside."

Pajamas are just one of many features of Moslem daily life that have been imported from Europe since the days of the medieval Crusades. The zero was borrowed from Moslem mathematicians, coffee was purchased from Moslem merchants, and the practice of putting carpets on the floor came to us from the Moslems.

When the first wave of Crusaders reached the Holy Land in 1099, they were amazed to see the Moslem infidels padding around on carpets that covered the floors of their homes and castles. The Europeans had been accustomed to hanging carpets on the walls as insulation against the draughts for which medieval castles were notorious. The floors of these castles were strewn with rushes to soak up the leftovers that fell — or were thrown over the shoulder from — the dining table. And like medieval vacuum cleaners, dogs rooted and snarled under the table for scraps of meat. All of this came to an end, of course, when the lord of the castle unrolled his first Persian carpet. Any dog taking liberties with that ended up in the doghouse.

1801 POLYTECHNIC

The French Revolution is considered by many historians to be the great watershed, or dividing line, of modern history. It separated the *ancien regime* of the eighteenth century, with its trappings of feudalism and monarchy, from the industrial ferment of the nineteenth and twentieth centuries, when the role of science in human affairs succeeded in reshaping the face of civilization. In the field of education, the French Revolution also represented a significant dividing line. Subjects studied in the eighteenth century tended to be classical in nature: ancient languages, history, theology, law and the like. By the 1790s far-seeing Frenchmen, including Napoleon, could see the value of an educational system that promoted the science of engineering, both civil and military. The National Convention, which served as the government of France for a few brief months in the middle of the 1790s, opened in Paris the very first *Ecole Polytechnique*, designed to produce civil and military engineers. The new word was picked up by Englishman W. Taylor in the *Annual Review* of 1801: "The polytechnic school has ... been distributing among select pupils, all the military sciences, through the best teachers." England was not slow in setting up similar schools, the value of which became very apparent in wartime.

1802 VODKA

Vodka, in Russian, means "little water," a term of endearment that reflects the fondness the Russians feel for this intoxicating beverage. Produced in Russia since the fourteenth century, *vodka* did not appear in print in English until an 1802 translation of *Pallas's Travels*: "The principal imports are ... Sekiskaya-Vodka, or brandy distilled from fruit." Consumption of vodka was almost totally confined to Russia, Poland and the Baltic states until after World War II, when vodka then spread to other countries around the world, especially the United States. Today, Russian vodka is distilled mostly from potato spirits, whereas most American vodka comes from grains. The Russians and Poles prefer to drink their vodka straight, but the Americans usually mix it with other beverages, thereby producing concoctions such as the screwdriver (orange juice and vodka), the Bloody Mary (tomato juice and vodka) and the Moscow mule (ginger beer with vodka).

1803 WATERSHED

When this word first appeared in print in 1803, it applied only to the line or ridge of land that separates different river systems. By 1839 it was also used for the slope, down which water flows, from a divide. And by 1874 it had acquired the meaning that is probably the most popular today: the entire area of land drained by a river or river system. If you want to look at three watersheds at the same time without leaving the ground, you should visit the Columbia Icefield in the Canadian Rockies, where the runoff flows in three different directions. If you pour a cup of tea onto the melting ice, some of it will flow north into the Arctic Ocean, some drops will flow west into the Pacific, and the balance will flow east toward Hudson Bay and thence to the Atlantic Ocean.

A new word gaining currency among geographers and urban planners is *commutershed*, no doubt coined on the analogy of *watershed*. A commutershed is the zone of bedroom communities drained and replenished each day by a large urban centre in which commuters work.

Also in 1803: *humph, asteroid*

1804 PEROXIDE

The science of chemistry was advancing on a wide front in the late eighteenth and early nineteenth centuries. In a short span of years, the words *oxygen, hydrogen, nitrogen, potassium, magnesium* and *aluminum* were added to the English language. A new compound, peroxide, so called because it was fully permeated with oxygen — from the Latin, *per*, "through" — was introduced in 1804 by the English chemist Thomas Thomson: "When a metal has combined with as much oxygen as possible, I shall denote the compound formed by the term peroxide." Although Thomson could have had no way of knowing, a closely related term joined the English language in 1924: *beautician*, a fancy word for someone working in a beauty parlour (see page 270). Many customers of such establishments go there to get their hair bleached with peroxide.

1805 OUTCROP

Merriam-Webster gives us two definitions: "a coming out of bedrock or of an unconsolidated deposit to the surface of the ground; the part of a rock formation that appears at the surface of the ground." The appearance of the word in 1805 reflects the growing interest in the geologic history of the Earth.

1806 VERMOUTH

Vermouth is a white wine flavoured with aromatic herbs and spices, used chiefly as an ingredient in cocktails. The word *vermouth* comes from the French translation of the German *Wermut*, meaning "wormwood," one of the more than forty ingredients added to vermouth to give it its special flavour and aroma. Other additives include nutmeg, hyssop, quinine bark, camomile and rose leaves. John Pinkerton introduced this word into the English language in 1806 in his *Recollections of Paris*: "A decanter of Jamaican rum, Wormword wine, or that of Vermouth."

Also in 1806: *cocktail, horsepower, hydrant*

1807 POTASSIUM

The Greeks and Romans used oil as a cleansing agent, and sometimes mixed it with sand to produce a scouring action, but this mixture was harsh to the skin. As time went by, people discovered that the ash of certain woods, when mixed with oil, made a much better cleaning agent. The ash was boiled in a pot and the dry, powdery residue that resulted was called *potash*. When this was mixed with oil, a new and better kind of soap was produced.

In 1807, the British chemist Sir Humphry Davy isolated a hitherto-unknown metal and, because he found it in potash, called it *potassium*. The Germans named it *Kalium* after the Arabic word for potash. As a result, the chemical symbol for this element is the letter K, even in those countries that use the word *potassium*.

Little did Sir Humphry Davy realize, when he found this new metal in 1807, that it would someday be used to study the origin of early man. In July 1959, the British anthropologist Louis Leakey and his wife, Mary, discovered two teeth and a jawbone of an ancient human-like creature embedded in East Africa's Olduvai Gorge. The Leakeys, convinced that early man originated in Africa, had been digging at that site for thirty years. The teeth and jawbone were sent to the University of California, where their age was determined by the potassium-argon dating method. The verdict: 1,760,000 years old — three times older than any previously discovered humanlike remains.

Also in 1807: *lasso*

1808 MAGNESIUM

The ancient Greeks knew of a black mineral that attracted iron, and Thales of Miletus apparently made a careful study of it. Because the mineral samples he was using came from Magnesia (a city in Asia Minor), he named the mineral *magnes*, and this word evolved into our word *magnet*. Later on, the Roman naturalist Pliny the Elder confused the *magnes* of Thales with another black mineral, which he also called *magnes*. Over succeeding centuries, the word was copied and recopied by hand until it became *manganese*, which is the name the mineral has today.

Still another mineral was known to the ancients: a white one that had been discovered in the area around Magnesia (not necessarily the same city as the one mentioned above, since three ancient Greek cities bore this name). The Romans called it *magnesia alba*, "white magnesia," to avoid confusing it with magnes, which is black. When Sir Humphry Davy obtained an impure sample of a new metal from *magnesia alba*, he called in *magnesium*.

For many years after 1808, magnesium had no obvious uses because it was difficult to isolate. It was first produced commercially in Germany in 1866, but it took the enormous stimulus of World War II to turn magnesium into a structural metal of strategic importance. After the war, it remained important in light of modern society's demand for strong, lightweight metals. Many of the "muscle cars" that squeal away at traffic lights owe their neck-snapping acceleration to lightweight body parts, including wheel rims made of magnesium (popularly known as "mag wheels").

Also in 1808: *bronchitis*

1809 AMBULANCE

According to the *OED*, the word *ambulance* was first used to describe "a moving hospital, attending an army as it moves, so as to succour the wounded without delay." It comes from French, *hôpital ambulant*, "walking hospital." The word appeared, with this definition, in 1809, but no one paid much attention to it until the Crimean War broke out in 1854. Thanks to the work of Florence Nightingale and the stretcher-bearers who dodged the bullets on the battlefield, the ambulance became the wagon, stretcher, or other conveyance used to carry the injured back to safety.

Modern ambulances have the word AMBULANCE printed backward across the front of the vehicle. That makes it easy to read when you see it approaching, with siren wailing, in your rear-view mirror.

1810 Thug

Up until about a hundred years ago, a professional band of killers terrorized the people of India, particularly people of property. When a wealthy man was about to leave on a journey, these murderers would hide at a lonely spot along his route, and when he passed by they would rush out to strangle and rob him. The Hindustani word *thag* means "a cheat," and from these brutal men who thought nothing of robbing and killing, we derive the word *thug*.

Also in 1810: *kilometre*

1811 Tourism

This word first appeared in *Sporting Magazine* in 1811 and now identifies a worldwide multimillion-dollar business. The word *tourist* had appeared in print eleven years earlier, in 1800, and signalled the beginning of the modern trend of travel for pleasure. The word *travel* itself comes from the French *travail*, meaning work, because much early travel was an arduous affair over bumpy roads and choppy seas. English aristocrats were fond of taking what they proudly called "the Grand Tour" of European capitals in the eighteenth century — but the masses were still stuck at home, awaiting the improvements in transportation and purchasing power that the nineteenth and twentieth centuries would bring. By 1843 they were on the march, as William Makepeace Thackeray noted while vacationing in the west of Ireland: "No doubt, ere long … the rush of London tourism will come this way." The travel business in the next century received a big boost from Burton Holmes, who earned five million dollars from his illustrated lectures and books on travel before dying in 1958 at the age of eighty-eight. He coined the word *travelogue* in 1903 and inspired thousands of armchair travellers to hit the road.

1812 ALUMINUM

The age we live in could well be called the Age of Aluminum because of the enormous variety of uses to which this metal is put. From kitchen pots and pans to rocket fuel, aluminum ranks with iron and steel as among the most useful metals ever fashioned by man. It is the most abundant metallic element on earth — yet it was discovered less than two centuries ago and has been manufactured on a commercial scale only half that long.

How did it escape detection for so long? The answer lies in the properties of aluminum. It does not occur naturally in metallic form, but only in combination with other elements, primarily oxygen, with which it forms a hard oxide known as *alumina*. As early as the 1700s, European chemists suspected the existence of an invisible metal in certain soils they were analyzing, but could not find a way to isolate it. Sir Humphry Davy of England was among those who tried and failed, but he did propose in 1812 that this mysterious substance be called *aluminum*. For the next thirteen years, that's all the world had of this element — just the name. Then, in 1825, the Danish physicist Hans Christian Oersted succeeded in finding a process for isolating it, and thus became the first person in history to see this magic metal with his own eyes — a powdery metal that "in color and luster somewhat resembles tin."

The next problem was to find a way to produce aluminum on a large scale. Napoleon III of France actively promoted research into aluminum, perhaps hoping that his armies could march faster if they carried aluminum weapons. But the big breakthrough did not come until 1886, when a young American inventor and a young French inventor, working independently, stumbled upon the solution at almost precisely the same time. Charles Hall of Ohio and Paul Héroult of Gentilly, France, developed a manufacturing process that is used to produce virtually all the aluminum throughout the world today.

1813 SAUTÉ

Louis Ude first used this word in an English sentence in 1813: "Mind, you must never let the sauté be too much done." It comes from the French *sauté*, "tossed [in a pan]," from *sauter*, "to leap," which comes from the Latin *saltare*, an offshoot of the Latin verb *salire*, "to leap." A whole cluster of English words has sprouted from that single Latin root, which takes the form of *sal*, *sil*, *sault*, or *sult*, depending on which English word it shows up in. If you *insult* someone, you are, in a manner of speaking, jumping on [*in*-] them. If you drop a rubber ball and it bounces back up into your hand, we say it is *resilient* because it jumps back [*re*-] at you. The *salient* points of an argument are the ones that jump or leap up at you. If you have just heard some good news and feel *exultant*, you feel like you are jumping out of [*ex*-] your skin. If you do a *somersault*, you are leaping or jumping by turning your heels over [*somer*, from *supra*, "above"] your head. And if you visit the cities of Sault Ste. Marie in northern Michigan and Ontario, you are visiting a city named after the St. Mary's Rapids, where the water jumps or leaps over the rocks on its way from Lake Superior to Lake Huron.

1814 NAPOLEON

When a person's name enters the English language without a capital letter, that person has achieved a special version of immortality. Napoleon Bonaparte was still ruling France in 1814 (after his escape from Elba) when his name became an eponym for "a former French 20-franc gold coin." Two later meanings are these: "an oblong pastry with a filling of cream custard or jelly; *cap*, one like Napoleon (as in ambition)" — Merriam-Webster.

1815 OCTOGENARIAN

An elderly woman recently received a birthday gift and card from her granddaughter, who lived in another city. The grandmother wrote to the little girl, thanking her for the card and gift and asking her why she thought her grandmother had an eight-sided figure. It turned out that the young girl had wanted to write on the card: "To my favourite octogenarian" — but didn't know how to spell it, and so instead wrote: "To my favourite octagon."

A person in his or her eighties is an octogenarian, but what do you call someone in their seventies or sixties? Those in their seventies are *septuagenarians* (from the Latin *septuaginta,* "seventy") and those in their sixties are *sexagenarians* (from the Latin *sexaginta,* "sixty"). When the veteran Theater Guild actress Helen Westley was working on a movie set in Hollywood, a young extra came gushing up to her and said, "Why, Miss Westley, what are you doing in this picture?"

"My dear, haven't you heard?" replied Miss Westley. "I furnish the sexagenarian appeal."

1816 SEMAPHORE

A semaphore is a post with a movable arm or arms, and sometimes lights, for signalling, often between ships and along railway lines. The word comes from the Greek *sema,* "sign," and *pherein,* "to bear," and first appeared in print in 1816: "The improved Semaphore has been erected on the top of the Admiralty" (implying there was an earlier, less-than-perfect, semaphore in use). Interestingly enough, the adjective *semaphoric* goes back to 1808, when a chap named Cochrane used it in *The Naval Chronicles*: "The newly constructed Semaphoric telegraphs ... have been blown up." Perhaps the noun *semaphore* was in use as early as that, but the editors of the *OED* have found no evidence to that effect.

In addition to signals for ships and railways, the term *semaphore* is also used for a special kind of flag signalling, which employs its own semaphoric alphabet. In the days before the semaphore, methods other than flags or levers were used to send messages. The Native Americans used smoke signals, the Romans used mirrors that reflected flashes of sunlight, and an ancient Greek actually delivered, behind enemy lines, a message that was painted on his scalp after his head had been shaved bald. He waited until his hair grew back in, then delivered the message to the party for whom it was intended. His head had to be shaved again before the message could be read.

1817 KALEIDOSCOPE

The kaleidoscope owes its name to the Greek roots *kalos,* "beautiful," *eidos,* "form," and *skopein,* "to view." It was named by its inventor, David

Brewster, in 1817. In no time at all, other people began using the word. A chap named Murray, writing to Lord Byron in 1818, said, "I send you a very well-constructed Kaleidoscope, a newly-invented toy." The following year, Byron wrote, "This rainbow look'd like hope — Quite a celestial kaleidoscope." Five years later, in *Miscellaneous Writings*, Lord Macaulay asserted, "The mind of Petrarch was a kaleidoscope." Forty years later, Jonathan Pusey complained about people who "allow truth and falsehood to be jumbled together in one ever-shifting kaleidoscope of opinions." In 1891, in *Life's Little Ironies*, Thomas Hardy used it as an adverb: "The long plate-glass mirrors ... flashed the gyrating personages and hobby-horses kaleidoscopically into his eyes."

You will notice that only one of those quotations refers to the instrument itself. All the others use *kaleidoscope* in a figurative sense. And therein lies the real power of this word: it can be used to describe any scene of constantly shifting colour, shape or mood. David Brewster, we thank you.

1818 Bureaucracy

When the first volume (A–Anat) of the *OED* was published in 1884, the earliest example of *bureaucracy* that had been found in print dated back to 1848, when John Stuart Mill, in his *Political Economy*, wrote about "the ... inexpediency of concentrating in a dominant bureaucracy ... all the power of organized action ... in the community." When a supplement (A–G) of the *OED* was published in 1972, the earliest example of *bureaucracy* had been rolled back to 1818. Such changes are commonplace at the *OED* headquarters in Oxford, England, as thousands of voluntary readers around the world comb through old books and letters to trace the history and development of every single word in the English language from the date of its first appearance. Many of the entries in this book may someday have to be backdated as new evidence of a word in print is brought to light.

The word *bureaucracy* literally means "rule by office," coming as it does from the French *bureau*, "office," and the Greek root *kratein*, "to rule." Because the word *office* refers to government offices and the verb *to rule* refers to the function performed by government, this word really means "government by government." The first use of the word in print in

English has been credited to Lady Morgan, who, in 1818, wrote: "Mr. Commissioner ... represented the Bureaucratie, or office tyranny, by which Ireland has been so long governed."

1819 KEYBOARD

Whether you play the piano or play with your computer, *keyboard* is an everyday word. *Key* dates back to before the twelfth century and *board* (traceable back to Old High German *bort*, "ship's side") is just as old.

Also in 1819: *fanlight*

1820 YOGA

Although the word *yogi*, describing a practitioner of yoga, entered the English language in 1619, it was not until 1820 that *yoga*, from Sanskrit *yoga*, meaning "union" or "yoking," began to appear in print in English, and then only to refer to the rituals of meditation and self-control practised by followers of Hinduism in India. The yoga boom in North America did not get under way until after World War II, and it was fuelled by two simultaneous trends: a growing familiarity, through trade and travel, with Eastern religious practices, and the emigration of Indians and Pakistanis to North America.

By the 1960s yoga classes were springing up in one city after another, and in many of them the religious component was secondary to the physical — yoga simply offered a sensible pathway to relaxation for people caught up in the stresses and strains of modern Western life. To be convincing, yoga instructors must themselves be living models of the relaxation and inner serenity they are trying to instil in their students. In one yoga class, the instructor was in too much of a hurry. She must have taken a crash course in fast yoga because she kept shouting at her class: "Relax! Relax!"

Also in 1820: *folderol, griot*

1821 MORGUE

In 1599 a French word of unknown origin, *morgue*, entered the English language as a synonym for a haughty pride or demeanour. In 1821 the same French word, but this time with the first letter capitalized — *Morgue* —

entered English to refer to the mortuary building in Paris where the bodies of victims of street accidents and other mishaps were taken to be identified. As time went by, *morgue* lost its capital letter and came to be applied to any building in any city where corpses are kept pending identification.

The late American author and man of letters E.B. White would never forget his first visit to a morgue. He had just been hired as a cub reporter for a Seattle newspaper and was told to go to the city morgue, where the body of a woman who had been brutally murdered was being examined. When White got there, a man the police hoped was the husband was being brought in to see if he could identify the body. The white sheet was pulled back and the man's face suddenly contorted in horror as he screamed: "My God! It's her!" White dutifully wrote the story and submitted it to his editor, who tended to be a stickler for proper grammar, even if it interfered with the natural rhythm of the sentence. The next day, when the story appeared, White discovered the scream at the morgue had been changed to "My God! It's she!" After telling the editor to look for another reporter, White moved on to bigger and better things.

1822 Aardvark

After the defeat of Napoleon at Waterloo in 1815, the English began migrating in large numbers to South Africa, attracted by the temperate climate and the fertile land. The original Dutch settlers resented the intrusion and finally, in 1836, decided to pull out altogether and move to the interior. Thus began the Great Trek, celebrated ever since in South African history and literature. The Dutch *voortrekkers* eventually settled on new land to the north and east and founded the Dutch republics of Transvaal, the Orange Free State and Natal. There they lived on their own until the 1880s, when the lure of gold and diamonds attracted the British once again and led in 1899 to the outbreak of the Boer War.

Between the defeat of Napoleon in 1815 and the start of the great trek in 1836, the word *aardvark*, from the Dutch *aarde*, "earth," and *vark*, "pig," passed from the Dutch language into English. Here is a quote from 1833: "The aard-vark is in all respects admirably fitted for the station which Nature has assigned to it." The aardvark is a burrowing mammal of southern Africa with a stocky, hairy body, large ears, a long, tubular snout, and powerful digging claws.

Today the aardvark is famous throughout the English-speaking world, not so much for what it does but because of how we spell it. The first two letters — *aa* — have guaranteed this humble animal a position of prominence on the first page of nearly every English dictionary now in print.

1823 BLACKBOARD

In *Contributions to the Cause of Education*, a fellow named Pillans wrote in 1823: "A large black board served my purpose. On it I wrote in chalk." As time went by, the two words *black* and *board* gradually joined to form *blackboard*.

This noun became an adjective in 1954, when American author Evan Hunter published his novel *Blackboard Jungle*, which told the story of juvenile delinquents attending a vocational school in New York City. The following year it was released as a motion picture starring Glenn Ford. So widespread did the term become that "blackboard jungle" is now a main entry in *The Barnhart Dictionary of New English Since 1963*, in which it is defined as "a school in which a condition of disorder and lawlessness exists."

Most blackboards now being installed in new schools are actually green boards designed for use with yellow chalk because the green-yellow combination is supposedly easier on the eyes than black and white. And many teachers ignore the blackboard (or green board) altogether in favour of overhead projectors.

Also in 1824: *adios, malaprop*

1824 REPLICA

This word entered the English language with a spelling mistake, when one Lady Morgan in 1824 wrote of an unknown artist: "He is said to have reproduced in numerous *replicos* [sic], the scenery of La Cave." Since 1824 the word *replica* has been applied chiefly to works of art — paintings, sculpture and the like.

By the mid-1970s, however, the word *replicar* (a contraction of *replica* and *car*) began popping up to describe the ever-growing selection of antique and classic automobiles that are now available in fibreglass reproductions, including the supercharged Auburn boattail speedster, the Excalibur (patterned after a Mercedes-Benz roadster of the late 1920s), and a fibreglass Model A Ford roadster, complete with running boards and rumble seat.

Also in 1824: *funambulism*

1825 Acrobat

Coming to English through French, *acrobat* first appeared in Fosbroke's *Encyclopedia of Antiquity*: "Acrobates ... were Rope Dancers of which there were four kinds." Fosbroke was referring to acrobats in ancient times, but as the nineteenth century rolled along this ancient art was revived and flourished under the "Big Top" of circus tents in Europe and North America, so much so that the London *Daily Telegraph* of May 30, 1879, was able to report: "The acrobat of today is a skilled professor of the trapeze and the parallel bars; he flies through the air, or comes careering from a hole in the ceiling."

Other words that use the same prefix as *acrobat* include *acrophobia* (fear of heights) and *acronym* (a word coined in 1943 for words made up of the initial letters of other words, such as *radar*, *scuba* and *laser*). *Acro-* comes from the Greek *akros*, meaning "extreme" or, as in the case of the above examples, "highest" or "first." *Acrobat* itself is originally from the Greek *akrobatein*, "to walk on tiptoe."

Also in 1825: *boomerang*

1826 Splashboard

Merriam-Webster gives two virtually interchangeable definitions: "dashboard; a panel to protect against splashes." This word reminds us of the days of horses and buggies, when the hooves of the horse would splash — or dash — mud all over the passengers if a board was not in front of them to protect them. *Splashboard* got into print sixteen years before *dashboard* (see 223).

1827 Omnicompetent

Lots of words begin with the first four letters of this one, including *omnibus* (a bus for everyone), *omnidirectional* (1927), *omnifarious* (1653), *omnificient* (1677), *omnipotence* (fifteenth century), *omnipotent* (fourteenth century), *omnipresence* (1601), *omnipresent* (1609), *omnirange* (1946), *omniscience* (circa 1610), *omnivore* (1887), and *omnivorous* (circa 1656). All these words are using the Latin *omni*, meaning "all." If you are *omnicompetent*, you are able to handle any situation. This word is seldom seen these days, perhaps because the complexity of modern life makes it almost impossible for anyone to be truly omnicompetent. The opposite would perhaps be, to coin another word, *omni-incompetent*.

1828 Morphine

The ancient Greeks had a god or goddess for practically everything. Even when they were asleep, there was a deity looking after them. Somnus was the god of sleep, and from him we derive words such as *somnolent* (sleepy), *somniloquence* (talking in one's sleep) and *somnambulance* (sleepwalking). Somnus was also called Hypnos, from which we derive *hypnosis* and *hypnotism*. He had an assistant named Phantasus, who regaled sleepers with hallucinations and fantasies, hence the word *fantasy*. He also had a son, Morpheus, the god of dreams, from whom we derive the name for morphine, a drug that kills pain by putting you to sleep.

The first big European war that made use of morphine (and choloroform as well) was the Crimean War, which broke out in 1854 and raged for two years on the north shore of the Black Sea before Britain and France managed to defeat Russia. Florence Nightingale made a name for herself for the work she did on the battlefield, tending to the wounded and dying. Painkillers were also used in the American Civil War, a bloody conflict that cost six hundred thousand lives. In an effort to force the South into an early surrender, President Lincoln banned all shipments of morphine and chloroform to the Confederate states. His strategy did not work, and the Old South had to be invaded and devastated before it was willing to lay down its arms.

Also in 1828: *ampersand, psychiatry*

1829 Blizzard

In 1829 a *blizzard* was a sharp blow or knock. That's what this word meant until 1859, when it acquired its current meaning (a raging snowstorm). Before that date, *blizzard* was commonly used to refer to the knockout punch delivered by a boxer. Then on March 14, 1859, a newspaper reporter in Iowa used the word to describe a raging snowstorm that had "knocked out" his city. By the end of the 1870s, the new usage had spread across the United States and into Canada, eventually elbowing the original meaning out of the dictionary altogether. Here's how the *Oxford American Dictionary* of 1980 defines blizzard: "A storm with wind-driven snow." No mention at all of a knockout punch. That Iowa snowstorm knocked that definition right out of the English language.

1830 Kleptomaniac

Most people have never met a genuine kleptomaniac, and yet nearly everyone knows what this word, from the Greek *kleptein*, "to steal," and *mania*, "madness," means. That's because it is often used in a lighthearted sense whenever you borrow something from someone and forget to return it. If you borrow someone's pen to write something down, you might then absentmindedly put it in your own pocket. When the pen lender asks for it back, you can always return it with a sheepish smile and mumble something about being a kleptomaniac.

But the English language has no word for the opposite of a kleptomaniac. What do you call people who are always forgetting to take their things with them, who leave coats and hats and rubbers and umbrellas and car keys and Lord-knows-what in restaurants, at the homes of friends, at work — everywhere. What mania do they suffer from? I've never heard of a word for it. If you know of one, let me know.

1831 THERMOSTAT

In 1660 a group of scientifically minded Englishmen formed the Royal Society for the purpose of studying the whole field of human knowledge. Such luminaries as Robert Boyle, Samuel Pepys, John Winthrop and Sir Isaac Newton were among its members. The *Proceedings of the Royal Society*, dated June 16, 1831, include a section on "the Thermostat or Heat Governor, a self-acting physical Apparatus for regulating Temperature." Thus began the development of the amazing device that now mounts on your living-room wall to regulate the temperature in your home. In an effort to save fuel in an energy-hungry world, thermostats — from the Greek *therme*, "heat," and *statikos*, "causing to stand" — are available that automatically lower the temperature of your house at night and raise it again in the morning shortly before you get out of bed.

1832 CLICHÉ

Two closely related words have come to the English language from the printing business in France: *stereotype* and *cliché*. *Stereotype* (from Greek *stereos*, "solid," and *typos*, "impression"), was coined by Firman Didot, one of a family of prominent French printers, to describe a solid plate for printing that had been made from a papier-mâché mould of a page of composed type. Because the printed matter produced by this stereotype was fixed and unchangeable, a stereotype has come to describe an over-simplified opinion or prejudice.

The French word *cliché* is simply a synonym for the stereotype plate used in printing. This word entered the English language in 1832 as a printer's term, but waited until the 1890s before it acquired its modern meaning: a trite, hackneyed word or phrase. In an attempt to prod their students into writing more originally, English teachers are constantly exhorting them to avoid clichés "like the plague."

Also in 1832: *lariat, proofreader, scrawny, toothpaste*

1833 Aardwolf

This nocturnal mammal is found in southern and eastern Africa, "resembles the related hyena, and feeds chiefly on insects and especially termites" (Merriam-Webster). Along with *aardvark* (1822), the aardwolf can be found on page one of just about every dictionary except the one you are reading now.

1834 Rodeo

When this word first entered the English language, it simply meant a cattle roundup, from the Spanish *rodear*, "to surround," which can be traced back to the Latin *rotare*, "to rotate." (The rotisserie in your backyard barbecue comes from the same root.) *Rodeo* was first used in print in 1834 by the great Charles Darwin himself, who wrote, "Once every year, there is a grand 'rodeo' when all the cattle are driven down, counted, and marked." Many years later, *rodeo* acquired the more popular meaning of a public entertainment featuring bucking broncos, lassoing contests, chuck-wagon races and cowboys trying to catch (and hold onto) a greased pig.

1835 Telephone

In the 1830s an American named C.G. Page discovered the principle of electronic sound transmission. Almost immediately dozens of scientists, electricians and would-be inventors began to look for a way of transmitting the human voice. Telegraph wires were carrying Morse code signals by 1844. Surely a means could be found to transmit spoken words. So convinced were people working on the problem that a solution could be found, that the coining of the word *telephone*, from the Greek *tele*, "afar," and *phone*, "sound," preceded its actual invention by a full forty years!

The father of the telephone himself, Alexander Graham Bell, was granted a patent for his device in February 1876, three days before he made his first call. Those first immortal words ("Mr. Watson, come here. I want you.") were also the world's first emergency call, because Bell had just spilled some battery acid on the crotch of his trousers.

Also in 1835: *cigarette, latex*

1836 Bowdlerize

Because he could not stomach the sight of human blood, Dr. Thomas Bowdler (1754–1825) abandoned his medical practice in eighteenth-century London and spent the next several years travelling through Europe on a chunk of money he had inherited. With the onset of middle age he settled down on the Isle of Wight and devoted his declining years to the task of erasing from the complete works of William Shakespeare all references to sex and immorality. His *Family Shakespeare* was published in 1818 in a ten-volume edition; the title page explained that "nothing is added to the text; but those expressions are omitted which cannot with propriety be read aloud in a family." Bowdler's book became a best-seller, despite the fact that he had so twisted the words of the Bard of Avon that several main characters, including Hamlet, Macbeth and Falstaff were mutilated beyond recognition, while others were simply bowdlerized right out of existence, including the nymphomaniacal Doll Tearsheet. Emboldened by his success, Bowdler then proceeded to take Edward Gibbon to the cleaners by laundering his literary masterpiece *The History of the Decline and Fall of the Roman Empire*. "All passages of an irreligious or immoral tendency" were ruthlessly rooted out, leaving the ancient Romans high and dry on a pedestal of moral purity.

Other great works of literature escaped similar treatment when Bowdler died in 1825. Eleven years later, his name became a verb meaning "to expurgate by omitting or modifying words or passages considered indelicate or offensive." Imagine how slim the Bible would be if he had ever gotten around to bowdlerizing the Holy Scriptures.

Also in 1836: *kibosh*

1837 Malayalam

This is "the Dravidian language of Kerala, southwest India, closely related to Tamil." The name itself is a palindrome because you can spell it the same way backward or forward.

1838 CHLOROFORM

First discovered around 1831, chloroform was given its name in 1834 by a Frenchman, J. Dumas. This new word first appeared in English in 1838. If you look at the etymology of this word, you will see that *chloroform* literally means "green ant," from the Greek *chloros*, "green," and the Latin *formica*, "ant."

But where in the world can you find green ants, and why would chloroform be named after them? The two Greek and Latin roots actually have no connection. *Chloros* refers to chlorine (a basic ingredient in chloroform), which got its name because of its greenish colour. *Form* is an abbreviation for formic acid, which was first discovered in the seventeenth century by an Englishman named John Ray who cooked up a batch of red ants and obtained a liquid which he (or someone else) called formic acid, from the Latin *formica*. The word *chloroform* is actually, therefore, simply an abbreviation for "chlorinated formic acid."

Incidentally, the word *formication* refers to the tickly feeling of ants crawling on your skin. It has nothing to do with *fornication*, except for the time when the Greek god Zeus, that lusty Olympian lover, changed himself into a swarm of ants in order to seduce the nymph Clytoris.

As an anesthetic, chloroform had a bright and busy future. In 1847 it was first used in childbirth, although some religious people objected to it by quoting the biblical passage that says children should be "brought forth in sorrow." Six years later and after six births "in sorrow," Queen Victoria tried chloroform and liked it. And in 1884 a Philadelphia professor chloroformed a woman at the request of her sterile husband, who wanted his wife to undergo artificial insemination with sperm donated by another man. It was the first such operation ever performed, and neither the husband nor the professor bothered to tell the woman what was about to be done to her.

1839 CAFETERIA

When *cafeteria* first appeared in English in 1839 it referred to a Turkish coffee shop. By the end of the nineteenth century the meaning was beginning to shift to what it is today. In 1923, *Modern Language Notes* stated categorically, "Everyone knows by this time that a cafeteria is a 'help-yourself' restaurant."

Even cheaper than a cafeteria, but far less appetizing, is the automat, which first appeared in a photograph in *Scientific American* as early as 1903. This type of fast-food outlet was sufficiently well established by 1909 for Webster's Dictionary to include it: "a café or restaurant in which orders are automatically delivered to customers, who place coins or tokens in slots."

Also in 1839: *sanatorium*

1840 CRONYISM

Soon after becoming prime minister of Canada in 2003, Paul Martin promised to reform government by stamping out cronyism ("partiality to cronies especially as evidenced in the appointment of political hangers-on to office without regard to their qualifications" — Merriam-Webster).

1841 DINOSAUR

The first dinosaur bones were dug up in a field in Sussex, England, in 1822. Nineteen years later, the British naturalist Sir Richard Owen coined the word *dinosaur* from the Greek *deinos*, "fearful," and *sauros*, "lizard," because these prehistoric monsters looked so terrifying. Over the years the digging continued, until the shovels of archaeologists unearthed the grand-daddy of them all — the mighty brontosaurus (from Greek *bronte*, "thunder"), a seventy-foot-long, hundred-ton leviathan that was so heavy it had to spend most of its time in the water to help support its huge bulk.

The first brontosaurus bones were discovered by a chap named Marsh in Colorado in 1879. Although the skeleton was virtually intact, the head was missing, and so Marsh attached a head he had found four hundred miles away, figuring it was the right one for that species. As time went by, other specimens of brontosaurus were dug up, all of them incomplete. Only recently was a complete specimen found, and it was then discovered that Marsh had used the wrong head. Museums all across North America had composite models of the brontosaurus on display, all with the type of head used by Marsh back in 1879. By now, most museums have switched to the correct head.

1842 DASHBOARD

That part of an automobile we now call the dashboard can be traced back to the days of horses and buggies. The *OED* defines dashboard as: "a board or leather apron in the front of a vehicle, to prevent mud from being splashed by the heels of the horses upon the interior of the vehicle." An early user of this word was John Lang in *Wanderings in India*, published in 1859: "He fell asleep, his feet over the dashboard, and his head resting on my shoulder."

In modern automobiles, the dashboard is where the instruments that tell you what your car and its engine are doing are mounted. Mud is still being splashed up, but usually by other cars instead of horses, and the mud does not splash against your dashboard because it hits your fenders first. Some auto buffs who pride themselves on precision in language prefer to call the dashboard the instrument panel, because that's more precisely what it is.

The dashboard is not the only part of your car that reminds us of the days of horse and buggies. Your headlights and taillights are so called because the carriages of old were pulled along by a power plant that had no spark plugs or pistons, but did have a head and a tail. And the axle comes from the old Scandinavian word for "tree," because the first axles were fabricated from long, slender tree trunks attached to the underside of old wooden wagons.

1843 HYPNOTISM

This word was coined by Dr. James Braid of Manchester, who in 1842 introduced the term *neuro-hypnotism* for "the state or condition of nervous sleep," then shortened it to *hypnotism* from the Greek *hypnos*, "sleep," in 1843.

Franz Mesmer (1734–1815) was an Austrian physician who was possibly the first to treat patients by the use of hypnotism. Because the word *hypnotism* was not coined until twenty-eight years after Mesmer died, and because the very nature of the process was scarcely understood at all during his lifetime, Mesmer mistakenly assumed that his magical powers were derived from magnets, with which he stroked his patients in order to heal them. He apparently was possessed with a natural ability to hypnotize, and when he set up his practice in Paris (he was thrown out of Austria) many prominent figures came to his office, including Lafayette, Montesquieu and Marie Antoinette. A scientific commission appointed by Louis XVI declared him to be a charlatan and imposter, however, and he was forced out of practice. He lives on today as the root of the eponym *mesmerize* — to fascinate or spellbind.

Also in 1843: *paprika*

1844 GOATEE

Goatee first appeared in print in 1844 to describe the short, pointed beards that resemble the tuft of hair on the chin of a goat. In 1856 Miss Isabella Bird took note of this new style of facial hair in her book *An Englishwoman in America*: "They [Americans] also indulge in eccentricities of appearance in the shape of beards and imperials, not to speak of the 'goatee.'"

When Abraham Lincoln was first elected to Congress in 1846, he was clean-shaven. But when he campaigned for the presidency in 1860, he was sporting not just a goatee but a full beard from ear to ear. Beards were all the rage at that time, a legacy of the Crimean War (1854–1856), in which British troops had found that a thick layer of hair around the face protected them from the wintry blasts of frigid air that swept across the Russian steppes.

Six weeks after Lincoln entered the White House, the American Civil War broke out. One of the generals who fought for the North was a military bungler and incompetent named Ambrose E. Burnside, the only man Lincoln knew who could, on the battlefield, "snatch defeat from the jaws of victory." Burnside sported a pair of bushy side whiskers during the war, and this led to a new fashion in facial hair for men. People called these whiskers "mutton chops" until someone thought of naming them after Burnside himself — by transposing the two syllables of his surname to produce the word *sideburns*.

Also in 1844: *kinky*

1845 ORCHID

Pliny the Elder, that great Roman author and naturalist who died in Pompeii when Mount Vesuvius erupted, noted the similarity in shape between the plant we now call the orchid and the male organs known as testicles: "*Mirabilis est orchis herba, sive serapias, gemina radice testiculis simili.*" This similarity does not apply to the shape of the flower itself, but rather to the double roots, which look like a pair of testicles (the Greek word for "testicles" is *orchis*). The fruit we call an *avocado* has the same shape, and that word similarly comes from a Native Mexican word for "testicle" (see page 131).

The orchid, obviously, was not discovered in 1845. People in England had known about this plant since the 1500s and even earlier, when it was called the *orchis*, a name that now applies to the whole family of plants of which the orchid, a name first used in 1845, is just one example.

Also in 1845: *coitus, overdraft, reincarnation*

1846 SAXOPHONE

It is a miracle that this musical instrument was ever invented. Adolphe Sax, the man who gave the world the saxophone, was lucky to reach adulthood, as Willard Espy explains in his fascinating book, *O Thou Improper, Thou Uncommon Noun*: "Adolphe Sax, born in Belgium in the early nineteenth century, grew up accident-prone: he was struck on the head by a brick, swallowed a needle, fell down a flight of stairs, toppled onto a burning stove, and accidentally drank sulphuric acid. None of this prevented him from perfecting, in 1835, the wind instrument named after him, which combined the reed mouthpiece of a clarinet with a bent conical tube of metal, equipped with finger keys." Sax patented his new instrument in 1846, thus lending his name and his invention to the English language.

Also in 1846: *lasagna*

1847 GYNECOLOGY

The nineteenth century was almost half over before medical science grudgingly recognized one of its newest branches: gynecology, the study and treatment of diseases and other ailments peculiar to women (from Greek *gune*, "woman," and *logos*, "study"). For women in the nineteenth century, such recognition was an uphill battle. The delivery of babies had been dignified with the term *obstetrics* earlier in the century, and in 1834 Professor William P. Dewees assumed the first chair of obstetrics at the University of Pennsylvania. However, he had to face the contempt and ridicule of his fellow doctors, who made much of the fact that the word *obstetrics* comes from the Latin *obstetrix*, meaning "midwife." If we look more closely at the Latin root, we find it comes from a Latin verb meaning "to stand before," no doubt in reference to the notion that the midwife stands in front of the delivering mother to catch the baby when it comes out. It was a standard joke in medical circles for many years that the only instrument an obstetrician needed was a large basket.

Toward the end of the nineteenth century, obstetrics and gynecology were fast becoming accepted branches of medical science, if only because practitioners in this field were now performing delicate operations that required instruments far more sophisticated than a large basket. The word *hysterectomy* dates from 1881, and by the 1890s that operation was fast becoming routine. The word itself, however, reminds us of the male-chauvinist influence on the English language, because both *hysterectomy* and *hysteria* come from the same Greek root: *hustera*, "womb." The man or men who coined *hysteria* no doubt believed that women were more prone to hysteria than men.

Also in 1847: *referendum*

1848 CANCAN

Beginning in Paris in the 1840s, the cancan soon became all the rage in musical revues, dance halls and operettas. Its electrifying high kicks and saucy, titillating movements inspired the great Jacques Offenbach to write music for it, and Toulouse-Lautrec vividly captured the dance in his energetic paintings. The origin of the word *cancan* is shrouded in uncertainty. It may be derived from the Old French *caquehan*, meaning "noise," "disturbance" or "rumpus," or it may come from the French *cancaner*, "to quack like a duck." In any event, H. Greville has the honour of using it first in English when he recorded the word in his diary in 1848: "Wearing a beard, smoking a short pipe, dancing the cancan."

1849 Mispunctuate

Although the noun *mispunctuation* appeared in print as early as 1807, no one, it seems, turned the noun into a verb until Edgar Allen Poe wrote these words in 1849: "The writer who neglects punctuation, or mis-punctuates, is liable to be misunderstood."

To stress the importance of proper punctuation, some English teachers write this statement on the blackboard: "King Charles the First walked and talked ten minutes after his head was chopped off."

Faced with this biological impossibility, the students are challenged to make sense of it — and all it takes is a semicolon after "talked" and a comma after "after."

1850 Pornographer

Ancient Greece had its share of prostitutes, one of whom apparently wore sandals that, when she walked, printed the Greek equivalent of "Follow me" on the ground beneath her feet. Another one (mindful, no doubt, of the Athenian Better Business Bureau) was famous for giving full refunds if she enjoyed herself more than her customers did. And still another, a very wealthy one, offered to donate a large chunk of her ill-gotten gains for the construction of a protective wall around the city of Athens, provided that the grateful citizens chisel her name in a prominent place on the wall (the Athenians refused).

These ladies of pleasure have long since gone the way of all flesh, and yet they live on in the English language today because the word *pornographer* and all its variations (*pornography, pornographic, porn, porno,* and *porno flick*) are based on the Greek root *porne,* meaning "harlot," "strumpet" or "prostitute."

The *OED* assigns John Leitch the honour of first using *pornographer* in print, which he did in 1850. *Pornography* itself popped up seven years later in Robley Dunglison's Medical Dictionary: "*Pornography*, a description of prostitutes or of prostitution, as a matter of public hygiene." In 1864 *Webster's Dictionary* defined pornography as "licentious painting employed to decorate the walls of rooms sacred to bacchanalian orgies, examples of which exist in Pompeii."

Ninety-nine years later, the New York publishing house of G.P. Putman's Sons released *Fanny Hill: The Memoirs of a Woman of Pleasure*, a book that had been banned for more than two hundred years. Although taken to court on an obscenity charge, the publisher won, and other books of *Fanny's* ilk quickly flooded the shelves of bookstores from Hoboken to Hollywood. Finding existing words inadequate to describe the huge new outpouring of smut that was spreading its salacious fingers across the country, *Time* magazine concocted a new word by taking *pornography* and *cornucopia* and shoving them together to produce *pornucopia*.

1851 PREHISTORIC

Throughout the Middle Ages, the literal interpretation of the Book of Genesis was generally accepted throughout Europe — God created the universe in six days and then rested, after breathing life into Adam and making Eve from Adam's rib. A seventeenth-century Anglican archbishop, James Ussher, decided to calculate the exact calendar date of the beginning of creation by working his way back through all the "begats" in the Old Testament. He finally arrived at what he claimed was the answer: 9 o'clock (although he wasn't sure if it was A.M. or P.M.) on October 23, 4004 B.C.

So widely accepted was Ussher's date that many Bible publishers printed it in the margin beside the story of creation, leading many readers to think the date had been there since the Bible was first written.

By the early nineteenth century evidence began to emerge suggesting that the Earth was much older than Ussher thought. The first dinosaur bones were found in a field in Sussex, England, in 1822, and so many similar ones were found over the next few years that Richard Owen, the British naturalist, was prompted to coin the word *dinosaur* in 1841. By 1851 the study of the distant past was attracting serious and widespread scientific attention. The time was ripe for the birth of a new word: *prehistoric* (from Latin *prae*, "before," and *historia*, "inquiry"), coined by Sir Daniel

Wilson, a Scots-born professor of history and English at the University of Toronto, who used the word in the title of his book *Prehistoric Annals of Scotland*, published in 1851.

As the veil of time was pushed further and further back, Ussher's date of 4004 B.C. began to seem like only yesterday. Modern science now estimates the age of the Earth to be around five billion years — a span of time so enormous as to be almost incomprehensible. A history text, *The Foundations of the West*, expresses this in terms that can be easily understood: "One scholar has calculated that if the life-span of the earth were compressed into a single year, the first eight months would be devoid of life and the next two would show only very primitive animal forms. Not until some time between 10 and 11 P.M. on December 31 would man appear, and only in the final minute of that last day would he learn how to grow grain. Into that minute, too, would be crammed the entire period of recorded history. The momentous developments of [the twentieth] century would all occur during the last second."

Also in 1851: *chintzy, chauvinist*

1852 KINDERGARTEN

The concept of kindergarten (from the German *kinder garten*, "children's garden") was introduced in 1837 in Blankenburg, Germany, by Friedrich Froebel (1782–1852), a German educator who strongly believed in the importance of providing a variety of stimulating physical and mental activities for your children. Although the king of Prussia banned kindergartens in that country in 1851 because they conflicted with the older, more authoritarian methods of instructing young children, the idea reached England in 1852 (the year of Froebel's death) and caught on not only there, but throughout the world. We can only hope that those first few kindergartens in England were interesting places to be, because the word *boredom* entered the English language in the same year.

1853 BADMINTON

The Duke of Beaufort must have been a big trendsetter in Victorian England because two items of pleasant living have been named after

Badminton, his country estate in Gloucestershire: a cooling summer drink ("that grateful compound of mingled claret, sugar, and soda water") was given the name *badminton* in 1853; and twenty years later a game of racquets and shuttlecocks was imported from India to England and called *badminton*. The beverage has long since been forgotten, but you can be reasonably certain that someone, somewhere, is right now playing badminton.

Also in 1853: *Braille*

1854 KEROSENE

The early prosperity of New England depended largely on shipbuilding and overseas trade, particularly in coffee, tea, sugar, molasses and whale oil. The whale oil was used for lamps and worked very well until the mid-nineteenth century, when whales became scarce. That's when the American inventor Abraham Gesner developed a way of producing fuel oil from coal tar or shale oil. Calling the new fluid *kerosene*, from the Greek *keros*, "wax" (because paraffin was used initially to manufacture kerosene), he began to manufacture it in 1854. Some was produced from petroleum, but not much, because petroleum was at that time only available in small quantities when it happened to seep up to the surface of the earth.

Five years later, in 1859, a retired railroad conductor named Colonel E. S. Drake had a brainstorm: why not drill for petroleum the same way we drill for water? With some partners, he built a wooden derrick thirty feet high near Titusville, Pennsylvania, where the Native Americans had skimmed oil off the ground for years. Known as Drake's Folly, the derrick used a steam engine and oak battering ram to pound an iron pipe into the ground. At sixty-nine-and-one-half feet they struck oil and ushered in the age of petroleum. From then on, kerosene was distilled from petroleum and became the major refinery product until its role as a lamplighter was replaced by electricity.

Also in 1854: *fiasco*

1855 STERN-WHEELER

In Mark Twain's immortal American classic, *The Adventures of Huckleberry Finn*, young Huck travelled down the Mississippi River on a raft. Those who could afford it travelled by steamboat — on board a craft with a paddle-wheel either at the back or on either side. The word *side-wheeler* predates *stern-wheeler* by one year.

Also in 1855: *croquet*

1856 PICCOLO

Music made great advances in the nineteenth century, thanks in part to the greater variety of instruments available. Amongst many others, the saxophone appeared in 1846 (see page 225), the piccolo in 1856, and the xylophone in 1866 (see page 235). The piccolo (from the Italian *piccolo*, "small"), is really a flute that plays an octave higher. And what do you call a person who plays a flute? You can call him or her a "flutist," but those in the know prefer to be called "flautists" (pronounce *flau* to rhyme with *bow*, as in the front of a ship).

Also in 1856: *igloo*

1857 SQUARSON

The typical parish priest of bygone centuries in England owned little or no land of his own, contenting himself with his devotion to the church and the prospect of heavenly reward in the afterlife. But not all sons of the church were so self-sacrificing; some of them used church funds to furnish their own ambitions in politics, land and commerce. By the early eighteenth century, all twenty-six bishops of the Church of England sat in the House of Lords, and those members of the lower clergy who were eager to climb the ladder of success found it helpful to kowtow to the government and make the right political connections. Benjamin Hoadly was an Anglican clergyman of the time who knew how to get ahead; for good and faithful service to the government of Sir Robert Walpole, Hoadly was given the bishoprics of Bangor, Hereford, Salisbury and Winchester, the latter two alone providing him with an annual income of £5,000 a year.

By the mid-nineteenth century, Anglican parsons who owned land and lived the life of country squires were sufficiently common to prompt someone to coin the term *squarson*. No one knows who that someone was, although credit has been given to Bishop Wilberforce (1805–1873) and Sydney Smith (1771–1845), a well-known London clergyman whose comment "Who reads an American book?" was not appreciated in the former colonies. *Squarson* is a word seldom heard today, but it flourished in Victorian England long enough to inspire the coining of a similar word to describe a squire who was also a bishop. That person was known as a *squishop*.

Also in 1857: *khaki*

1858 PAPERWEIGHT

The word *paper* comes from papyrus, the reed plant in ancient Egypt and elsewhere that was used in making paper thousands of years ago. The eastern Mediterranean port of Byblos imported papyrus from Egypt to make books, hence the Greek *biblion*— "book." And that's how the Bible got its name.

1859 ABUZZ

The last four letters of this five-letter word were formed through onomatopoeia (a buzzing sound). Your cottage might be on a lake abuzz with outboards. Or, if you have your ear to the ground, you might discover your workplace is abuzz with rumours of impropriety.

1860 DEADLINE

Back in 1860 when this word first appeared, it was used by anglers to describe a fishing line that does not move or run. By 1868 a deadline was a line drawn around a prison beyond which an inmate could be shot down. It was not until the late 1920s that *deadline* acquired its current familiar meaning, a time limit for the payment of a debt or the completion of a task. In one of the earliest examples of this usage, *Publishers Weekly* reported on July 27, 1929: "[The] deadline for *Poetry's* $250 prize poem contest is September 1."

Also in 1860: *billionaire, massage, plebiscite, flatfoot*

1861 Slob

Merriam-Webster defines this word as "a slovenly or boorish person" or "an ordinary person (just some poor slob)."

However, the verb *slobber* has been dated as far back as 1607, that being the fourth year of the reign of King James I of England. At least one high school history text describes James as a sloppy drinker, with the beverage running out of both sides of his mouth.

1862 Dynamite

The earliest known explosive was black gunpowder (a mixture of powdered charcoal, sulphur and potassium nitrate), used by the Chinese to make firecrackers two thousand years ago. Marco Polo learned how to make it when he visited China in the thirteenth century. Less than a hundred years later, the English used gunpowder in wooden cannons to defeat the French at the Battle of Crecy.

In 1846 an Italian chemist named Ascanio Sobrero made the world's first batch of nitroglycerin. In minute quantities it is useful as a heart stimulant, but in larger volumes it is so unstable that a slight jolt can make it explode with devastating violence.

Meanwhile, a young lad named Alfred Nobel was growing up in Sweden. His father was in the explosives business; in fact, Alfred's younger brother was killed by an accidental explosion of nitroglycerin. Alfred then set to work to find a way of harnessing this dangerous material. He found the answer in *kieselguhr*, a porous substance which, when combined with nitroglycerin, can be moulded into sticks that are safe to handle but can be detonated from a safe distance by an electrical spark to produce an explosion of tremendous power. Alfred patented his new invention in 1862 under the name *dynamite*, from the Greek *dynamis*, meaning "power."

Dynamite was put to so many uses that when Nobel died in 1896 he was a multimillionaire. He left over nine million dollars to establish the Nobel Foundation, which annually awards prizes throughout the world to those people who have made outstanding contributions to the arts and sciences. Awards are given in five categories: physics, chemistry, medicine, literature and world peace.

Nobel's turn for an award came in 1957, when the Nobel Institute discovered element #102. It was named *nobelium* in his honour.

1863 VINYL

The word *vinyl* first entered the English language as a chemical ($CH_2=CH$) in Watts's *Dictionary of Chemistry* in 1863 and comes from the Latin *vinum*, "wine," perhaps because vinyl in its liquid form looks like wine. No one made much of a fuss when this word first appeared, and yet it's difficult to imagine a substance with a greater range of uses in modern life. Made from natural gas, petroleum or salt, vinyl plastics (often simply called *vinyls*) can be found in windbreakers, electrical insulators, toys, upholstery, water pipes and hundreds of other everyday items. Vinyl can be given the stiffness of wood or the flexibility of cloth; it can be made in any colour — or simply transparent — will not break or tear easily, burns slowly, and can be fashioned into any shape. All vinyl plastics contain the chemical substance we call vinyl, but by combining that substance with several others, manufacturers can produce a wide range of vinyl plastics. A big breakthrough occurred in 1927, when PVC (polyvinyl chloride) was first manufactured commercially. By 1973 the United States was producing 4.6 billion tons of vinyl plastics every year.

1864 GUSHER

When you recall that the first oil well in the United States was drilled at Titusville, Pennsylvania, in 1859, it seems logical to assume that this word, appearing five years later, would be used to describe a gusher of an oil well. But it wasn't. In *Broken of Harness*, published in 1864, Edmund Yates was writing not about oil wells but about "the enthusiastic gusher who flings his or herself upon our necks, and insists upon sharing our sorrow." The petroleum-based definition did not appear for another twenty-two years, when *Pall Mall* reported it on October 13, 1886: "Tagieff's 'gusher' beats out and out every previous record in the oil regions of the two hemispheres."

1865 GASOLINE

No one was interested in gasoline when the first oil well began gushing in Pennsylvania in 1859. Kerosene is what the oil refiners wanted in those early days, and gasoline was simply a dangerous and explosive by-product that had to be thrown away. The word itself first appeared in *Appleton's Annual Encyclopedia* in 1865: "Many refiners [of petroleum] separate first of all the lightest naphtha; ... to this the name of gasoline has been given." For the next quarter-century, gasoline was simply dumped on the ground or burned, while kerosene reigned supreme. Then, around 1892, the first gasoline-powered horseless carriages began chugging along the streets of America. Suddenly the waste product could be put to good use.

When will the world run out of gasoline? No one knows, but Jack Stockton of radio station WIND in Chicago is fond of telling what happened at a Chicago gas station during the 1979 U.S.–wide gasoline shortage. Just as the shortage began, the big GASOLINE sign over the station lost its letter *O* in a windstorm; thus the sign read GAS LINE, the perfect description for the long lineups at the pumps.

1866 XYLOPHONE

A xylophone (from the Greek *xylon*, "wood," and *phone*, "sound") is a musical instrument consisting of a row of wooden blocks of resonant wood which produce notes when struck with two small hammers. The earliest quotation illustrating the use of this word shows us just how new it was in 1866. It appears in quotation marks, in a sentence that describes what it looks like, presumably because the readers of the *Athenaeum* had never seen a xylophone: "[He is] a prodigy ... who does wonderful things with little drumsticks on a machine of wooden keys, called the 'xylophone,' almost five octaves in compass."

If you have been reading this book from page one, you will notice this is the first entry beginning with the letter *x*. If you press on, you'll find one more: the trade name Xerox, in 1937.

1867 ANGLOPHILE

An Anglophile is a person who loves England and English culture (from the Angles, who settled there after the fall of Rome, and from the Greek *philos*, "loving"). The word first appeared in print in 1867, a year in which England had much to be proud of: London had become the financial capital of the world and the Colonial Office presided over an empire on which the sun never set. Exotic goods from the far corners of the globe crowded into the berths on the London docks and the transatlantic cable had just been laid the previous year, giving England up-to-the-minute communication with Canada and the rest of North America. Poet laureate Alfred Lord Tennyson saw an even brighter England coming in the years ahead: "For I dipt into the future, far as human eye could see,/Saw the Vision of the world, and all the wonder that would be;/Saw the heavens fill with commerce, argosies of magic sail;/Pilots of the purple twilight, dropping down with costly bales."

Because the Industrial Revolution erupted first in England, it gave the English people a headstart in the worldwide scramble for material wealth. Small wonder that the England of 1867 was envied and admired. In an issue of *Contemporary Review* published that year, we find this line: "The *Revue des deux Mondes* [is] a thoroughly 'Anglo-phile' periodical."

1868 BICYCLE

The forerunners of the modern bicycle can be traced back to the manumotive wagons and coaches of the Middle Ages, which had power supplied by paddling with feet along the ground. The first two-wheeled vehicle of which we can document the existence was the *draisienne*, invented by Charles Baron Karl van Drais de Sauerbrun in Paris in 1818. According to C.F. Cauntier in *The History and*

Development of Cycles, it was constructed with "a ... partially triangulated wooden frame, a steerable front wheel (the first of its kind), a padded saddle, and an arm rest which provided a greater purchase for the purpose of thrusting at the ground with the feet." When Drais put his vehicle on display in Paris, the word *velocipede* (from the Latin *velox*, "swift," and *pes*, "foot") was coined to replace the earlier *velocifere*, which had superceded the still-earlier *celerifere*, itself a replacement for the medieval *manumotive vehicle*.

The first self-propelled two-wheeler was built in 1839 by the Scottish blacksmith Kirkpatrick Macmillan, who used wheels rimmed with iron and transmitted the power through two swinging cranks mounted at the front. In 1868 the word *bicycle* was coined (*tricycle* appeared in the same year), and this is the term that caught on and doomed to oblivion such synonyms as *draisienne, swiftwalker, dandy horse, hobby horse* and *pedestrian curricle*. But it took more than a catchy new word to get the bicycle industry rolling. The wheels were rimmed with iron or steel, and early cyclists complained about the hard ride. Finally a Scottish veterinarian living in Belfast decided to do something about it. His name was John Dunlop and in February 1888 he introduced the pneumatic bicycle tire. By the 1890s bicycles were everywhere.

1869 Agnostic

The word *atheist* (see page 54) first entered the English language in 1571 to describe someone who denies the existence of God. For the next three centuries, you were either a believer or an atheist; the English language recognized no position in between.

Then along came Thomas Huxley (1825–1895), the great English biologist who defended the theory of evolution with such vigour that he became known as "Darwin's Bulldog." Sick and tired of being called an atheist by members of the Church of England, Huxley is said to have coined the word *agnostic*, from the Greek *agnostos*, "unknowing," at a party in 1869 to describe all those people who simply do not know whether God exists. The word quickly spread and began popping up in dictionaries. It's been there ever since.

1870 Kilo

This abbreviation for *kilogram* has been dated back to at least 1870. Another abbreviation arising from the metric system is *klickage*, referring to your car's rate of fuel consumption (instead of the Imperial *mileage*). But even though Canadians have now lived with the metric system for more than a quarter-century, most of them, it seems, still talk of mileage when discussing fuel consumption.

1871 Hoodlum

The story is probably untrue, but it's an interesting one nonetheless. A gang of thugs reportedly terrorized the good citizens of San Francisco in the early 1870s, and they were led by an Irish fellow named Muldoon. A newspaper reporter wrote a series of articles about them, and, fearing for his life at the hands of Muldoon, spelled his name backward: Noodlum. Somewhere along the way, the *N* changed to an *H*, giving us *hoodlum*.

1872 Sadism

This word is an eponym — a word based on someone's name. In this case, Count Donatien Alphonse François de Sade (1740–1814), an eighteenth-century French novelist whose books are filled with sexual fantasies based on the torturing of one's sexual partner or partners. De Sade was condemned to death by the French in 1772 for "an unnatural offence," but he beat the rap by escaping to Italy. The rest of his life was a revolving door of perversions, arrests, imprisonments, escapes and re-arrests. He was finally incarcerated in the Charenton Lunatic Asylum, where he died in 1814. The sexologist Kraft-Ebbing coined the term *sadism* fifty-eight years later, thus giving this prince of perverts a dubious kind of immortality. See *masochism*, page 248.

Also in 1872: *chortle, galumph, extrasolar*

1873 Atchoo

Atchoo, an onomatopoetic interjection for the sound of someone sneezing, is also spelled *atcha, atichoo,* and *atishoo.* In 1873 a chap named Broughton wrote, "I sneeze loudly and irrepressibly. Atcha! Atcha!" Five years later, on January 26, 1878, *Punch* magazine ran a sentence written by someone in desperate need of a handkerchief: "A cough tears your lungs, but a sneeze tears you through — A'd — goodness! — it's cubbi'g — a'tschoo — A-tischoo!" On November 30, 1910, *Punch* carried another sneeze: "There, that's all right. A-a-a-tishoo!"

Apparently, none of these sneezes were responded to with "Gesundheit," because the earliest recorded use of that Germanic blessing in English did not take place until 1914.

Also in 1873: *oleomargarine, switchboard*

1874 Pistol grip

We encountered the word *pistol* in 1570 (see page 53). By 1874, that noun was turned into an adjective modifying "grip," a very old word dating back before the twelfth century (that is to say, the 1100s), to Old English *grippan.*

The term *pistol grip* came to be applied in the twentieth century to at least two parts of an automobile. On the very early cars — say, prior to the 1920s — the emergency brake was operated by a long lever that the driver usually pulled back on to operate. These levers were often mounted on the floor just ahead of the front seat.

By the 1950s, pistol-grip emergency brake handles were common on most North American cars. They were mounted just under the dashboard, to the left of the steering column. The handle was shaped, for quick and easy grasping, like the handle of a gun — hence "pistol grip."

In the 1940s, many motorists jazzed up their cars by mounting a pistol-grip spotlight to the windshield post on the driver's side (some cars had these on the other side, too). The handle was similar in shape to the parking/emergency brake handle, hence a new use for the term *pistol grip.*

These spotlights came in handy when one wanted to look for a house number at night, or to play spotlight tag with other cars by shining them at the screen at a drive-in movie theatre.

1875 SUDAN

The year 1875 marked a turning point in Britain's relations with Africa. The name *Sudan* (the Arabic word for "black") first appeared in print in English as the name for all those African lands between the Sahara and the equator. Later, the name came to be applied to the Republic of Sudan, a nation that covers nearly one million square miles directly south of Egypt. Also in 1875, British Prime Minister Benjamin Disraeli paid a visit to the Rothschild family in London to ask for a loan of four million dollars because he had just got wind of the fact that the Khedive of Egypt was about to sell his controlling shares in the Suez Canal, which had opened for traffic just six years earlier. Disraeli, ever mindful of the need to bolster British holdings in India, wanted to buy the canal shares before they were snapped up by a hostile foreign power. The Rothschilds lent him the money, which Parliament, at its next sitting, voted to pay back. And thus the Suez Canal in 1875 fell into British hands, and the journey from England to India was now four thousand miles shorter.

Also in 1876: *geothermal*

1876 BULLDOZER

As a noun, this word has been traced back to 1876. As a verb, it has been traced back to the same year. Merriam-Webster gives three definitions for *bulldoze* as a transitive verb (one that takes an object): "1) to coerce or restrain by threats: bully; 2) to move, clear, gouge out, or level off by pushing with or as if with a bulldozer; 3) to force insensitively or ruthlessly (*bulldozed* the program through the legislature)." Two more definitions are given when the verb is used intransitively: "1) to operate a bulldozer; 2) to force one's way like a bulldozer. For synonyms, see INTIMIDATE."

1877 PONDAGE

Pondage is the capacity of a dam or pond to hold water. But where does this word come from? Well, if the dogcatcher takes your mutt to the *pound*, he is putting him, her or it into an enclosure. If the police *impound* your car because you are double-parked, they are hauling it away to an enclosure. And if you dig a big hole in the ground, fill it with water, and call it a *pond*, you are using the word based on the Middle English word for enclosure (*ponde* or *pounde*), because the ground around it encloses the water it contains.

The suffix *-age* of which *pondage* makes use is a popular one in the English language. It means "state of," "result of," "collection of," and "function." Some other words that contain it are: *carriage, courage, dotage, damage, envisage, forage, marriage, mirage, pillage, sabotage, salvage* and *storage*. And if you use too many words to get the idea across, you are guilty of *verbiage*.

1878 ALEXIA

Alexia is a form of aphasia marked by the loss of ability to read. *Aphasia* has been traced back to 1867 and describes the "loss or impairment of the power to use or comprehend words, usually resulting from brain damage" (Merriam-Webster). In both cases, the Greek prefix *a-* means "not." That prefix also begins the word *atom*, because atoms were at one time believed to be so small they were unsplittable (*tom* in Greek meaning "cut" or "split").

1879 CLAUSTROPHOBIA

The word *claustrophobia* (from Latin *claustrum*, "bar" or "bolt," and Greek *phobia*, "fear") first appeared in an article in the *British Medical Journal* on September 6, 1879. Although other phobias have been identified since then, including *acrophobia* (fear of heights), *agoraphobia* (fear of wide open spaces) and *phobophobia* (inspired by Franklin Roosevelt, who as president of the United States, said, "The only thing we have to fear is fear itself"), *claustrophobia* is still the best known.

One chap I know suffers an attack of claustrophobia every time he has to ride in a crowded elevator, and one day when he was jammed into a corner at the back, he decided he just had to have more room. Just before the elevator reached the next floor, he feigned illness by announcing, in a quavering voice, "I think … I'm going … to vomit." Then the doors opened and everyone else — on the verge of panic — quickly stepped out. Then the doors closed and he rode the rest of the way in elbow-room comfort.

1880 ASTRONAUT

Most people added *astronaut* to their vocabulary after the space flights of John Glenn and Yuri Gagarin in the early 1960s, but the *OED* has traced this word as far back as 1880, when it referred to the spaceship itself and not the occupants. It comes from the Greek roots *aster*, "star," and *naus*, "ship," and was first used by Percy Greg in *Across the Zodiac*, a book about an imaginary space flight to Mars: "In shape my Astronaut somewhat resembled the form of an antique Dutch East-Indiaman."

By 1929 *astronaut* was shifting its meaning to apply to someone who travels through space. In that year, the *Journal of British Astronomical Association* examined "that first obstacle encountered by the would-be 'Astronaut' … terrestrial gravitation." When the race for space got under way after the launch of *Sputnik* in 1957, the Americans gave the word *astronaut* worldwide exposure, but the Russians chose to use the term *cosmonaut* (from the Greek *kosmos*, "universe").

Also in 1881: *municipalize* (localized version of *nationalize*), *gonad* (*gonads*)

1881 PASTEURIZE

Louis Pasteur was a forty-two-year-old French chemist who discovered a means of sterilizing milk in 1864. The problem he tackled was how to make milk last longer on the shelf before going sour. After some success in the sterilization of beer and wine, he heated up some milk and then let it cool under carefully controlled laboratory conditions. The result was milk that would stay fresh and free of contamination much longer.

That was in France in 1864. His name was not applied to this process by the English until 1881, when *pasteurize* first appeared in print (according to the *OED*). Pasteur, who was not a wealthy man, resisted the urgings of his wife and friends to cash in on his new scheme and instead gave pasteurization to the world. He placed his discoveries in the public domain and published carefully illustrated treatises to show others how to pasteurize milk. He died in 1895, after having enriched the world far more than he enriched himself.

Also in 1881: *aquanaut, jackpot*

1882 DACHSHUND

Merriam-Webster describes these lovable little canines as "any of a breed of long-bodied, short-legged dogs of German origin that occur in short-haired, long-haired, and wirehaired varieties." That dictionary dates the word back to 1882, but it may have entered the English language before that. Margaret Baltzer of Leamington, Ontario (the woman who diskified this dictionary — see page 311), owns a dachshund named Reuben who always starts barking whenever a visitor knocks (Reuben takes his watchdog duties very seriously). According to *Dogs in Canada* magazine, the dachshund was introduced to Britain by Prince Albert, Queen Victoria's German consort. He died in 1861, so he must have done the introducing while he was still alive. When the next edition of this dictionary (God willing) comes out, you might find that "dachshund" has been backdated to 1861 or earlier. And so goes the English language, which is always revealing something new about its past.

1883 DUDE

Merriam-Webster lists the etymology of *dude* as "origin unknown," and this description applies to quite a number of words in the English language. Suddenly a word appears in print somewhere, perhaps for the first time, but without any clue as to where it came from. Such a word is *dude*: "1) a man extremely fastidious in dress and manner: DANDY, 2) a city dweller unfamiliar with life on the range, especially an Easterner in the West, 3) FELLOW, GUY — sometimes used informally as a term of address (hey, *dude*, what's up?)."

The term *dude ranch* (for Easterners wanting to experience the West) goes back to 1921.

1884 HAMBURGER

According to the *OED*, the hamburger made its debut in the English language on January 5, 1889, in a newspaper in Walla Walla, Washington: "You are asked if you will have portchopbeafsteakhamandegghamburgerssteakorliverandbacon…" If they talked that fast, it must have been a fast-food outlet. Merriam-Webster dates *hamburger* to 1884.

The hamburger itself originated on the steppes of medieval Russia, where Tartars ate raw meat seasoned with salt, pepper and onion juice. German sailors on the Baltic brought it home to Hamburg, where it was broiled on the outside and came to be known as hamburger steak. German immigrants brought it to America, and when a chef at the St. Louis World's Fair in 1904 began slapping beef patties between buns, the modern hamburger was born.

The worldwide icon for the hamburger today is the pair of golden arches that stand over every McDonald's restaurant from Hoboken to Hollywood. The first golden arches were erected over a hamburger stand in San Bernardino, California, when Maurice and Richard McDonald decided to go into the hamburger business. Along came a milk-shake-mixer salesman named Ray Kroc, who saw the potential in fast-food hamburger stands and bought out the brothers in 1960. Twenty years later, the business was, by anyone's yardstick, a sizzling success: eight million patties a day sold from more than forty-three hundred restaurants on five continents with an annual gross of more than three billion dollars.

If you want to join the McDonald's management team, the company will send you to Hamburger University in Chicago, where you can specialize in Hamburger Sciences and pick up a degree in hamburgerology, with a minor in French fries. And when you graduate, you can play around with the English language as you serve to your hungry customers a dazzling array of McRibs, McChicken and McMuffins.

1885 DELICATESSEN

This word of German, and perhaps Italian, origin describes one of the earliest versions of the fast-food outlet, with the typical delicatessen featuring sliced meat at room temperature in sandwiches (see page 174) and salads. The word *salad* dates back to at least the fourteenth century and comes from Latin *sal*, meaning salt. It's hard to imagine a salad without any lettuce, and this word also goes back to the fourteenth century. Its etymology is interesting. It comes from Latin *lactuca*, from *lact-* and *lac*, "milk," because of the milky juice of the lettuce plant.

1886 Gadget

Although possibly in use as early as the 1850s, this word's earliest known appearance in print dates back to 1886, when a chap named Brown used it in *Spunyarn and Spindrift*: "Then the names of all the other things on board ship! I don't know half of them yet; even the sailors forget at times, and if the exact name of anything they want happens to slip from their memory, they call it a chicken-fixing, or a gadjet, or a gillguy, or a timmey-noggy, or a wim-wom — just *pro tem*, you know."

The *OED* does not know from where this word comes, but suggests it may be derived from the French *gachette*, which has often been applied to various mechanical parts, or from the dialect French *gagée*, a tool or instrument. Regardless of the etymology, it was certainly a word whose time had come. The Industrial Revolution was by then in full swing in Europe and North America, and people were quickly being surrounded by all manner of newfangled contraptions full of strange parts with funny names. Why bother learning all those new names when a single all-purpose noun, *gadget*, fits them all?

Also in 1886: *kimono, leotard*

1887 Gramophone

The word *phonograph* — from the Greek *phone*, "sound," and *graphein*, "to write" — was first used in 1835, when the principles of electronic sound transmission were first being discovered. In 1877 Thomas Edison applied this word to his latest invention: a machine that could record the human voice and other sounds on a rotating metal cylinder, over which was fastened a layer of tin foil, on which the sound was recorded. Ten years later, in 1887, the U.S. Patent Office *Gazette* reported on the "Gramophone [patented by] Emile Berliner, Washington, D.C." Berliner's new machine did everything Edison's did, but instead of using a rotating cylinder, it used grooved disks that revolved on a turntable, exactly like the phonograph of today. By the early 1890s Berliner was manufacturing his machines under the trade name of Gramophone (from the Greek *gramma*, "letter," and *phone*, "sound").

It's interesting to note that the word *phonograph* survived longer in popular usage than *gramophone*. Both terms were eventually elbowed out by *record player*, but in an era of compact discs and MP3s, the device, by any name, might be considered a museum piece.

Also in 1887: *sideburns*

1888 KODAK

George Eastman did for photography what Henry Ford did for the automobile: he brought it within reach of the masses. Before the Kodak camera came along, you were at the mercy of your local photography studio, but Eastman set out to change all that. Working in his Rochester, New York, laboratory, he introduced the world's first simple and inexpensive camera in 1888 with the slogan, "You push the button; we do the rest." If you could cough up the purchase price of twenty-five dollars (a hefty sum in those days), you found yourself holding a rectangular box camera already loaded with film and with focus and shutter speed pre-set at the factory. After taking all your pictures, you shipped the entire camera off to Kodak, and for ten dollars the company developed the photos and returned them, along with your camera, which was again loaded with film.

But how did Eastman hit upon the name *Kodak*? He made it up himself, starting with the letter *K* (a "strong, incisive sort of letter") and then playing around with vowels and consonants until he had a name he liked. He knew what he was doing and said so: "A trademark should be short, vigorous, incapable of being misspelled to an extent that it will destroy its identity; and — in order to satisfy trademark laws — it must mean nothing."

Indeed, it *must* mean nothing. General Motors learned this lesson the hard way when it tried to market its Chevrolet Nova in Latin America. *No va* in Spanish means "no go."

Also in 1888: *doodad, larvicide*

1889 TUXEDO

This semiformal jacket for men (in black or bluish-black) takes its name from Tuxedo Park, New York. Also appearing that same year: *milk shake*, which, according to Merriam-Webster, is two separate words. But many roadside diners spell it MILKSHAKE, perhaps to leave room on the sign for the price.

Getting back to *tuxedo*, Townsend Haines was the school president at Northern Secondary School in Toronto, Canada, a few years ago. He attended an event somewhere downtown that required him to wear a tux. To get there, he rode the Yonge Street subway — and judging by the reaction of the other passengers, none of them had ever before seen a man in a tuxedo riding the subway. Taxis, yes, but the subway?

1890 GRADE CROSSING

Here is Merriam-Webster's definition: "a crossing of highways, railroad tracks, or pedestrian walks or combinations of these on the same level." It's easy to see why this term cropped up around 1890. By then, the countryside was becoming criss-crossed with roads and railways — and where traffic was heaviest, bridges and underpasses were constructed.

Before this time, a crossing was just a crossing. But with the proliferation of crossings at different levels, it became necessary to come up with a term for crossings at the same level. The word *grade* fit the bill because it comes from Latin (*gradus, gress* — "step"). At a grade crossing, you can step or walk across it instead of going over a bridge or through an underpass.

Grade crossing is a *retronym*, a word coined by someone a few years ago to describe a noun that now needs an adjective to distinguish it from other variations modified by a different adjective. Remember when a guitar was just a guitar? Then along came electric guitars, giving rise to the term "acoustic guitar" to set the original apart from the new invention. In this case, *acoustic guitar* is a retronym.

1891 SOUTHPAW

Left-handed people have been called *southpaws* since 1891, when the word first appeared in a Chicago newspaper. It originated in a baseball park on Chicago's west side, where home plate was west of the pitcher's mound, and so a left-handed pitcher had to use his "south paw." Had the pitcher's mound faced a different direction, the new word could just as easily have been *northpaw, eastpaw* or *westpaw*.

Also in 1891: *fedora, plankton*

1892 MASOCHISM

This word is based on the name of Leopold van Sacher-Masoch, an Austrian novelist who was fascinated by the sexual pleasure certain individuals derive from being physically and emotionally abused during, or in lieu of, copulation. This emotional sickness became such a recurring theme in his books that his name was eventually applied to the malaise he described. He died in 1895, three years after his name became immortalized.

Sacher-Masoch (pronounced za-kur-ma-zok) did not invent masochism; he merely drew attention to a perversion as old as the human race itself. One of the more popular forms of masochism passed down through the ages has been whipping, or flagellation. In the early 1700s a machine was invented that could whip forty persons at a time, and an English madam, Mrs. Berkeley, made £10,000 in eight years from a brothel that specialized in flagellation.

Sadism, or sexual pleasure derived from inflicting pain on others, was coined in 1872; you can find it on page 238. Somebody once explained the difference between sadism and masochism this way: a masochist says, "Hurt me! Hurt me!" while a sadist says, "No, I won't!"

Also in 1892: *heterosexual, rookie*

1893 FERRIS WHEEL

These large and well-known attractions at amusement parks are named after G.W.G. Ferris, an American engineer who first designed and built them in the 1890s.

A few years ago, a collector of automotive and other memorabilia who lives in southwestern Ontario bought a full-size Ferris wheel and brought it home. When he tried to operate it, with one passenger on board, it wouldn't work properly. Then he discovered that you need another passenger on the opposite side to give it the proper balance. The only other passenger available at that moment was a neighbour's billy goat, which was promptly conscripted for a test spin. The Ferris wheel now worked properly, and that goat probably soared higher off the face of the earth than any other goat before or since.

Also in 1893: *homosexual*

1894 DIESEL

When German Chancellor Otto von Bismarck declared war on France in 1870, he was unwittingly paving the way for the invention of the diesel engine. Rudolph Diesel was a young lad of German parents living in Paris at the time, and the outbreak of war forced him and his family to flee to England. No sooner had they arrived than Rudolph's uncle in Germany offered to take care of the boy until the war was over. He was put on a train with his uncle's address on a card tied around his neck; because of the war, the trains were not running on time, and the journey took eight long and lonely days. When he grew up, Rudolph was determined that the clumsy and inefficient steam engines that carried him to Germany should be replaced with something better.

As a young man he conducted numerous experiments — one of which nearly killed him, when his first diesel engine exploded. Undaunted, he improved upon it and, after trying everything from alcohol to peanut oil, hit upon a cheap, semi-refined crude oil as fuel for his diesel engines. Ocean-going vessels quickly adopted his new power plants, and in the years that followed diesel engines were used to power zeppelins, locomotives and even automobiles.

Diesel himself became rich and famous, but he died under mysterious circumstances. He was travelling to England with two colleagues on the cross-Channel steamer *Dresden* on September 29, 1913, and he strolled along the deck with his travelling companions before retiring for the night. He did not appear the next morning for breakfast, and ten days later the crew of another boat fished his corpse out of the water. Suicide or murder? No one knows.

Also in 1894: *cholesterol, honky tonk*

1895 BRUNCH

The August 1, 1896, issue of *Punch* tells us how brunch was born: "To be fashionable nowadays we must 'brunch.' Truly an excellent portmanteau word, introduced, by the way, last year, by Mr. Guy Beringer, in the now defunct *Hunter's Weekly*, and indicating a combined breakfast and lunch."

A *portmanteau word* is a word formed by taking two existing words and shoving them together. The term was first used by Lewis Carroll, who coined many such words, including *chortle* (a cross between chuckle and snort) and *galumph* (a cross between gallop and thump). The three best-known portmanteau words in the English language today are *brunch, smog* (a cross between *smoke* and *fog*) and *motel* (a contraction of *motor hotel*). It's interesting to note that each of these three words first appeared in the very middle of the decade in which each was coined. *Brunch* was coined in 1895, *smog* in 1905 and *motel* in 1925.

A new portmanteau word now struggling to be born is *lupper*, a midafternoon meal eaten in place of lunch and supper. I included it as a main entry in my 1979 dictionary, *Brave New Words*, and I have been both amazed and delighted to see it in print elsewhere.

Also in 1895: *appendectomy*

1896 MARATHON

The first recorded Olympic Games were held on the western side of the Peloponnese in ancient Greece in 776 B.C. Every four years thereafter for nearly twelve hundred years, the Olympic Games were held on the same site.

They finally came to an end in the year 394 A.D., when the Roman Emperor Theodosius I, a Christian, abolished them because they were considered a pagan festival. For the next fifteen hundred years, the Olympic Games were all but totally forgotten.

The modern revival of the Olympics was brought about by the enthusiasm of a young Frenchman, Baron Pierre de Coubertin, who visited the ancient site and then persuaded the Athletic Sports Union in Paris to bring them back to life. The first modern Olympics were held in Athens in 1896. The marathon foot race of twenty-six miles and 385 yards was not part of the original games, but a Frenchman suggested it be included in the modern games to commemorate the run by the Athenian Pheidippides from Marathon to Athens to tell his fellow citizens of their victory over the Persians. He managed to gasp: "Rejoice! We conquered!" before he fell over dead.

And so the word *marathon* entered the English language — 2,386 years after the battle from which it takes its name. And it has inspired a rash of related words: *swimathon, walkathon, readathon, bike-a-thon* and *dance-a-thon*. You can probably think of several more.

Also in 1896: *carburetor, face-off, limerick*

1897 TURTLENECK

In the 1950s the standard attire for business and professional men was a suit with a white shirt and tie — and when outdoors, a fedora sat on the head.

When John F. Kennedy won the U.S. presidential election in November 1960, millions of American and Canadian men stopped wearing fedoras because Kennedy preferred to go hatless. He set the style for the new look — and even though hat manufacturers begged him to start wearing a fedora to save them from bankruptcy, he continued to be bareheaded.

Later that same decade, in June 1968, Pierre Elliot Trudeau became prime minister of Canada. He disliked neckties as much as Kennedy disdained the fedora, and he opted to wear turtlenecks instead, thus setting off another fashion craze.

1898 OVERSEXED

This adjective was coined to describe people who have a greater than normal interest in sex (whatever that may be). Which brings to mind the elderly couple who went to the doctor with a sex problem:

> Couple: "Doctor, we've been married for sixty years, and
> we're losing our interest in sex."
> Doctor: "When did you first notice this problem?"
> Couple: "Last night and first thing this morning."

1899 VASECTOMY

Many adult males have opted for a vasectomy as a form of birth control. The operation usually takes about half an hour (fifteen minutes per testicle), and most patients quickly return to their daily routine. In 1984 a vasectomy was performed on a man at Sunnybrook Hospital on Bayview Avenue in Toronto, Ontario. While he was recuperating from haemotoma (a temporary complication), he composed the following sonnet (with apologies to William Shakespeare):

Ode to My Vasectomy

> O scabrous flesh, so vile and festering,
> What brought thee to this low estate?
> Was it perchance the hand of God
> Or just a strange, cruel twist of fate?
> Mere days ago, yon swollen sac
> Hung contented from thy crotch
> And held within its hairy grasp
> Two orbs of flesh we seldom watch.
>
> Ouch! What knife thru yonder scrotum breaks?
> What blood runs forth upon thy groin?
> Snip! Stitch! Snip! Stitch!
> The deed is done without a hitch.

And when will I ever love again?
As soon as the pleasure exceeds the pain.

The composer mailed a copy to the doctor who performed the operation. He was so impressed that he posted it in the scrub area of the operating room.

Also in 1899: *paperback, taxicab, tonsillectomy*

The 1900s

And Beyond

In many ways, the details of our daily lives have changed radically since the arrival of the twentieth century, and our language has reflected these changes. In the realm of clothing and personal appearance, consider *brassiere, zipper, nylon, bikini, beautician, zit* and *nudist,* all of which were unheard of when Queen Victoria was alive. The struggle between the sexes has given us *macho, Ms., chairperson, personhole, suffragette, heterosexual, palimony* and *covivant.* Our changing work environment has given us *flextime, nitpicker, gofer* and *workaholic.* And the way we spend our leisure time has helped to spawn *posh, motel, bistro, gatecrasher, crossword, whodunit, karate* and *Astroturf.*

Life in the twentieth century has been profoundly reshaped by two world wars and the terrifying possibility of a third and final one. In the pages ahead you will meet *bomber, blimp* and *camouflage* from World War I; *Gestapo, fascism, flak, blitz, Jeep, radar, genocide* and *kamikaze* from World War II; and *fallout* and *nuke* to remind us of the war we would all like to avoid. The peaceful use of atomic power has made all of us familiar with the dangers of a *meltdown,* and our dwindling reserves of fossil fuels have prompted us to start using words like *chillout, gasohol* and *downsize.* One word, first coined in 1831, has been used more in the last ten years than in the previous one hundred: *thermostat.*

Science has continued to multiply the number of new words, many of which have stayed in the lab because they are so technical. But the impact of applied science on everyday life has brought sweeping changes to our vocabulary. Consider *speedometer, smog, television, penicillin, insulin, cortisone, Xerox, microfilm, liftoff, splashdown, spinoff, anchorman, Sputnik, moped, bionic, aquanaut, cosmonaut, retrorocket, space shuttle, Breathalyser, software, courseware, computerese, catalytic converter, aerosol, fluorocarbons, supersonic, nylon, rayon, videotape, word processor, pocket calculator, Styrofoam, polyurethane, polyester, plexiglass* and *polyunsaturated.*

And with two rovers on the surface of Mars at the time of this writing (May 2004), we can add *Marsiphobiphiliac* to our space age vocabulary. That's an astronaut who would love to go to Mars but is afraid of never returning home.

1900 ESCALATOR

The world's first escalator was patented in March 1892 by Jesse W. Reno and was called Reno's Inclined Elevator. It carried passengers up and down between floors electrically at one and a half miles per hour and first went into operation in a building at Coney Island, New York, in 1896. Two years later, Harrods of London installed one of Reno's sliding stairs and stationed a butler at the top to serve brandy to any passengers who felt faint from the ride.

In the same year (1898), Charles Seeberger developed another version of a moving staircase and persuaded the Otis Elevator Company of New York to manufacture it. Seeberger's staircase was exhibited at the Paris Exposition in 1900, and that was where the name *escalator* was adopted. Gimbel's Department Store in Philadelphia installed the first commercial model the following year.

The elevator and escalator represent the most widely used forms of mass transportation in North America today. Most of us take them for granted, but not everyone: a little girl recently had her first ride on an escalator, which took her and her mother to the lower level of a shopping mall, where she looked up at her mother and asked: "Mommy, what happens when the basement is full of steps?"

Also in 1900: *coitus interruptus, tractor, undies*

1901 EYEBALL

As a noun, *eyeball* goes back at least as far as 1582, and is probably even older. As a verb (to look at something with great interest), it dates back only to 1901. The author of this dictionary used *eyeball* in this sense when reminiscing about the purchase of his first car in June 1959: "The janitor at the local high school owned it and I eyeballed it for a whole year before I bought it. I didn't have the six hundred dollars the owner insisted it was worth (I was sixteen and still in school) so I polished cars in my spare time and saved my money, hoping I would have enough before he sold it to someone else. Every time I saw him driving it around my home town of Leamington, Ontario, I stopped and stared at it: a sunset-orange 1940 Mercury convertible, nosed and decked and lowered, with air scoops in the hood. I had to have it.

"The following spring, when I had almost enough money, the price suddenly dropped. The owner had taken out the engine (a '51 Studebaker V-8) and put the '40 Merc up for sale 'as is.' I offered $100. He refused. Then I offered $150 and he said 'yes'! I had to tow it home, but it was finally mine."

1902 TEDDY BEAR

In September 1901 an anarchist at the Pan-American Exposition in Buffalo, New York, shot President William McKinley, who was taken to a nearby hospital in an electric ambulance, only to die a few days later. The bullet that felled McKinley put the impetuous and flamboyant vice president, Teddy Roosevelt, into the White House. Roosevelt was a great sportsman and big game hunter — and that's what put his name in the dictionary. *Time* (December 5, 1969) tells us how it happened: "The name [Teddy Bear] was attached to a new line of stuffed bruins manufactured by the forerunner of the Ideal Toy Corp. and by Germany's Steiff Co. after President Theodore Roosevelt, on an expedition to Mississippi in 1902, refused to shoot a bear cub. Washington *Star* cartoonist Clifford Berryman instantly made the cub a symbol for Roosevelt, and the country went for the notion lock, stock, and bear jokes. (If T.R. is President when he is fully dressed, went one kneeslapper, what is he with his clothes off? Answer: Teddy Bare.)"

Also in 1902: *garage*

1903 SPEEDOMETER

In the *Times* of London on August 4, 1904, you can find this sentence: "His 'speedometer' … showed he was going at only ten miles an hour." If you reverse the last two digits of that date, you will get 1940, the year of manufacture of the Buick coupe that the author owned for thirty years. Its speedometer went up to 110 miles per hour (on the dial, not on the road), and the following year the 1941 Buick's speedometer went up to 120. That's where it stayed for most big American cars until the rush for fuel economy and pollution controls brought top speeds below 100 miles per hour for the first time in over forty years.

Many of the early cars had no speedometer at all, and you judged your speed by how much the fenders were rattling. Up until 1914 the Model T Ford came with a speedometer as standard equipment. The dial went up to an incredible 60 miles per hour, and the car could actually hit that speed if you were going downhill. After 1914 the Model T was sold without a speedometer because Henry Ford wanted to lower the price of the car. It was not until the debut of the Model A in December 1927 that Ford once again offered a speedometer as standard equipment.

Today the numbers on your speedometer are much higher than the ones on the Model T, especially if you're driving a car that measures its speed not in miles but in kilometres. And if you aren't driving such a vehicle but wish you were, you can buy a decal that converts your old speedometer to metric. Why cruise at 65 when you can tear along at 110?

1904 PELYCOSAUR

The word *dinosaur* was coined in 1841 (see page 222). Since then, many varieties of these fearsome creatures have been added to the English language, including *brontosaurus* (1892), *stegosaurus* (1892), *triceratops* (1892) and *tyrannosaur* (1924). The pelycosaur was a quadraped reptile of prehistoric (Permian) times, often with enlarged dorsal vertebrae. It may have been a forerunner of the dinosaurs.

1905 SMOG

The following sentence appeared in the London *Globe* on July 27, 1905: "The other day at a meeting of the Public Health Congress, Dr. Des Voeux did a public service in coining a new word for the London fog, which was referred to as 'smog', a compound of 'smoke' and 'fog'."

The good doctor was thinking only of London when he coined his new word, but the filthy atmospheric conditions that arose over other cities around the world guaranteed that this word would spread to the four corners of the English-speaking world. The U.S. city of Los Angeles is practically synonymous with smog, while Tokyo also had a reputation for badly polluted air for many years. Tokyo policemen directing traffic had to return periodically to their home station to breathe fresh air from a machine to avoid being overcome by the fumes out on the street. And ships were known to collide in Tokyo's harbour because of thick smog. Currently, the *Guinness Book of World Records* cites Mexico City and Beijing as having the worst air quality in the world.

1906 SUFFRAGETTE

When the word *suffragette* (based on the Latin, *suffragium*, "a vote") first appeared in London's *Daily Mail* on January 10, 1906, it was used with quotation marks around it to indicate it was a new word. But the feminist movement it stood for was not so new. During the last quarter of the nineteenth century, women in Britain and North America began moving out of the kitchen and into the offices, shops and factories. When these formerly male bastions had been breached, women began demanding suffrage — the right to vote. And because they agitated for female suffrage, they became know as *suffragettes*.

The most famous leader of the suffragette movement in Britain was Emmeline Pankhurst, who, with her two daughters, formed the Women's Social and Political Union in 1903 to work for the goal of female suffrage. During the 1906 election, female hecklers disrupted scores of political meetings and gained the attention of the Liberals, who were voted into office. But the new prime minister did nothing but offer advice. "Go on pestering," he told the suffragettes, who took his advice with a vengeance.

Over the next few years the more militant suffragettes smashed windows, set fire to empty buildings, hooted and jeered from the House of Commons gallery, cut telephone wires, disrupted the mail and used acid to burn the slogan "Votes for Women" into the grass on golf courses. The men of Britain, with the police backing them up, refused to budge, and dozens of suffragettes were regularly dragged off to jail.

By the spring of 1914 the women of Britain were no closer to getting the vote than they had been in 1906. Then, on June 28, in a city in the Balkan peninsula, the heir to the Austrian throne was shot dead by a Serbian nationalist. Six weeks later the continent of Europe was ablaze with war. By the end of World War I, thousands of women in Britain and North America had worked in factories and hospitals and even seen action as ambulance drivers on the battlefield. The men were now convinced that women were capable of doing a man's job — and the right to vote was extended to all adults, in Britain, the United States and Canada, regardless of sex.

Also in 1906: *psychoanalysis, sidekick*

1907 TELEVISION

Like the word *telephone* in the previous century, the word *television* was coined many years before its actual invention. The new term consisted of a Greek root *tele*, "afar," and a Latin root *visio*, "sight," prompting a language purist of the time to remark, "Television is a bastardized word. Nothing good will ever come of it."

The world's first television transmission took place in a London attic on October 30, 1925, when John Logie Baird of Scotland broadcast the first faint images using a primitive contraption made of cardboard, piano wire, darning needles, old electric motors, wire, glue, string, wax and lenses. When he saw that it actually worked, Baird rushed downstairs in search of a live performer and returned with William Taynton, a fifteen-year-old office boy. And thus Taynton became the first person in the world to be seen on television.

Baird's device was slow in catching on. The 1939 edition of *Compton's Encyclopedia* pessimistically predicted that television had no chance at all of commercial success in the United States. To serve the entire nation would require a chain of stations fifty miles apart, and "the expense would be enormous, and neither the sale of receiving sets nor advertising revenue offers sure prospects of paying a profit on the investment."

1908 DÉTENTE

Although the name Henry Kissinger usually springs to mind as the architect of *détente* (a relaxation of tension between countries formerly hostile to one another, particularly between the United States and Soviet Union), the term itself goes back to August 17, 1908, when the *Times* of London reported: "A change in the European situation ... had ... set in.... The characteristic feature of this transformation may be called a *détente*." Europeans had good reason to heave a collective sign of relief in 1908: the tension that had flared up in 1905 and 1906 over disputes between Germany and Morocco was subsiding; the shock of the Russo-Japanese War (in which, for the first time in modern history, an Asiatic nation had defeated a European one in battle) was beginning to fade; there was growing hope that the nations of Europe might indeed be able to settle their differences without resorting to war. That hope was sustained for six more years.

The term *détente* was revived in the early 1970s, when it was adopted as virtually the cornerstone of U.S. foreign policy for the entire decade. The *Manchester Guardian Weekly*, on July 10, 1977, explains the term: "Kissinger's solution was détente (he wasn't the first to come up with the idea, but he was the one to get it implemented). Détente, as the French writer Andre Fontaine neatly put it, was not the same as peace or else it would have been called peace. It was an arrangement whereby a combination of political, military, technical and commercial agreements were reached for the expressed purpose of preventing the sort of confrontation that would end in mutual annihilation. For a time, roughly between the summers of 1972 and 1975, the process was working."

Also in 1908: *panties, powerboat*

1909 JOYRIDE

Merriam-Webster defines this as "a ride taken for pleasure (as in a car or aircraft); especially an automobile ride marked by reckless driving (as in a stolen car)." Car thieves began plying their trade as soon as automobiles began to be manufactured back in the 1890s. Because these early cars were mostly open cars with primitive technology, they were relatively easy to steal. One anti-theft device available back then was an inflatable man. You blew him up and positioned him behind the steering wheel whenever you parked your car and left if for a while.

1910 Joystick

Popping into the language just one year after *joyride*, a *joystick* is the lever in an aircraft that controls its motion up and down and side to side, and was probably so-called because of the thrill of flying, especially in early aircraft with an open cockpit. Thirty-one years later, a young pilot named John Gillespie Magee Jr. immortalized the joy of flying by composing a poem he scribbled on the back of an envelope containing a letter from his mother. It was found among his personal belongings after he was shot down and killed in 1941:

High Flight

Oh! I have slipped the surly bonds of Earth
And danced the skies on laughter-silvered wings;
Sunward I've climbed, and joined the tumbling mirth
of sun-split clouds, — and done a hundred things
You have not dreamed of — wheeled and soared and swung
High in the sunlit silence. Hov'ring there,
I've chased the shouting wind along, and flung
My eager craft through footless halls of air

Up, up, the long, delirious, burning blue
I've topped the wind-swept heights with easy grace
Where never lark or even eagle flew —
And, while with silent lifting mind I've trod
The high untrespassed sanctity of space,
Put out my hand, and touched the face of God.

1911 AUTISM

Leah Myers of Pickering, Ontario, is the mother of an autistic child. Leah has written a handbook for teachers to help them be more aware of the special needs of autistic children, and because of her personal connection with this topic, I asked her to write the commentary for this entry.

When the Swiss psychiatrist Eugen Bleuler first coined the term in 1911 (from the Greek *auto*, meaning "self"), he undoubtedly had in mind the disorder's distinguishing feature of the afflicted individuals' appearing to "live in their own little world." Individuals with autism often appear unresponsive to people around them, and this lack of responsiveness can take the form of silence, gaze aversion, rocking, covering their ears or any number of other behaviours.

Formerly called "childhood psychosis" or "childhood schizophrenia," autism is now understood to be a distinct medical, rather than a psychological, disorder. While it is still considered somewhat mysterious, much more is now understood about the varying degrees of sensory impairment to which many of the disorder's unusual behaviours and mannerisms can be attributed. Although behavioural and other therapies may help individuals to overcome some of their challenges and reduce maladaptive behaviours, there is, as yet, no cure for autism.

1912 BRASSIERE

According to *The People's Almanac* by David Wallechinsky and Irving Wallace, the brassiere was first invented by an American named Otto Titzling (yes, that was his real name) in 1912. It seems that in 1910 Titzling had heard a young opera singer named Swanhilda Olafsen complain that her corset did not adequately support her huge breasts. Rising to the challenge, Titzling designed a chest halter to provide uplift and shapeliness for Swanhilda's bosom.

But Titzling didn't cash in on his brainstorm because he never bothered to get a patent. Then, around 1929, a French dress designer and former World War I flying ace named Philippe de Brassière arrived in New York and began marketing a glamorized version of Titzling's plain chest halter. Because of Philippe's flair for flogging his wares (his *under*-wares, if you will), his name became a household word.

But Philippe de Brassière named himself after the fact because, according to the *OED*, the word *brassiere* appeared in print as early as 1912. Perhaps Philippe Whoever-He-Was adopted the name Brassière in the hopes of replacing the term *chest halter* with its more glamorous sounding synonym. If so, he certainly succeeded.

1913 CROSSWORD

The first crossword puzzle in the United States appeared in the *New York World* on December 21, 1913. By the end of the decade, crossword puzzle fever was rampant on both sides of the Atlantic and reached such epidemic proportions in England in the 1920s that the London Zoo refused to answer any more questions about the names of unusual animals. English libraries began blotting out the crosswords in all their newspapers because crossword puzzle addicts were monopolizing all the papers. And during a crossword puzzle contest in Liverpool, one contestant had the gall to go to the dictionary in his local library and black out a key word needed to complete the contest so as to discourage others from horning in on his prize.

Also in 1913: *gumshoe*

1914 GESUNDHEIT

The earliest entry in the *OED* for *Gesundheit* is February 1914, when *Everybody's* magazine contained the sentence: "'Saved your life,' he murmured mechanically, as one suffixes 'Gesundheit' to a sneeze." That quote suggests that *Gesundheit* had been a follow-up for sneezes for quite some time already. Perhaps it was only part of spoken English for a number of years, or perhaps the readers who helped the Oxford people research their mammoth dictionary simply did not find whatever earlier examples of *Gesundheit,* from the German for "health," exist in print.

A similar interjection is "Skol!", used as a toast to your health, from the old Scandinavian word for *skull.* This word got its start back in the days of the Viking invasions in the eighth, ninth and tenth centuries. Whenever an enemy was defeated, the leader's head would be chopped off and his skull would be used as a drinking vessel by the Vikings, who swallowed his blood while it was still warm so that his strength would be added to theirs.

1915 WHIZBANG

Merriam-Webster defines this word as "one that is conspicuous for noise, speed, excellence, or startling effect." It may have been inspired by an automobile of that era. Some of them were fast and noisy by 1915.

Several decades later, Roland Drake, a student at North Toronto Collegiate, coined the term *quizbang* for a surprise test.

Also in 1915: *persnickety*

1916 BLIMP

When the Wright brothers took to the air at Kitty Hawk, North Carolina, on December 17, 1903, in the world's first heavier-than-air flying machine, the rest of the world was amazed, but not entirely convinced that this was the way to move across the sky. Ever since the Montgolfier brothers had flown over Paris in a balloon in 1783, numerous experiments had been conducted to make the balloon a useful mode of transportation. The secret lay in making the balloon *dirigible,* or capable of being steered. When the Wright brothers were busy with their work, other inventors in Europe and the United States were solving this problem. Out of their experiments emerged three types of airships: rigid, semirigid and nonrigid. The British referred to the nonrigid ones as "limp airships," and some etymologists claim the Type B-limp, a model widely used during World War I for aerial reconnaissance, was contracted to *blimp.*

On July 27, 1918, the *Illustrated London News* identified the brilliant neologist who first began using the new term: "Nobody in the R.N.A.S.

[Royal Naval Air Service] ever called them anything but 'Blimps', an onomatopoeic name invented by that genius for apposite nomenclature, the late Horace Shortt."

Horace has been dead a long time now, but if he came back to life and plunked himself in front of a TV set tuned to a major sports event, he would be delighted to see his word living on in the Goodyear blimps that provide aerial television images.

1917 CAMOUFLAGE

Although camouflage in one form or another has been practised since ancient times (for example, the Trojan horse in Homer's *Iliad*, or the shrubbery of Birnam Wood in Act V of *Macbeth*), the word itself did not enter the English language until World War I, when soldiers needed protection from aerial reconnaissance. According to the *OED*, the first newspaper to use the term was the London *Daily Mail* on May 25, 1917: "The act of hiding anything from your enemy is termed 'camouflage'." A couple of months later on July 16, that same paper reported that "the King paid a visit to what is called a camouflage factory." By the end of the war *camouflage* was a household word, and the May 23, 1919, edition of *Athenaeum* claimed that "'camouflage' [is] a word that ... has met with more wear and tear in a few months than many receive in a century."

By the outbreak of World War II, the airplane was such a highly developed weapon of destruction that camouflage had to be employed on a massive scale. According to the *Encyclopaedia Britannica*, "in World War II everything from individual soldiers and vehicles to whole cities was given protective coloration. Uniforms, helmets, trucks, tanks and guns were painted or covered with leaves and brush; airfields were blacked out while neighbouring areas were set ablaze with lights; dummy harbours, shipyards, fleets, manufacturing plants, armies, and cities were constructed with pneumatic decoys and other materials. Smoke-screens were also used on a large scale..." And so it is not surprising to discover that *camouflage* has its roots in the French *camouflet*, "a puff of smoke."

But one type of camouflage became obsolete by 1942 when the advent of radar made camouflage paint no longer effective or necessary for airplanes and submarines.

1918 Posh

Some books on the origin of words will tell you that *posh* became a word when Peninsula and Oriental steamship liners travelled regularly between England and India. Well-to-do passengers booked passage on the shady, or port, side of the ship while travelling to India, and on the starboard side when returning home, in order to avoid the discomfort of the blazing-hot sunlight in their staterooms. To facilitate this change of cabins, round-trip steamer tickets were stamped P.O.S.H. — for *Port Out, Starboard Home.* Eventually the letters lost their capitalization and *posh* became a synonym for luxurious.

But not everyone agrees with this origin. The 1980 edition of the *Oxford American Dictionary* says, "This word is sometimes said to have been derived from the initials of 'port out, starboard home,' referring to the more expensive side for accommodation on ships formerly travelling between England and India. This suggestion lacks foundation. The origin of posh is uncertain."

Be that as it may, there is no dispute over the origin of *port* and *starboard.* These two terms go back to the days of the dragon-prowed Viking ships that ravaged the coast of Europe in the eighth, ninth and tenth centuries. Because these ships were pointed at both ends, they were steered not by a rudder mounted in the middle of the stern but by a steerboard (an old Viking word) mounted to the right of the stern. When coming into port, the helmsman would dock on the left side of the ship to prevent the steerboard from hitting the side of the dock. And that's why today port is on the left and starboard is on the right.

Also in 1918: *extrovert, kerflooey, keypunch, red cap, three-point landing*

1919 Supersonic

In 1919 this word had nothing to do with airplanes that flew faster than the speed of sound. *Supersonic* simply referred to sounds that are at a frequency too high for the human ear to hear. A publication called *The Electrician* was the first to make mention of it: "The French have experimented with a system in which a continuous wave signal is heterodyned to a supersonic frequency." Not until 1945 did the word *supersonic* take on the additional meaning that is so familiar today.

As World War II neared its end, the aviation industry was on the brink of exciting new developments, including the jet engine. The prospect of flying at speeds far greater than ever before was now a distinct possibility, and that dream was soon realized. It was on October 14, 1947, that U.S. Air Force Captain Charles Yeager flew the experimental Bell X-1, accelerating beyond the speed of sound and thus becoming the first supersonic pilot in history.

Because of their high cost, supersonic aircraft remained the exclusive preserve of the military until 1968, when the Soviet Union tested the Tu-144, its first SST (supersonic transport). One year later, two prototypes of the Anglo-French Concorde were test-flown; despite the vociferous protests of environmentalists who objected to the sonic booms and predicted they would do permanent damage to the ozone layer of Earth's atmosphere, commercial flights of the Concorde began in January 1976. These flights finally ended in 2003 for a very old-fashioned reason: Concorde service had become a massive money-loser.

1920 PARANORMAL

This word can be used as a noun or adjective and is a synonym for "supernatural" (that which is not scientifically explainable).

The word *normal* goes back to circa 1696, and is probably older than that. The noun *normalcy*, the state of being normal, goes back to 1857. During the 1920 U.S. presidential election, Warren Harding campaigned by promising a "return to normality," even though that word was not yet in any dictionary (it is now). He won the election.

1921 FASCISM

In one of Aesop's fables, which were written in the sixth century B.C., a father shows his three sons a bundle of sticks. He breaks three sticks one by one, then tries to break the whole bundle at once, but cannot. The lesson is clear: if his three sons stood united, no one could break them. If they stood alone, they would fall.

The ancient Romans were very impressed with this fable — so much so, in fact, that they used a bundle of sticks (or *fasces* in Latin) to symbolize the authority of Roman magistrates. Hoping some of the glory of ancient Rome would rub off on his own political party, Benito Mussolini adopted the *fasces* as the symbol for his newly formed Fascist Party of Italy. He carried this symbol with him in his famous March on Rome in 1922, when he seized power and became dictator of Italy.

Mussolini's word outlasted him. He was overthrown during the Allied invasion of Italy in 1943, then later captured and hanged upside-down with his mistress, in a public square, while an angry crowd of his countrymen finished him off. The word *fascism* is now used to describe any political movement that smacks of autocracy or dictatorship.

1922 GIMMICK

In their *Wise-crack Dictionary*, published in 1926, Maines and Grant include this entry: "Gimmick, device used for making a fair game crooked." Apparently at that time, this word applied to an apparatus used to dishonestly regulate a gambling game. Later in the same year, *American Speech* magazine carried this sentence: "Every snipe endeavors to impress the poor swabbos with his talk of gillguys, gadgets, and gimmicks!"

Most dictionaries describe the etymology of this word as either "uncertain" or "unknown"; but the November 1936 issue of *Words* magazine claims to have the answer: "The word *gimac* [earlier spelling of gimmick] means 'a gadget'. It is an anagram of the word *magic*, and is used by magicians the same way as others use the word 'thing-a-ma-bob'."

Advertising executives would agree with that. If you have the right gimmick for the product or service you're flogging, your sales charts will go straight up as if by magic. One of the greatest advertising geniuses of all time was the circus magnate P. T. Barnum, who was fond of saying, "There's a sucker born every minute." He once used the word *egress* (a fancy word for "exit") as a gimmick to keep his business booming. In his early days, Barnum operated a museum of natural history in lower Manhattan; visitors would linger so long to look at the exhibits that others couldn't get in. Alarmed at the loss of potential business, Barnum put on his thinking cap and decided — in a stroke of pure genius — to make the *exit* one of the attractions. Over the cage that housed the mother tiger and her cubs, he installed a big sign that said, "TIGRESS."

Then, over a nearby doorway, he put a sign reading, "TO THE EGRESS." Expecting to see yet another exotic creature, many spectators in the crowded museum pushed their way through the door, only to find themselves out on the street.

1923 ZIPPER

The history of the zipper stretches back to 1891, when a Chicago inventor named Whitcomb Judson designed and patented a series of hooks and eyes with a sliding clasp to open and close them. But it was many years before a reliable sliding fastener was developed. The man most responsible for perfecting it was a Swedish engineer named Gideon Sundback, whose Hookless #2 appeared in 1917 and became the zipper we know today.

In 1921 the B.F. Goodrich Company decided to market a new model of galoshes with hookless fasteners. The company coined the brand name *Zipper* for the new overshoes in 1923. They were an instant success — so much so that the word lost its capital letter and entered the popular lexicon as the name for the fastener instead of the galoshes.

Also in 1923: *aerosol, robot, hijack*

1924 BEAUTICIAN

The 1920s generated a host of new words and phrases to reflect the time and money Americans were now spending on having a good time: *speakeasies, hip flasks, bathtub gin, Tin Lizzies, raccoon coats* and buying stocks *on margin*. Some of that money flowed into the pockets of the proprietors of beauty parlours as the women of America, inspired by the specimens of female pulchritude that flashed across the silent movie screens, sought to improve upon the raw material supplied by Mother Nature. Beauty parlours set their prices by that old American standby: whatever the traffic will bear. And if you wanted to charge fancy prices, you stopped calling yourself a *hairdresser* and started calling yourself a *beautician* (in much the same way, several decades later, that barbers transformed themselves into hair stylists).

Two years after *beautician* broke into print, *cosmetician* appeared on the scene, surfacing first in *American Speech* magazine in a report on "a Missouri law ... [that] speaks of hair-dressers as cosmeticians and cosmetologists." Both *beautician* and *cosmetician* were patterned after *mortician*, the fellow who makes your Uncle Harry look better dead than alive. *Mortician* came into circulation in the 1890s to replace the more mundane *undertaker*.

Also in 1925: *rayon, penis envy*

1925 MOTEL

The world's first motel, appropriately named the Motel Inn, opened in San Luis Obispo, California, on December 12, 1925. The owner, Robert Heineman, concocted the new word, and it caught on — but not exactly overnight. Heineman's new word was not granted official recognition by dictionary publishers until 1950, a full twenty-five years after he coined it.

Why did it take so long to catch on? Partly because of the popularity of tourist homes and tourist cabins, which dotted the American landscape until after World War II. And possibly because the word *motel* was competing with two other words — *autel* and *autotel* — for the honour of describing this new automobile-oriented overnight accommodation.

1926 GATECRASHER

What better decade than the Roaring Twenties for *gatecrasher* to break into print? These were the days of flappers, the Charleston, and roadsters with rumble seats. We usually use *gatecrasher* today to describe someone attending a private party uninvited, but the first example in print, from the London *Daily News* of June 28, 1927, had a slightly different emphasis: "'One-eyed Connolly' [is] the champion American 'gate crasher' (one who gains admittance to big sporting events without payment)." In the following year the *Sunday Dispatch* used the word somewhat differently: "He was arrested for 'gate-crashing' over the frontier from Canada to America without a passport." But this quote from 1931 has a decidedly familiar ring: "Geoffrey Hays is giving a party tonight — shall we gate-crash?"

If you throw a party at your home and someone arrives uninvited, we call that person a *gatecrasher* whether or not you have a front gate through which the guests have to pass to reach your front door. The word *gate* refers back to the first quote cited above, with "One-eyed Connolly" breaking into sporting events without paying. Because such events use a gate where tickets are collected, the term *gatecrasher* fits perfectly. If an uninvited guest darkens the door to your party, he or she should really be called a *doorcrasher* — but this term has already been snapped up by department stores with on-sale merchandise priced so low that the customers crash through the front door to get their hands on it.

Also in 1926: *stablemate, steroid*

1927 PARATROOPER

The word *parachute* goes back to 1785, and *trooper* to 1640. But troops apparently didn't start jumping out of airplanes (with a parachute) until 1927. That's the same year that Charles Lindbergh made his famous solo flight across the Atlantic in *The Spirit of St. Louis*, now displayed at the Smithsonian in Washington, D.C.

Also in 1927: *nova, paradiddle, upchuck*

1928 PENICILLIN

The wonder drug we call *penicillin* was discovered in 1928 by a Scottish bacteriologist named Alexander Fleming. He named it from the Latin root *penicillium*, "a painter's brush," because the moulds from which the drug is extracted produce tiny tufts of filaments that look like a painter's brush. The Latin *penicillium* in turn comes from the Latin *penis*, meaning "tail." This description is entirely fitting when you consider that penicillin has been used in the treatment of venereal disease, an ailment that can produce great discomfort in the penis.

For several years, Fleming's discovery attracted no widespread attention because it could only be produced in very small quantities. After the outbreak of World War II, a research laboratory in Peoria, Illinois, began searching for a way to mass-produce it. Every day, a woman from the lab was sent to the local markets to gather rotting produce. She soon became known as "Mouldy Mary" and one day returned with an overripe melon that produced a culture in which penicillin flourished. Allied troops were soon being supplied with penicillin, and by 1944 it was available for civilian use as well. Much of today's penicillin can be traced directly back to the rotting melon found by Mouldy Mary.

Also in 1928: *downtime, macho*

1929 NUDIST

Several great historical figures are known to have paraded around in the nude. In 334 B.C., in full view of all his troops, Alexander the Great ran naked three times around the city walls of Troy. In medieval England, Lady Godiva mounted her horse and rode naked through the streets of her hometown to protest the latest increase in taxes. Giacomo Casanova, the greatest lover and lecher of the eighteenth century, must surely have been naked nearly all the time.

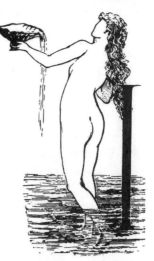

But it took the Roaring Twenties to bring out nudists (from the Latin *nudus,* "naked") in large numbers. On July 1, 1929, *Time* reported: "Much publicity has been given the Nudist colony on an island in the Seine near Paris." The article then proceeded to expose what these nudists were all about: "Made in Germany, imported to France, is the cult of Nudism, a mulligan stew of vegetarianism, physical culture and pagan worship." The fad soon crossed the English Channel, where the *Daily Express* stood ready to cover it (if you'll pardon the pun): "Nudist camps have sprung up all over England in the past fortnight, in which happy families disport themselves in the sunshine."

Also in 1929: *foreplay, spermicide*

1930 WHODUNIT

Whodunit was coined in 1930 by Donald Gordon in *American News of Books* as a slangy new term for detective stories, especially those in which several characters are likely suspects and the one guilty of the crime is not exposed until the last few pages. It was entirely fitting that this new word was coined at the outset of the Great Depression, because one of the cheapest forms of entertainment during the 1930s was a visit to the local library to read the latest murder mystery.

A main entry in *The Second Barnhart Dictionary of New English* is *whydunit*: "a mystery novel, play, or motion picture which deals primarily with the motivation for the crime." First breaking into print in the *Manchester Guardian* on August 7, 1971, *whydunit* was carried by *Time* on June 4, 1973: "Connery takes over the interrogation and in the process beats the man to death. This much we know almost from the beginning, so the film is less of a whodunit than a whydunit."

1931 LOW-SLUNG

The American Underslung was an automobile built from 1905 to 1914. Its low profile was achieved by having the frame slung under the axles. The term *underslung* itself dates back to 1903.

In November 1929, the Auburn Automobile Company of Auburn, Indiana, introduced the L-29 Cord, a styling sensation with a height of only 61 inches, the low-slung stance made possible by front-wheel drive, thus eliminating the driveshaft usually found under the floor of the passenger cabin. Merriam-Webster dates *low-slung* to 1931, but it was probably in use before that.

1932 NYLON

According to a popular misconception, the word *nylon* was coined by abbreviating New York (NY) and London (LON). The true story behind the birth of this word can be found in the February 9, 1940, issue of *Women's Wear Daily*, in a letter written by John W. Eckelberry of the du Pont Company, which invented the new fabric: "The word is a generic word coined by the du Pont Co. It is not a registered name or trademark.... We wish to emphasize the following additional points: First, that the letters n-y-l-o-n have absolutely no significance, etymologically or otherwise.... Because the names of two textile fibers in common use — namely 'cotton' and 'rayon,' end with letters 'on' ... it was felt that a word ending in 'on' might be desirable. A number of words ... were rejected because it was found they were not sufficiently distinct from words found in the dictionary, or in lists of classified trademarks. After much deliberation, the term 'nylon' was finally adopted."

Nylon stockings were available by 1940, when *Woman* magazine advised, "Dunk your nylons in rich suds of neutral soap." Twenty-five years later, on May 16, 1965, the *New York Times* reported: "By 1964, silk and rayon stockings were almost unknown in the United States, while production of nylons had risen to 83,900,000 dozen pairs."

Incidentally the founder of the du Pont Company was a French-born aristocrat named Eleuthère Irénée du Pont de Nemours who, in his spare time, was an amateur naturalist and birdwatcher. He was also a little eccentric, and proved it in 1807 by compiling two unusual dictionaries, *Crow-French* and *Nightingale-French*, which offered to the reader the French translation of the various calls of those two birds.

Also in 1932: *greenbelt*

1933 SUPERMARKET

At first, we had grocery stores, where you bought your groceries. Gradually, these stores got bigger and bigger, and added product lines (such as lawn furniture) that were totally inedible. To let customers know how special these bigger stores were, *supermarket* was coined as early as 1933.

Now here we are in the twenty-first century, and some supermarkets have grown so big and fancy that a new term was begging to be coined: *superstore*.

1934 GESTAPO

This word first came to the attention of the English language in 1934. It was the name for the German Secret Police established by Herman Göring in Prussia in 1933 and then extended to all of Germany the following year. The name itself is an acronym assembled from the first letters of **Geheime Staats-Polizei**, or Secret State Police. The power of the Gestapo in Nazi Germany was virtually unlimited. In addition to its role in quashing all political opposition, the Gestapo controlled the concentration camps where Jews and other unfortunates were exterminated by the millions. Gruesome medical experiments were also conducted at those places, and lampshades were fashioned out of human skin.

When Adolf Hitler came to power in Germany in 1933, almost no one could foresee the terror he would later unleash upon the world. In retrospect we can pinpoint three words that perhaps best sum up what Nazi Germany was all about: *Gestapo, blitzkrieg* (which joined the English language when Hitler attacked Poland on September 1, 1939; see page 279), and *genocide* (which entered English in 1944; see page 282).

Also in 1934: *face-lift, one-off, streamliner, winterize*

1935 CRACKDOWN

A crackdown is a strict enforcement of the rules or law, especially after a period of permissiveness, and is probably based on a combination of *crack the whip* and *lower the boom*. The first publication on record to use this word was the *Washington Post*, which on May 18, 1935, reported on the "threat of a 'crack-down' by the middle class group against those who put forward the legislation for abolishing public utility holding companies." Over the years since then, *crackdown* has been printed with or without a hyphen — and this raises an intriguing question: How do you know when to use a hyphen and when not to use it? Shakespeare himself probably wondered about it: To hyphenate or not to hyphenate — that is the question.

You can find the answer in the *Harper Dictionary of Contemporary Usage* by William and Mary Morris (who call themselves *co-authors*, not *coauthors*). They tell you the story of what happened a few years ago "when a major reference-book publisher decided to set the record straight on hyphenation by having an entire book written on the subject. The author chosen for the task was a woman who was chief judge of commas and hyphens for a major government department. Who else could possibly be better qualified to settle the matter once and for all?

"The book was finally published, at considerable expense, and proved to be an embarrassment for all concerned. The publisher discovered too late that almost no one in the fields of writing or editing books, newspapers, or magazines agreed with the rules on hyphens laid down by this author who, it turned out, for years had been single-handedly battling all other government departments because she preferred to hyphenate a whole range of words that everyone else preferred to write solid, and vice versa." John Benbow perhaps said it best when he wrote in the style book of the Oxford University Press: "If you take hyphens seriously, you will surely go mad."

In other words, there's no use trying to crack down on hyphenation.

1936 STRIPTEASE

The entertainment industry enjoyed unparalleled prosperity all through the Great Depression as people went to the movies or listened to the radio for a brief escape from the harsh economic realities of daily life.

Travelling burlesque shows always included some *stripteasing*, a word dated by Merriam-Webster to 1936. But those who perform the act, *stripteasers*, got their name back in 1930. And in an apparent attempt to make that profession respectable, the word *ecdysiast* (a synonym for stripteaser) appeared by 1940. It's based on the Greek *ekdysis*, which also gives us *ecdysis*, a molting or shedding of an outer layer of skin.

1937 XEROX

When an American manufacturer of outdoor toilets for construction sites wanted to label its latest model Heee-r-r-r-r-r-re's Johnny!, it was prevented from doing so by a court opinion that those two words, expressed in that particular fashion, were the exclusive property of Johnny Carson and his television program, *The Tonight Show*.

Brand names and trademarks constantly run the risk of being pirated by entrepreneurial imitators, especially if a brand name becomes so popular that it turns into just another word in the English language. The Xerox Corporation sent to all its stockholders a letter pointing out that *aspirin* started out as a brand name but soon became a generic term — in the public domain — because so many people used it as a synonym for headache pill. The corporation went on to explain that the name *Xerox* could become another *aspirin* if people use it as a synonym for "photocopy." Other names that have fallen off the brand-name wagon or are in danger of doing so include Kleenex, Coke, Levis, Band-Aid, Scotch tape, Frigidaire and Linotype. It's ironic that companies spend a great deal of money on advertising to popularize their brand names, and then often have to spend additional sums of money to protect those names if they become too widely used.

And if the company doesn't run ads in magazines or send letters to editors or broadcasters who treat the brand name as a generic term, it becomes very hard to defend the brand in court once a competitor starts using it. The onus is on the company that originated the brand name to prove that it has done everything within reason to protect it. And that's why the Xerox Corporation tells its stockholders, "Copy things, don't 'Xerox' them."

The name *Xerox*, incidentally, comes from the Greek *xeros*, "dry," because Xerox photocopiers use a dry method of production — as distinct from the older spirit duplicators that rely on fluid.

Also in 1937: *carhop, fibreglass, neoprene*

1938 FLAK

World War II was responsible for the introduction of hundreds of new words and phrases to the English language, including *blitz, gremlin, Jeep, radar, gung-ho, fifth column, quisling, Quonset hut, antipersonnel, panzer, luftwaffe, blockbuster, expendables, genocide, kamikaze, atomic bomb* and *iron curtain*. Some words engendered by World War II entered English even before the war itself broke out; a prime example came along in 1938 to describe antiaircraft fire: *flak*. It was coined by contracting the German *Fliegerabwehrkanonen*, which means "aviator defence guns," and it first appeared in a book called *Jane's Fighting Ships*: "[On a German vessel] A .A. guns, 4.1 inch, 3.5 inch on H.A. mounts ('Flak')." Two years later, this new word was part of everyday English, as *The Times* of September 16, 1940, reveals: "The word 'Flak' is probably used in every Bomber Command pilot's report after a raid on Germany." Three days later, Flight carried this line: "One of the British bombers which raided Berlin ... had been damaged when diving through heavy *Flak* fire." The use of quotation marks and italics by these publications reminds us of the newness of the word when it appeared back then. By the end of the war, it had lost both its capital letter and its quotation marks, a sure sign that it was considered part of regular English.

Some new words born in or around World War II died after the war came to an end, but *flak* was not one of them. It is used today as a synonym for argument ("Don't give me any flak") and as an adjective for the protective clothing worn by British soldiers in Belfast, who put on their *flak jackets* before going out on patrol.

Also in 1938: *babushka, googol*

1939 Blitz

On August 23, 1939, a stunned world heard the news that Hitler and Stalin had just signed the Nazi-Soviet Non-Aggression Pact which removed the final obstacle that lay in the path of Hitler's plans for the invasion of Poland. Just over one week later the German forces, both on land and in the air, suddenly invaded Poland and overran the country in three short weeks. The Germans called it *Blitzkrieg*, or "lightning war," because of the speed with which it was carried out. The shortened form, *blitz*, quickly entered the English language.

As World War II dragged on, other German terms joined the English language, prompting a Mrs. Faning to write a letter of protest to the *Daily Telegraph* in October 1941:

> Sir — I view with concern the increasing introduction of German words into our language — such words as "blitz," "panzer," "luftwaffe" and others.
>
> Surely it is sad to reflect on the ease with which Germany can invade our language, if not our shores!
>
> If no check is put upon this practice these horrible words

will become incorporated into our English vocabulary. German is uncouth and hardly fit for a civilized nation."

It's unfortunate that King George I of England was unavailable for comment at the time (he died in 1727). When he became king of England in 1714, he had lived in Germany all his life and couldn't speak a word of English!

Also in 1939: *addictive, Disneyesque, walkie-talkie*

1940 JEEP

The Jeep, as everyone knows, is a small, lightweight military vehicle widely used during World War II and now often employed as a recreational vehicle. Joe Frazer, the president of Willys-Overland from 1939 to 1944, claims to have coined the name from the initials G.P., a military abbreviation of General Purpose Vehicle. Soldiers and test drivers had lots of names (some of them unprintable) for the vehicle, too, including *Bantam, Blitz Buggy, Bug, Gnat, GP, Midget, Pygmy* and *Peep*. Gradually *Peep* was elbowed out by *Jeep*, and when the Washington *Daily News* reporter Katy Hillyer rode in one in February 1941, she asked what it was called. Someone said "Jeep," and that's what she put in her story. The name stuck.

Also in 1940: *extraordinaire, quisling*

1941 RADAR

Radar was not invented overnight. Heinrich Hertz first demonstrated in 1888 that electromagnetic waves can be reflected, yet when Marconi presented a paper to the Institute of Radio Engineers in New York on June 20, 1922, describing the feasibility of providing ships with radio beams for detecting other ships in fog or darkness, the first radar sets still lay several years in the future. In the late 1930s, scientists in the United States and Britain began constructing the first rudimentary radar sets and installing them on an experimental basis on ships and planes. These experiments were still in progress when World War II broke out in September 1939. After the fall of France in June 1940, the full fury of Hitler's military might was unleashed against Britain as

German planes tried to bomb the island into submission. British fighter planes scrambled to meet the invaders, guided to their points of interception by the magic of radar, a weapon that the Germans did not yet have. By the spring of 1941, Hitler realized his projected invasion of Britain would have to be postponed indefinitely.

Meanwhile, in the Pacific, Japan and the United States were heading toward a fateful rendezvous. On the morning of December 7, 1941, Private Joseph P. Lockhard detected the approach of planes on the radar equipment at Pearl Harbor and flashed a report to his superior officer. Because some American planes were due to arrive from the mainland that very morning, no action was taken. Radar had issued the warning, but it went unheeded. Shortly thereafter, Japanese bombs began falling on American forces stationed at Pearl Harbor.

The word *radar* (an acronym based on *ra*dio *d*etection *a*nd *r*anging) may have been coined before the year 1941, but the *OED* has found no evidence of it. The development of this invention had been a carefully guarded secret until the Japanese attack on Pearl Harbor. By the end of 1942, thousands of radar sets were in use by the Allies and *radar* had become part of everyday English. And before the end of the 1950s, radar was being used to catch speeding motorists.

Also in 1941: *prang*

1942 WHITEOUT

A blizzard that reduces visibility almost down to zero is a whiteout. The word was coined as early as 1942 as a variation on *blackout*, which goes back to 1913. *Blizzard* itself goes back to 1829. Many new words appeared in 1942, including *all-wheel*, *dozer* (for *bulldozer*), *fanzine*, *geoscience*, *harrumph*, *king-size* (probably in reference to cigarettes) and *spelunker*.

1943 ACRONYM

An acronym is a word formed from the first letter or letters of other words (from the Greek *akros*, "at the top," and *onoma*, "name"). It's easy to understand why this word appeared when it did: Franklin Roosevelt's New Deal legislation in the 1930s spawned a plethora of Depression-fighting programs that were known by their initials alone: CCC (Civilian Conservation Corps), WPA (Works Progress Administration), AAA (Agricultural Adjustment Act), TVA (Tennessee Valley Authority), and many more. When World War II got under way, the trend continued, with many initials now being pronounced as actual words, including *WAC, WAVE, radar* and *snafu* ("situation normal, all fouled up"). The February 1943 issue of *American Notes and Quotes* took notice of the new word coined to describe these new words: "Words made up of the initial letters or syllables of other words ... I have seen ... called by the name *acronym.*"

With the formation of the United Nations in San Francisco in October 1945, UNESCO (United Nations Educational, Scientific and Cultural Organization) and UNICEF (United Nations International Children's Emergency Fund) joined the ranks of acronyms. The National Biscuit Company also jumped on the acronymic bandwagon by calling itself Nabisco. A scuba diver is someone who uses a *s*elf-*c*ontained *u*nderwater *b*reathing *a*pparatus. And one of the most popular TV series of all time bases its title on an acronym formed from the initials for Mobile Army Surgical Hospital, better known as a MASH unit.

Also in 1943: *cannibalize, chino, falsie, pinup, pizzeria*

1944 GENOCIDE

The most gruesome word to emerge from World War II has to be *genocide* (from Greek *genos,* "race," and Latin *caedere,* "to kill"), first used by Dr. Raphael Lemkin in his book *Axis Rule in Occupied Europe*: "By 'genocide' we mean the destruction of a nation or of an ethnic group." He was referring of course to the Holocaust — the extermination of six million Jews in the death camps of Nazi Germany. The persistence of the Nazis in tracking down Jews all over occupied Europe has been poignantly immortalized by the author of *The Diary of a Young Girl*: Anne Frank.

Thanks to aerial photography, the Allied leaders were aware of the death camps before the end of the war, but they refused to authorize the bombing of rail lines leading into them, claiming that other targets had greater priority. Once Germany was defeated, the full horror of the death camps was made known to the world — and *genocide* quickly became part of the English language. The *Sunday Times* of London heralded its arrival on October 21, 1945: "The United Nations indictment of the 24 Nazi leaders has brought a new word into the language — genocide: … the extermination of racial and national groups."

1945 KAMIKAZE

In August 1281 a Mongol navy was attempting to invade Japan when a mighty wind came along and destroyed their ships. Japan was spared the invasion, and ever since, its people have referred to the *kamikaze* (divine wind) that saved the island nation from the enemy.

Toward the end of World War II, and especially after the surrender of Germany in May 1945, Japan once again faced the prospect of invasion, this time from the opposite direction. It was time again for a *kamikaze*, but rather than wait for the wind to blow the Americans away, the Japanese air force decided to create one of its own. Fighter pilots were urged to crash their fighter planes onto the decks of American warships in one last heroic bid to prevent the GIs from setting foot on Japanese soil.

The kamikaze raids, however, were no match for the atomic bomb that fell on Hiroshima. Three days later, on August 9, 1945, a similar bomb fell on Nagasaki. The Japanese warlords quickly indicated their willingness to surrender, and that took place on the deck of the U.S.S. *Missouri* in Tokyo Bay on September 2.

1946 BIKINI

On July 1, 1946, a joint U.S. Army–Navy task force detonated an atomic bomb on Bikini Atoll in the Pacific. Four days later, the French fashion designer Louis Reard unveiled his latest creation at a Paris fashion show: a skimpy, two-piece bathing suit. The atomic explosion at Bikini and Reard's new bathing suit captured world attention almost simultaneously, so Reard named his new brainchild the *bikini*. The first one was modelled by French designer Micheline Bernardi, and photographs of her explosively stunning figure were carried in newspapers around the world. She received fifty thousand fan letters.

By sheer coincidence, the first two letters of bikini are *bi*, the Latin word for "two." With the debut of the topless bikini in the mid-1960s, two words were coined to describe it: *monokini* (from the Greek *mono*, "one"), and *unikini* (from the Latin *uni*, "one"). So far, no dictionary publisher has seen fit to legitimize either. The most likely label these days for the lower half of the bikini would be "the bottom line."

Also in 1946: *fail-safe, kerfuffle, Latino, wolf whistle, twi-night*

1947 UNPUTDOWNABLE

This word is an adjective describing a book that's so fascinating the reader just can't put it down. American humorist Mark Twain (a.k.a. Samuel Clemens) wrote many books that still make people laugh nearly one hundred years after his death. And yet Twain himself claimed that his funniest book was never published — typesetters began reading it and died laughing before they could get it into print.

Also in 1947: *eyeliner, flying saucer, kickstand, Polaroid, retro-rocket, tranquilizer, transistor, gamesmanship*

1948 FAX

"Send me a fax!" That's a sentence heard every day nowadays, and it actually goes back to 1948, long before fax machines could be seen in every office. The word "fax" is a contraction and alteration of *facsimile* (a copy), and that word comes straight out of ancient Latin: *fac simile* — "to make similar." If Julius Caesar were alive today, he'd be proud to know that his native tongue is still being used to add new words to our language.

Also in 1948: *fast-forward, privatize*

1949 MS.

It will come as a surprise to many people to discover that this term, which really gained widespread use only during the 1970s, is more than fifty years old. An early example appeared on January 4, 1952, in *The Simplified Letter*, published by the national office of the Management Association in Philadelphia: "Use abbreviation Ms. for *all women* addressees. This modern style solves an age-old problem." In the revised edition of June 4 of the same year, it states, "Use abbreviation Ms. if not sure whether to use Mrs. or Miss." This new term got a big boost when the first issue of *Ms.* magazine appeared in January 1972.

But years before the women's libbers began burning their bras, the American humorist Ambrose Bierce (1842–1913) tackled the problem of linguistic sexism from the opposite direction. In *The Devil's Dictionary,* a collection of humorous definitions which appeared in his newspaper columns beginning in 1881, he explains how he would straighten things out: "Miss, *n.* A title with which we brand unmarried women to indicate that they are in the market. Miss, Missis (Mrs.) and Mister (Mr.) are the three most distinctly disagreeable words in the language, in sound and sense. Two are corruptions of Mistress; the other of Master. In the general abolition of social titles in this our country they miraculously escaped to plague us. If we must have them, let us be consistent and give one to the unmarried man. I venture to suggest Mush, abbreviated to Mh."

Unlike the modern term *Ms.,* which does not betray the marital status of the female, Bierce's Mush sought to reveal that of the male. If women's libbers and male chauvinists want to take Bierce to task over this, they're too late. He headed down to Mexico to cover a political revolution in 1913. After writing to a friend from Chihuahua on Boxing Day of that year, he was never seen or heard from again.

Also in 1949: *cortisone, falafel, flash-forward*

1950 PAPERBOUND

With the popularity of paperback versions of hardbound (or hardcover) books, nearly everyone can afford to have a personal library of good books. Synonymous with *paperback* is *paperbound,* which appears on the front cover of the *Oxford American Dictionary* (1980), "the most authoritative paperbound dictionary." But by a curious oversight, the word *paperbound* is not listed within that dictionary!

Also in 1950: *name-dropping,, spin-off, snowblower*

1951 NITPICKER

The *OED* gives *Collier's* magazine the credit for first using this word on November 24, 1951: "Two long-time Pentagon stand-bys are *fly-speckers* and *nit-pickers*. The first of these nouns refers to people whose sole occupation seems to be studying papers in the hope of finding flaws in the writing, rather than making any effort to improve the thought or meaning; nit-pickers are those who quarrel with trivialities of expression *and* meaning, but who usually end up without making concrete or justified suggestions for improvement."

Five years later this new word had made it all the way to the White House, as *Time* magazine notes on January 16, 1956: "The members of the Cabinet commented on the draft of the message, then commented on one another's comments. 'No nit-picking,' Vice President Nixon adjured his colleagues, but the Cabinet eventually sent out to the President a file of verbatim reaction that piled 1½ inches high."

Also in 1951: *globalization, knee-jerk, nerd, orbiter, whirlybird*

1952 CENTREFOLD

This word has been indelibly linked to *Playboy* magazine, launched by Hugh Hefner in the early 1950s. No volume number or date appeared on the first issue because Hefner wasn't sure at the time if there would be a second.

Also in 1952: *downrange, landfill, one-upmanship*

1953 COUNTDOWN

Although the act of performing a countdown must surely date back to at least July 1945, when the United States tested its first atomic bomb in the

New Mexico desert, the *OED* has found no evidence of the word itself in print before June 4, 1953. On that day the Birmingham (Alabama) *News* carried this sentence: "Observers on the mountain were able to hear the count-down on the [parachute] drop from the control tower."

One month later, on July 4, *Monsanto Magazine* wrote: "Time on the range is expressed in minutes before a missile is to be fired. This is called a 'count down.'"

The countdowns that have captured the most public attention are the ones at Cape Canaveral just prior to a spaceshot. Other words that have entered the English language as a result of those spaceshots include *liftoff, blast-off, nose cone, retrorockets* and *splashdown*. The advent of the space shuttle, which can be used over and over again because it can land, like an airplane, on a runway on solid ground, means that the word *splashdown* may well be on the road to obsolescence.

Also in 1953: *flyby, labour-intensive, retrofit, UFO, videotape, gay* (new meaning)

1954 Acetazolamide

If this word (pronounced a-se-ta-ZOL-a-mid) looks unfamiliar to you, you're lucky, because you have probably never suffered from convulsions or glaucoma or ever needed a diuretic. This drug, introduced in 1954, is used to treat all these conditions, each of which has an etymology worth looking at. *Convulsion* comes from the Latin *convellere* or *convulsus*, "to pull violently," and bears a striking resemblance to the Latin *vultur*, which gives us the word *vulture*, the name of a bird that pulls or pecks at a carcass. *Glaucoma* comes to us unchanged from the Latin *glaucoma*, "cataract," and is, according to the *American Heritage Dictionary*, "a disease of the eye characterized by high intraocular pressure, damaged optic disk, hardening of the eyeball, and partial or complete loss of vision." Its resemblance to the word *coma* is apparently only a coincidence, with *coma* coming from the Greek root *koma*, "deep sleep" or "lethargy." A *diuretic* is anything that increases your flow of urine, and it comes from the Greek *diourein*, "to pass urine," a root formed from *dia*, "through," and *ourein*, "to urinate." It shares the same prefix as *diarrhea* (from the Greek *dia*, "through," and *rheein*, "to flow").

Another drug whose name rhymes with *acetaxolamide* is *thalidomide*, which achieved widespread notoriety in the early 1960s when it was linked to birth defects after being given to expectant mothers.

Also in 1954: *far-out, fastback, repro*

1955 KARATE

In 1945, as World War II drew to a close, Japan donated a deadly word to the English language: *kamikaze* (see page 283). In the ten years that followed, America's foreign policy on the Far East concentrated on the containment of communism and the turning of Japan from a wartime enemy into a peacetime ally. With a large American army of occupation in Japan, it was inevitable that the two cultures would begin to mingle. One feature of Japanese culture that was eagerly adopted by many Americans was an interest in the martial arts, particularly *karate* (from the Japanese *karate*, "empty hand").

In *The Fighting Spirit of Japan*, published in 1955, E.J. Harrison reported: "Karate resembles both jujutsu and judo … A single karate technique is capable of inflicting fatal injury upon its victim." By the next decade, the power of karate was well known, as shown by this 1966 exchange from *The Crying of Lot Forty-nine* by Thomas Pynchon:

> "I'm unarmed, you can frisk me."
> "While you karate-chop me in the spine? No, thank you."

Also in 1955: *exurb, spinout*

1956 MELTDOWN

Some new words make a big splash as soon as they are coined. Others live in relative obscurity for several years, then suddenly become famous because of a dramatic event. Such a word is *meltdown*, which appeared in print as early as 1956, but did not become a household word until the end of the 1970s. *Time* used it in quotation marks on March 8, 1976, indicating that the word even then was still in its infancy: "What concerns these nuclear engineers … is not any possibility that a conventional nuclear power plant will blow up in a mushroom cloud and wipe out a city. What they do fear, however, is a 'meltdown,' which can occur if a reactor loses the water used to control the temperature of its uranium core."

Meltdown lost its quotation marks and became a full-fledged member of the English language in March 1979, when an accident at the nuclear power plant at Three Mile Island near Harrisburg, Pennsylvania, led to the leakage of dangerous radioactive gas, and resulted in a partial meltdown of the reactor. Although the danger soon subsided, the incident raised once again the perennial question: How safe is nuclear power? Looking on the brighter side, the Three Mile Island accident was a publicity agent's dream because it coincided with the release of a motion picture called *The China Syndrome*, which dramatized a massive meltdown in a nuclear power plant. The film took its title from the fact that a meltdown can create a nuclear lava flow of intense heat that would burn through the floor of the reactor and deep into the ground beneath, like the childhood fantasy of digging through the earth to reach China.

Also in 1956: *dune buggy, psychedelic*

1957 Sputnik

In his book *The Story of the Dictionary*, Robert Kraske tells us how *Sputnik* joined the English language in less than twenty-four hours: "Perhaps the fastest entry of a word into a dictionary happened in 1957. On October 4 of that year, the Russians sent the world's first satellite, *Sputnik I*, into orbit around the earth. An editor in New York saw the word in a newspaper delivered to his desk. He grabbed the phone and called a printing plant in the Midwest where his company's new dictionary was just about ready to be printed. 'Stop the press!' he shouted. Over the long distance phone, he dictated a definition of the word. One day later, *Sputnik* appeared in a dictionary and became part of the English language."

That was forty-seven years ago. When I asked my students at North Toronto Collegiate for a definition of *Sputnik* (a Russian word meaning "fellow traveller"), only a small minority could tell me what the word meant (several thought it was a Russian potato). These students were born in the mid-1960s and grew up in a world where terms like *lunar, moon rover* and *space shuttle* were pushing the word *Sputnik* out of the newspapers and into the history books. But all of my students know and use another word that joined the English language in 1957: *Frisbee*. It showed up in *Newsweek* magazine on July 8 of that year and owes its name to the Frisbie bakery in Bridgeport, Connecticut, the employees of which were fond of spinning the company's pie tins through the air.

1958 BEATNIK

When Jack Kerouac wrote his best-selling *On the Road* in 1957, it became the new bible for a whole generation of young Americans who were fed up with the "suffocating conformity of conventional society." Kerouac himself spoke of the Beat Generation (a term he may have derived from the Beatitudes of the New Testament), and became what we today would call the guru of the new movement. The followers of this new lifestyle at first called themselves *beats*, but shortly after the Soviet Union launched *Sputnik I* in late 1957, *beat* picked up a Russian suffix and became *beatnik*. On July 23, 1958, the London *Daily Express* took note of this new word: "San Francisco is the home and the haunt of America's Beat generation and these are the Beatniks — or new barbarians." By the mid-1960s, the term *beatnik* was becoming passé, and the rising tide of protest against the war in Vietnam set the stage for a new word to describe the rebels of society: *hippie* (from the expression "Are you *hip*, man?" — meaning "with it" or "in the know").

Incidentally, *beatnik* was not the only new word inspired by the launching of Sputnik, as witness the emergence of *peacenik*, *fitnik* and *nogoodnik*. In his weekly column on language in the *New York Times* Sunday magazine, William Safire makes mention of *plusniks* (people fond of starting sentences with "Plus…") and *whomniks* (those who feel strongly about the differences between *who* and *whom*). All these sound slightly Russian, which prompts me to add one of my own: *jollyoldsaintnik* — a street-corner Santa Claus fond of drinking vodka.

Also in 1958: *software*

1959 NUKE

Lots of words in our language have been shortened and streamlined by common usage. *Plane* is short for *airplane* or *aeroplane*, *bus* for *omnibus*, and *taxicab* for *taximeter cabriolet*. Fourteen years after the world's first nuclear explosion, the term *nuke*, a slangy contraction of *nuclear*, from the Latin *nucleus*, "a kernel," began appearing in print. Looking ahead to the day when pocket-sized nuclear bombs will be available, the *New York Times Magazine* on February 1, 1959, reported, "Soon there may be 5-inch nuclear shells and portable Davy Crockett 'nukes' for the infantry-man." The following year, on July 4, *Time* magazine reported, "Nuclear submarines — called 'nukes' — can cruise underwater for weeks at top speed." On September 29, 1969, *Life* carried a story on how attitudes toward nuclear energy were changing: "Once communities vied for nuclear power plants ('nukes') as passports to prosperity." *Look* used the word as a verb on July 11, 1967: "I remember in Saigon how disturbed General Westmoreland was after talking to a group of American editors … who told him they favoured 'nuking' (A-bombing) China." On December 23, 1972, the *Japan Times Weekly* used the verb twice in a single sentence: "I asked how he could be sure that the Soviet Union would nuke us if we nuked China." And on April 13, 1973, the *Daily Telegraph* decided to tell its readers once and for all what this word meant: "'Nuked,' for those unfamiliar with modern war-parlance, means to let off a nuclear bomb."

Today, it's not only a household word, but a verb used in the household whenever you nuke something in your microwave oven.

Also in 1959: *ombudsman, splashdown*

1960 BIONICS

In 1960, J. E. Keto introduced a new word in the *Procedures of the National Aeronautical Electronics Conference*: "The title of this session is Bionics. This is a new term referring to a relatively new but rapidly expanding area of activity — the study of systems which function after the manner of or in a manner characteristic of resembling living systems." Bionics is based on the Greek *bios*, "life," and *electronics*, because it is a combination of these two ingredients.

Back in 1960, the name Steve Austin would have meant nothing at all to J. E. Keto. Austin was the central character of television's *Six-Million-Dollar Man*, an astronaut brought back from the brink of death by having a dazzling array of electronic gadgetry implanted in his body. Touted by the dramatic series' creators as the "world's first bionic man," Colonel Austin performed wonders that rivalled the powers of Superman. His female counterpart was Jaime Sommers, who had her own TV series as *The Bionic Woman*. She co-starred with Max, another marvel of mechanical engineering who happened to be — are you ready for this? — a bionic dog.

1961 ZIMBABWE

In 1900 nearly every part of Africa was a colony of some European nation. By 1960 most of the continent had either gained its independence or was well on the road to achieving it. The name *Zimbabwe*, an African term for the land occupied by Rhodesia, first came to the attention of the English language in 1961, the same year in which the Union of South Africa, in a dispute with Britain over its racial policy, withdrew from the British Commonwealth and declared itself an independent republic. Rhodesia itself at the time seemed to be heading in the same direction, as a white minority forcibly maintained its grip on a large and subjugated native black population.

Between 1972 and 1979, however, thousands of black guerrillas took up arms and, at a cost of twenty-seven thousand lives, brought an end to nearly ninety years of white minority rule. As a sign of the changing times, the old name of Rhodesia (named after Cecil Rhodes, the British imperialist who first opened up the land to European colonists in 1890) has now been replaced with the native African name, Zimbabwe.

Also in 1961: *biodegradable, touch-tone, trade-off, geostationary*

1962 RUMBLE STRIP

You see them on many four-lane (or wider) highways today — a strip of corrugated pavement at the edge of the highway designed to produce a rumbling noise when driven over, thus awakening a driver who might be falling asleep.

Also in 1962: *multi-media, optical fibre, papovavirus, picosecond*

1963 PANTYHOSE

As the pace of life speeded up, women no longer had time to don panties *and* nylon hose as well. Enter pantyhose, the great time-saver and a far cry from Grandma's day when clips and buckles held up her stockings. A cure for apnea: put three tennis balls inside a pair of pantyhose and tie it around your waist with the balls at your back. This will prevent you from lying on your back, the sleeping position most conducive to apnea.

1964 PANTSUIT

Tired of wearing skirts, many women in the 1960s opted for a pantsuit, the new fashion craze which is still with us today. By the way, what does a dog do that people step into? It's not what you think. No need for the pooper-scooper because the answer is … pants.

Also in 1964: *gentrification, prioritize*

1965 MINISKIRT

The miniskirt caught on like wildfire in the mid-1960s; it was tremendously popular both with the women who wore them and the men who admired them. It was banned inside the Vatican, but many Italian women wearing a miniskirt still worshipped there by pulling a string, which dropped the hem of the skirt down to the accepted length, as they entered.

Around 1967 the *Toronto Star* conducted a "mini-meter" to see which high school in the Toronto area had the shortest miniskirts. The winner was Northern Secondary School, at 851 Mount Pleasant Road, where the average miniskirt's hemline rested eight-and-a-half inches above the knee.

Also in 1965: *aerobrake, extravehicular, pseudosophistication, spacewalk*

1966 ASTROTURF

What do the words *book, food, guitar, performance, play, transmission* and *turf* have in common? They have all become part of a *retronym*, a word coined by Frank Mankiewicz, the president of National Public Radio, for all those nouns that take on adjectives to survive in our rapidly changing world. *Hardcover book* is a retronym ever since the paperback, or *soft-cover* book made the plain, old word *book* inadequate. Health food stores sell *natural foods* (no preservatives added), something that everyone used to eat before additives came along. A guitar is no longer just a guitar. It's either an *electric guitar* or the old-fashioned kind, now called an *acoustic guitar*. All performances at one time were live, and so there was no need for an adjective. But with the advent of recorded performances, the word *live* is now *de rigueur* if the performance is in fact live. (We don't hear much about *dead* performances because they usually close after the first night.)

At one time, a play was a play was a play. Not anymore. Now it's a *stage play* to avoid confusion with *radio play* or *television play*. The transmission in your car is now either manual or automatic, and no longer just a gear-box. And *natural turf* is now part of our language to prevent confusion with *Astroturf*, the artificial grass used for playing fields. *Astroturf* is a trade-mark formed from the Astrodome, the indoor stadium in Houston, Texas, where this surface was first used.

Also in 1966: *crashworthy, duh, fallaway, knee-slapper, kung fu, paparrazo, zit*

1967 GOFER

Many new words enter the stream of spoken English before they appear in print, and an outstanding example is *gofer*, an office assistant who runs errands for the rest of the staff, based on a contraction of *go for* (coffee, newspapers, etc.). It may be impossible to ever determine who first coined it, but we can figure out when it started to catch on. In an article about the *Mary Tyler Moore Show*, *Time* used it on September 28, 1970, with quotation marks to indicate it was a word of dubious legit-imacy: "She plays an inadvertent career girl, jilted by the bounder she put through medical school, and working as a 'gofer' at a Minneapolis TV station."

The *American Heritage Dictionary* was published in September 1969 and became the biggest-selling hardcover book of that year, with 440,000 copies sold in the first four months. But you will look in vain to find *gofer* between its covers. The *Doubleday Dictionary* was published in 1975, but still no *gofer*. Even the 1980 edition of *Webster's New Collegiate Dictionary* doesn't include it. But if you look at the top of page 279 in the *Oxford American Dictionary* (also published in 1980), here's what you'll find: "gofer (goh-fer) *n.* (informal) a person who runs errands for another." Congratulations, gofer. You made it after all!

Also in 1967: *fast-track, parasailing, preppy, scumbag, tween, one-on-one*

1968 WORKAHOLIC

One of the quickest ways of getting a new word into circulation is to write a book and use the new word in the title. That's what happened in 1971, when Wayne E. Oates, a professor of psychology of religion at Southern Baptist Theological Seminary in Louisville, Kentucky, wrote *Confessions of a Workaholic*. Oates himself was a former workaholic who kicked the habit and wrote a book to tell others how to get unhooked, too. The blurb on the back cover tells what it's all about: "*Workaholic* doesn't appear in any dictionary. Wayne Oates uses it here to describe anyone who is so involved in work that it disturbs or interferes with his bodily health, personal happiness, interpersonal relations, and social functioning.

"There are workaholics all around you — and what's more, society approves of this addiction, industry fosters it, and religion appears to favour it."

Workaholic has since inspired a rash of related terms, including *beefaholic, bookaholic, golfaholic, spend-aholic, chocoholic,* and *wordaholic* (a member of the target audience for this book).

Also in 1968: *Breathalyzer, dweeb, reggae, sexism, goombah*

1969 AIR BAG

Ralph Nader's best-selling book, *Unsafe at Any Speed*, was published in 1966; at that time, five thousand Canadians a year were killed in traffic accidents, as were fifty thousand Americans. Nader's book led to many improvements in automobile safety. Air bags were talked about in 1969, but many more years passed before they became mandatory on all new vehicles.

Margaret Baltzer (the Leamington woman who diskified this dictionary), reports, "When I was married in November 1969, the car that my brother, a GM engineer, was using to take me to the church was a car that had experimental air bags in it."

Also in 1969: *doo-wop, homophobia, laid-back, paperless, paralegal*

1970 WHISTLE-BLOWER

This is a person who reports wrongdoing in a business or organization, often putting their own job at risk in doing so. The sponsorship scandal in the Canadian federal government in 2004 prompted the government of Prime Minister Paul Martin to pass legislation protecting whistle-blowers from being fired.

Also in 1970: *granola*

1971 AUDIOCASSETTE

Reel-to-reel tape recorders in the 1950s were big, heavy items that required the tape to be threaded by hand before it could be played. The arrival of the audiocassette greatly streamlined the playing of tapes, which were now far more compact. Like radio to television, it was only a matter of time before videocassettes became available.

Also in 1971: *pimpmobile, pronuclear, libber*

1972 FLEXTIME

Traditional office hours, for many years, have been from 9 A.M. to 5 P.M., spawning the term *nine-to-fiver* for anyone thus employed. But with everyone arriving and leaving at the same time, enormous traffic congestion on streets and subways is the inevitable result. In Tokyo, special "subway stuffers" are hired to shove passengers onto subway trains so that the doors will close. On the San Francisco–Oakland Bay Bridge, a special car-pool lane was set aside to help relieve the crush at peak travel times. And Toronto has experimented with special car-pool parking lots.

By the early 1970s many North American cities began to encourage flexible or staggered hours of work as an inexpensive alternative to building more roads and subways. *Flextime* (also called *flexitime, flexible time, gliding time* and *variable hours*) has other advantages as well. It allows parents to get home earlier to meet their children when the school day ends. It helps drivers to conserve gasoline (some people now work a four-day week of ten hours per day to reduce their weekly motoring costs by twenty percent). And fitness buffs prefer the flexible hours in order to play golf or tennis in the early morning or late afternoon.

Time magazine, on January 10, 1977, reports another advantage to flextime: "Supervisors report that productivity generally improves under Flextime — since employees can work at the hours they feel most alert — and that absenteeism drops."

Also in 1972: *bottom-line, courseware, lowrider, slamdunk, speed bump*

1973 CHILLOUT

Blackouts were common during World War II, especially during the Battle of Britain when German bombers were trying to flatten London in the hopes of breaking the British will to resist. Automobile headlights were fitted with black covers with narrow slits that directed a faint beam of light directly onto the road ahead — enough light to navigate by, but not enough for the vehicle to be seen by enemy aircraft.

When the war ended in 1945, blackouts seemed to be a thing of the past. Then came the big blackout of November 1965, when a vast segment of eastern North America, populated by millions of people, was without electricity for several hours — and nine months later, maternity wards kicked into overdrive ("With no TV, what else was there to do?" asked one new mother rather sheepishly). Later, *brownouts* became a fact of life in those cities where electrical voltage had to be reduced during peak demand periods in order to prevent the power distribution grid from becoming overloaded.

After brownouts came *chillouts*, as the oil business began to feel the energy squeeze. On April 16, 1973, *Time* reported: "There is one major hitch: if refineries produce enough gasoline to meet peak demand this summer, they may have to curtail heating-oil output enough to threaten more chillouts next winter." Although homeowners grumbled about having to turn down their thermostats to make their furnace fuel stretch until the next delivery, a chillout was far preferable to running out of fuel altogether. If that happened, the chillout would become a *freeze-out*.

1974 GASOHOL

Gasohol is both a generic term and a trademark. Under the heading "Gasohol Takes to the Road," *Science News* (on October 19, 1977) talked about the trademark: "Nebraskans just completed two million miles of on-road testing of Gasohol — a trademarked blend of 10 percent ethyl (or grain) alcohol and 90 percent unleaded gasoline." The *New York Times* of January 14, 1979, used the generic sense: "Supporters of gasohol say that its use will conserve scarce petroleum supplies and also reduce surplus farm crops, which can be used to produce alcohol."

The blending of gasoline and alcohol as fuel is not new. It was first developed in the United States in the 1930s and marketed in the Midwest under the trade name Agrol (from *agri*cultural alcoh*ol*). *Gasohol* joined the English language when the energy crisis of 1973–74 forced North Americans to look for alternatives to conventional gasoline.

Also in 1974: *full-bore*

1975 DOWNSIZE

Future historians will probably choose October 1973 as the most significant month and year of the twentieth century. It was in that month that the members of OPEC (the Organization of Petroleum Exporting Countries) imposed their first oil embargo against the industrialized nations of the Western world. As fuel prices began their relentless climb, American motorists turned increasingly to small, fuel-efficient cars from Japan. Detroit, the North American automotive capital, eventually got the message — and began trimming the fat from its corpulent gas guzzlers. A new word was needed to describe what was happening, and *Time* was one of the first magazines to use it on September 13, 1976: "All the automakers are already at work down-sizing their cars for 1978 and later years." When the 1978 models appeared, many of them had the lean — but not hungry — look. The four intermediate cars from General Motors had been downsized by about eight inches and had lost up to eight hundred and twenty-five pounds of superfluous tonnage.

But, as the *Second Barnhart Dictionary of New English* points out, not everyone was happy with this new word: "Technically to *downsize* means to reduce the exterior dimensions of an automobile while the passenger area and trunk remain the same or are increased. Car manufacturers and others in the industry prefer the older word *resized* to describe the new generation of smaller cars, claiming that *downsized* suggests a degrading of the product's appearance or quality."

Now that we have entered the twenty-first century, *downsize* has taken on a new primary usage: as a euphemism for corporate decisions to lay off or fire large numbers of people at once.

Also in 1975: *co-payment, garbology, keypad, psychobabble, sesquilingual*

1976 POOPER-SCOOPER

Here's the definition that Merriam-Webster supplies: "The device used for picking up the excrement of a pet (as a dog) for disposal."

1977 COVIVANT

In a *Newsweek* article entitled "Living in Syntax," writer Jan Otten surveys a surfeit of terms that seek to address the problem of what to call an unmarried person living on intimate terms with a member of the opposite sex: *cohabitor, companion, consort, friend, fiancé, lover, suitor, swain* or *mate*. "What's really needed," David Behrens of *Newsday* points out, "is one new word that will capture all the elements of blissful unmarried cohabitation. The word must at least blend a reference to residency, a suggestion of sexuality, a shading of emotional care, a hint of permanence and a dash, perhaps, of economic sharing."

When I appeared as a guest on a nationwide television talk show early in 1977, I mentioned a letter I had received from a woman wanting to know what word to use for "someone who is living with, but not married to, a member of the opposite sex" (the letter, incidentally had been sent from a motel in North Dakota). As a result of that broadcast, I received another letter, this one from Shirley Yamada of Toronto, who gave me the perfect word: *covivant* (from Latin *co*, together, and *vivere*, to live). It rhymes with *bon vivant* and it even boasts a romantic French flavour. Its Latin roots suggest a hint of permanence (ancient Rome lasted over a thousand years) and it sounds so much more endearing than *cohab* (the abbreviated form of *cohabitor*).

No one seems to know who first coined it. Shirley Yamada passed it along to me from an unknown and forgotten source, and her letter of April 4, 1977, is the earliest example I know of this word appearing in print. I included it as a main entry in my dictionary, *Brave New Words*, published by Doubleday in 1979, and I have seen it in print several times since then. The Swedes have been using the word *sambo* (Swedish for living together) since the 1960s, and it's time now for the English language to catch up.

The big breakthrough for covivant came in 1981 with the publication of Lynn Fels' best-selling book, *Living Together*. When she sat down to write the book, Fels had to decide what to call the people she was writing about. She looked at the possibilities — *boon companion, live-in lover, significant other, roommate, old man, cohab, inamorata* and even the acronym *POSSLQ* (pronounced PAW-sul-kyoo, it stands for Persons of the Opposite Sex Sharing Living Quarters), invented by Arthur Norton for the 1980 U.S. census. Fels rejected all of these in favour of *covivant*, which she uses throughout her book.

Much less romantic is the recognized Canadian census term, *common-law spouse*.

Also in 1977: *download, just-in-time*

1978 PERSONHOLE

In an effort to eliminate supposedly sexist language, the city council of Woonsocket, Rhode Island, decreed in 1978 that all manholes within Woonsocket city limits were henceforth to be called *personholes*. Although this new word might forever remain confined to large, round, manmade (sorry, person-made) holes dug in the middle of streets to gain access to the sewer system, a similar word — *chairperson* — has made it all the way to the *Oxford American Dictionary*, first published in 1980. You'll find this sexually neutral word in the blurb on the back cover of the *OAD*: "... in the long-awaited OXFORD AMERICAN DICTIONARY ... hundreds of notes on usage clarify grammatical points and words that are easily confused: Should you use *chairperson* or *chairwoman*? Is *disinterested* an acceptable way of expressing lack of interest? Is it correct to say the media *is* doing anything? Can one *catch* a movie? The OXFORD AMERICAN DICTIONARY is completely up-to-date and establishes a firm standard for all lovers of our language."

If you then look inside the *OAD*, you will discover you don't have to use *chairperson* or *chairwoman* if you really don't want to: "The word *chairman* may be used of persons of either sex, but *chairperson* is increasingly heard in this sense." In other words, it boils down to this: Do you want to be trendy or conservative?

Tackling the problem of sexist language from another direction, Don Sternbergh of York, Pennsylvania, has come up with a sexless new salutation to replace Sir, Miss, Mrs., Ms., and Madam. The new word is *SM* (pronounced sim), a contraction of *sir* and *madam*. It will save you, Sternbergh points out, from the awkwardness of "writing a letter to a stranger named Lee Jones or Kim Smith or Marvel Miller. You are able to solve the gender problem by writing, 'Dear SM.'"

Sternbergh sees other possibilities as well: "A policeman has halted a motorist in a tiny car. He cannot tell his victim's gender, but can see only a mass of curls on the head of the driver. 'SM, you failed to observe the red light you just drove through.'"

SM also comes in handy when talking with or writing to an hermaphrodite. And because it has only two letters, it can help you win your next game of Scrabble.

Also in 1978: *paragliding, SUV*

1979 Palimony

When the actor Lee Marvin began living with Michelle Triola, the couple had no idea they would end up contributing a new word to the English language. When the romance went sour after six years, the two lovers split up — but, in an unprecedented move, Triola (who called herself Michelle Triola Marvin) sued for $1.5 million, even though she and Lee Marvin had never married. The court case that followed attracted widespread publicity and prompted someone to call it a *palimony* case (a contraction of *pal* and *alimony*).

Other palimony cases followed, including a $4 million demand by Kayatana Harrison against the comedian Flip Wilson, who, she said, was a longtime, live-in boyfriend.

But dictionary publishers are cautious when it comes to new words, and the editors of the *Oxford American Dictionary*, published in 1980, saw fit not to include *palimony*. A similar word that has appeared in print is *galimony* — for alimony payments between former lesbian covivants.

Also in 1979: *karaoke*

1980 GRIDLOCK

Many are the commuters who have tossed and turned in the wee small hours, all caught in the grip of the same nightmare: What if so many cars try to enter the city core tomorrow morning that all traffic is brought to a grinding halt, with no room to move anywhere? The New York *Daily News* has already brought this word to the attention of its readers: "As most traffic-jammed New Yorkers found out ... gridlock (a term used by traffic engineers) exists when traffic suffers paralysis and all vehicle movement stops." *Newsweek* on July 12, 1982, used it in the caption of an article on a British labour dispute in the transportation industry: "British unions try a little gridlock." And the *Oxford American Dictionary* in 1980 includes *gridlock* as a main entry with this definition: "An urban traffic jam caused by continuous lines of intersecting traffic." When the Oxford editors grant recognition to a word, you can be sure it's legit.

Also in 1980: *flatline, NIMBY, spell-check*

1981 CAMCORDER

Now a common everyday item, the camcorder was hailed as the latest and greatest technological breakthrough when the first few came on the market in the early 1980s. Wow! Imagine taking home movies and then viewing them on your TV screen! Makes every member of the family feel like a star.

Also in 1981: *snowboard*

1982 KINDERKIN

In his weekly column "On Language" in the *New York Times Magazine*, William Safire asked his readers to suggest a new word to mean "the in-laws of your children." Although most of the mail was full of ways to describe "an ex-wife with whom one is having an affair," Safire did get some answers to his question. Gene Fried and Arnold Lewin, both of New York state, pointed out that Spanish has already solved this problem with *consuegros* (*suegros* are your in-laws, and once removed — through your children — they become *consuegros*). In Yiddish these relatives are called *machetunim*, from the Hebrew *mechatanim*, "related by marriage." Safire seemed impressed, but kept looking through the mail: "Most suggestions included outlaws, but that is not conducive to good relations with the kid's new in-laws; they might respond by calling you a horse thief.

"The best idea for a name for your children's relatives was submitted by a neologenius who demands anonymity: *kinderkin* [from the German *kinder*, children, as in kindergarten + kin]. Let's see if it flies…"

Also in 1982: *yuppie, email*

1983 Hip-hop

In the late 1970s, a new form of music began to emerge from New York's African-American neighbourhoods. It was similar to Jamaican dub music, in which disc jockeys at dances began speaking over the records they played, but with a twist: the New York DJs began manipulating their turntables to alter the rhythm of the music — a technique known as "scratching" — thus transforming the record player into a musical instrument in itself. Meanwhile a separate performer (or group of perfomers) called MCs would speak, or *rap*, in rhyming lines set to the DJ's concocted rhythms. The music came to be known as rap, while the culture surrounding it — which involved spray-painted graffiti, breakdancing, slang and, eventually, clothing fashions — acquired the name *hip-hop*.

Merriam-Webster suggests that *hip-hop* is a combination of *hip* — meaning "with it" or "cool" — and *hop*, perhaps because of the syncopated dancing that rap music inspired. In addition to the surrounding culture, *hip-hop* has also become synonymous with the music.

1984 LAPTOP

You see them everywhere now — on the subway, on the bus, on the commuter train. The portable personal computers we call *laptops* are the perfect tool for people on the move. No longer tied to a desk at the office, you can do all your keyboarding in the back seat of a limo taking you to the airport at sixty miles an hour, and you can keep doing it while jetting across the sky at six hundred miles an hour at thirty thousand feet.

The word *lap* dates back to before the twelfth century and comes from the Old English *laeppa*, akin to the Old High German *lappa*, "a flap." Among the several definitions of *lap* in the dictionary, this is the one that applies here: "the front part of the lower trunk and thighs of a seated person" (*Merriam-Webster's Collegiate Dictionary*).

In other words, your lap is the only part of your body that disappears when you stand up and reappears when you sit down.

The word *top* comes also from Old English, akin to Old High German *zopf*, a tip or tuft of hair. And speaking of hair, you often hear the following sentence in a barbershop: "Just a little off the top, please."

No one would be surprised to see someone using their laptop while getting a haircut. These new gizmos are rapidly becoming ubiquitous! (That adjective, incidentally, goes back to 1830, and the noun *ubiquity* to 1579.)

Also in 1984: *cell phone*

1985 INTERNET

Now a word heard everyday, Merriam-Webster defines it as "an electronic communications network that connects computer networks and organizational computer facilities around the world."

It's interesting to note that the word coined to describe this worldwide web consists of two language components dating back many hundreds of years. *Net* comes from Middle English *nett*, from Old English akin to Old High German *nezzi* ("net"), and predates the twelfth century ("an open-meshed fabric twisted, knotted, or woven together at regular intervals" — Merriam-Webster).

Inter- is a prefix meaning "between" or "among," and words beginning with these five letters fill almost five entire pages of the latest edition of

Merriam-Webster's Collegiate Dictionary (published in 2003). These *inter-* words take up so much room that nearly two hundred of them are listed without definitions. Among them: *interbed* (the space between twin beds?)

Inter- can be traced back to Latin *inter,* akin to the Old High German *untar,* "among," and the Greek *enteron,* "intestine." And why not? Your intestines are located *between* your stomach and your rectum.

Which brings to mind the old story about the fellow who was butted over a fence by a charging billy goat: "The goat slammed right into his ass!"

"You mean 'rectum.'"

"Wrecked him? It nearly killed him!"

1986 Farch

A new month to replace February and March. First overheard at Irene Tysall's house party in Toronto in the middle of Farch 1986. Later that year, a Farch calendar was published by Slopp Shirts at 2468 Yonge Street in Toronto. Only a few were sold, making that calendar a collector's item today.

Why *Farch*? Well, for those who hate winter, Farch would make the winter go faster because there would now be only one month between January and April instead of two. And because "Farch!" sounds slightly vulgar and distasteful, it's a perfect match for the mood that many people experience during the long, dreary winter months.

Shakespeare could have used this word: "Now is the Farch of our discontent made glorious summer by this son of York."

If the soothsayer had warned Julius Caesar to "beware the Ides of Farch," Big Julie might still be alive.

Worshippers in church could sing a new tune: "When the Saints Go Farching In."

If Yasser Arafat celebrates his birthday during the winter, he could change his name to Yasser Arafarch.

Groundhog Day would fall on the second of Farch. The 14th of Farch would be Valentine's Day. George Washington's birthday: 22nd of Farch. And Lincoln was born on the 12th of Farch in 1809.

The new month would have fifty-nine days (60 in a leap year). Easter Sunday would sometimes fall near the end of Farch, and the arrival of spring could be celebrated right around the 59th of Farch!

1987 THIRTY-SOMETHING

For certain things or concepts, you need two words (for example, *ice cream*). For others, two words have been joined to form one (*laptop*). And in other cases, two words heretofore unrelated have been joined together by a hyphen to form a new word. Such is the case with thirty-something.

The hyphen is useful in delineating where the two words have been joined together. And that way, when you see it in print, you know exactly how to pronounce it. Take away the hyphen and you have "thirtysomething," which at first glance someone might pronounce "thur-TIS-o-meth-ing." Long live the hyphen!

However, Merriam-Webster lists it without the hyphen. Which is correct? It may have begun with a hyphen, or maybe not. You can use a hyphen if you wish, or you can leave it out. Either way, the meaning is clear. It's usually used as an adjective ("my thirty-something daughter-in-law"). It comes in handy for people near the end of their thirties who wish to fuzzicate (a new word!) their actual age. The late comedian Jack Benny — he's always late now, because he's dead — often joked about being only thirty-nine (there's a hyphen for you) when it was obvious he was nearly twice that age.

1988 AUDIOBOOK

Another name for *talking book*. Audiobooks are very popular with the elderly, whose eyesight prevents them from reading off the printed page. Also known as *e-book*.

1989 FARTTAGE

A farm inhabited only on weekends, which therefore makes it, in effect, half a *farm* and half a *cottage*. Coined by Eric Skeoch, a retired high school principal, to describe his family property north of Toronto, which isn't entirely a farm and not entirely a cottage. The sign out front says it all: "Welcome to the Farttage."

1990 Husband-in-Law

How does a man refer to his wife's ex-husband? And how does the ex-husband refer to his ex-wife's current husband? *Husband-in-law* is the perfect answer, because both men have been legally married to the same woman — although not at the same time. That would be bigamy.

The word *husband* is of German origin and means "house-bound" because a married man is expected to spend a good part of his time at home.

1991 Cybersex

Merriam-Webster gives two definitions: "online sex-oriented conversations and exchanges; sex-oriented material available on a computer (as on the Internet and on CD-ROMs)." It's only a matter of time before someone coins *cybergasm* (an orgasm induced by on-line sex-oriented conversations).

Also in 1991: *latte*

1992 Cyberporn

Merriam-Webster gives this definition: "pornography accessible online especially via the Internet." See Merriam-Webster for *cybernaut* (1989), *cyberpunk* (1983) and *cyberspace* (1982).

Also in 1992: *Gen X, home page*

1993 DVD

DVD is the abbreviation for "digital video disk." The letters DVD shorten those words from seven syllables down to three. Merriam-Webster (the eleventh edition, published in 2003) offers two definitions: "a high-capacity optical disk format; *also*: an optical disk using such a format and containing especially a video recording (as a movie) or computer data."

Digital is derived from the Latin *digitus*, "finger" or "toe," taking us back to the days when people used fingers and toes for counting. *Video* is derived from the Latin *videre*, "to see" —*television* (see page 260) comes from the same root.

Disk also comes from Latin *discus*, "disk" or "dish," and the Romans got that word from the Greek *diskos*, from another Greek word *dikein*, "to throw."

This leads us to the word *discus* (dating back to 1656), which Merriam-Webster defines as "a heavy disc (as of wood or plastic) that is thicker in the center than at the perimeter and that is hurled for distance as a track-and-field event, *also*, the event."

Frisbee has a capital letter because it is a trademark "for a plastic disk for tossing between players."

It's interesting to note that an item as modern and recent as a DVD is derived from linguistic roots reaching back two thousand years. The ancient Greeks and Romans would be proud to know that their words are being used to create new words at least twenty-one centuries later.

1994 SPAM

Long familiar as the trademark for a canned meat product, *spam* without a capital letter refers to unwanted email (the electronic equivalent of junk mail in an old-fashioned mailbox). It apparently derives from a skit on the British television series *Monty Python's Flying Circus*, in which the chanting of the word *spam* drowns out other dialogue.

The popularity of email has created the term "snail mail" to show how slow traditional mail is, compared to the speed of email.

But snail mail has not always been as slow as a snail. About eighty years ago, a man in Pickering, Ontario, wrote a letter one morning before breakfast to a friend up north and mailed the letter at the local railway station.

The letter went north on the morning train and was dropped off in a mailbag at the Kirkfield station (about sixty miles north of Pickering). The local mailman picked up the morning mail and proceeded to deliver it along his dead-end route. The letter from Pickering was delivered to a mailbox in front of a farmhouse about halfway along that route.

The fellow in the farmhouse looked out and saw by the little flag sticking up on the box that he had mail. He read the letter from Pickering, then wrote a reply and put it in his mailbox in time for the mailman to pick it up on his way back to the Kirkfield station, where the letter caught the afternoon train heading south.

That evening, the man in Pickering was reading the reply from his friend to the letter he had mailed that same morning. And they say email is fast…

1995 WEBCAM/WEBCAST

A webcam is "a camera used in transmitting live images over the World Wide Web." A webcast is "a transmission of sound and images (as of an event) via the World Wide Web." Both these definitions appear in the eleventh edition of *Merriam-Webster's Collegiate Dictionary* (published in 2003). And according to M-W, both words can be dated from 1995.

Also in 1995: *proteome*

1996 AIR RAGE

Road rage appeared in print as early as 1988, eight years before rage apparently bore wings and took to the skies. Other rages are no doubt on the horizon as more people get angry in more places: *train rage, boat rage, ship rage, canoe rage, hot air balloon rage, gas pump rage, restaurant rage, waiting-in-line-at-the-bank rage* and *motorcade rage* — suffered especially by those in a hurry who have to stop to let a funeral procession go by. We might even see *rage rage* if people get angry at others for getting angry...

1997 JOB-LAG

A variation of *jet lag* (1969). Coined in 1997 by the author of this dictionary. When I retired in June 1997 from thirty-one years teaching history to high school students, I enjoyed my new-found freedom but occasionally missed the excitement of teaching a spellbinding history lesson. To cope with this period of adjustment from work to retirement, I volunteered to return once or twice a month to where I taught and re-teach some of my favourite lessons. The urge to do this continued into the spring of 1998, then came to a sudden end on a warm and sunny school day in early May. A couple of friends (Paul and Vern) phoned to invite me to go with them to a vintage auto wrecking yard out in the country east of Toronto (something I love doing). I had to turn down the invitation because I had promised an art teacher I would teach a lesson on automotive design the next day. That final lesson cured me of my job-lag and I never went back to school again.

Also 1997: *proteomics*

1998 CARCHEOLOGIST

In addition to being a lexicographer (see page 109), the author of this book is also a *carcheologist*, a word that appeared in the *Toronto Star* on August 8, 1998, in an article on my other career as Bill "Sherlock" Sherk, the "Old Car Detective" for *Old Autos* newpaper (call 1-800-461-3457 to subscribe).

A carcheologist tracks down and attempts to reconstruct the "auto"-biography of old cars as they passed from owner to owner many years ago. This digging into automotive history closely parallels the work of an archaeologist excavating a long-lost city. A carcheologist interviews current and former owners (if still alive) and tries to round up documents (such as the original bill of sale from the dealer who sold it new, as far back as 1940 or even earlier). Old photos are also helpful, and if the licence plate is legible, the year the photo was taken can be determined. In the case of my first car, a 1940 Mercury convertible, I found nineteen people (including myself, twice!) who owned it between 1951 and the present day. I still hope to learn who bought the car sixty-four years ago, when it was new.

1999 CANUBA

The name of the new country that would be formed if Canada and Cuba were to join together. Their citizens would be Canubians. Canada would gain a new province in the tropics, and people in Cuba would have the benefit of a distinctly Canadian social safety net. Overheard fleetingly on television while the author was channel-surfing.

2000 BARFARRHEA

Overheard on a Toronto subway in early January 2000. Two young men were comparing notes on how they celebrated New Year's Eve 1999. One fellow stayed home watching TV and fell asleep before midnight. The other fellow drank and partied all night, then suffered what he described as "an attack of barfarrhea" the next day. "Barfarrhea?" asked his friend, apparently unfamiliar with this word. "Yeah, barfarrhea," said the party-goer. "I was going at both ends at once."

According to Merriam-Webster, *barf* as a synonym for "vomit" goes back to 1957, *upchuck* to 1929, and *puke* to circa 1600. *Vomit* itself is much older, dating back to Roman times.

Diarrhea has been around since the fourteenth century as a word. The activity itself goes back even further, maybe all the way to Adam and Eve.

2001 PHILAMBULIST

Coined by the author of this dictionary in the year 2001 while walking around his hometown of Leamington, Ontario. A philambulist is someone who loves to walk. This word now joins *philatelist* (a stamp collector), *philanthropist* (one who helps others, often with financial donations), and *philodendron* (a plant that loves shade).

2002 REINTRUCKNATION

The restoration of antique trucks. The author of this dictionary first coined this word in 2002 in response to the growing popularity of restoring old trucks — a phenomenon that closely parallels the popularity of new trucks, especially pickups.

Old pickups are often rescued from automotive graveyards and totally rebuilt, often at a cost exceeding the original price of the truck when new.

2003 DISKIFY

Diskify is a verb meaning to transfer a handwritten manuscript to digital form, so that it may be saved on a computer disk. This word was born on Tuesday, August 5, 2003, when the author of this dictionary, Bill Sherk, composed the "Special Thanks" page for his previous book, *60 Years Behind the Wheel* (published by Dundurn Press in October 2003):

> I wish to thank many fine people for helping to make this book a reality. Toronto historian Mike Filey set the ball rolling by recommending me to Dundurn Press, where I met Tony Hawke, editor extraordinaire! Tony, Beth, Kirk, Andrea, Jennifer, Barry, and indeed the whole gang at

Dundurn tackled the project with unbridled enthusiasm and carried this author on their shoulders all the way to the finish line. Any errors, flaws, weaknesses, shortcomings, defects, and examples of human frailty are mine. All mine.

I still don't own a computer, and don't even know how to use one (hence my nickname, "Dinosaur Bill"). Imagine my shock when Tony told me the manuscript for this, my fifth book, had to be delivered to Dundurn on a disk. A computer disk. I could feel the blood draining from my face. At sixty-one I'm too old, I muttered to myself, to be dragged into a high-tech twenty-first century.

Marg Baltzer to the rescue! Marg lives here in Leamington and is a computer whiz. She agreed to "disk-ify" my manuscript, and even contributed a computer-enhanced photo of her dad, Neil Quick, behind the wheel of his 1927 Model T Ford roadster.

2004 MARSIPHOBIPHILIAC

The coining of this word was inspired by the landing of two U.S. rovers, *Spirit* and *Opportunity*, on the surface of Mars in January 2004. The subsequent discovery that liquid water existed on the surface of Mars sometime in the past caused great excitement throughout the scientific community. Where once there was water, there may have been life.

President George W. Bush has already spoken in favour of a manned mission to Mars within the foreseeable future. And astronauts willing to take the risk will surely volunteer.

The journey there and back would probably take about two years, with no guarantee of success. Each person on board would go with the awareness that they might never see Earth again. A Marsiphobiphiliac is a person who would love to explore Mars but is afraid of never returning home.

This new word is easy to pronounce: MARZ-i-FOB-i-FEEL-ee-ak). It has two Greek roots: *phobos*, meaning "fear," and *philos*, meaning "loving," as well as the name of Mars, the Roman god of war.